DOWN THE VOLGA IN A TIME OF TROUBLES

•

A journey revealing the people
and heartland
of post-perestroika Russia

•

By MARQ de VILLIERS

HarperCollins*PublishersLtd*

First Edition

Canadian Cataloguing in Publication Data

de Villiers, Marq
Down the Volga in a time of troubles

ISBN 0-00-215689-X

1. Volga River (R.S.F.S.R.) — Description and travel. 2. Volga
River Region (R.S.F.S.R.) — Description and travel. I. Title.

DK511.V65D48 1991   914.7'8   C91-094556-X
91 92 93 94 95 RRD 5 4 3 2 1

*For Alla, who taught me to
love her country as she did,
for all its grievous faults*

Special Thanks

To Sheila Hirtle, who knows what it's like, for pertinent advice and rigorous early editing; to Peter Herrndorf, publisher of *Toronto Life* magazine, for his generous and unwavering support; to J.D. MacFarlane, for sending me to Moscow in the first place, more than two decades ago.

CONTENTS

PREFACE

History, that prisoner of politics, has always been a confusing discipline for Russians, and in Russia today Soviet history — the real Soviet history, with all its brutal energy, all its manifest guilt — is hardly taught at all; the textbooks have been scrapped and the new ones not yet printed. What are they to say? What to make of Stalin? Of the show trials and orgies of self-incrimination? Of the genocidal famines? Of the human meat-grinder called the Great Terror? Of Khrushchev the Stalin toady, the buffoon who became a reformer, the "partial man," as the poet Yevgeny Yevtushenko called him? And Brezhnev the bureaucrat, whose rule led to sloth and cynical corruption? What, indeed, to make of Mikhail Sergeievich Gorbachev, the man who wanted to force his country to be free, but who became mired in the bog of bureaucratic centralism, the poisoned muck of Stalinism?

But while teachers cancel exams, hide the few textbooks they still have, and pass in shamed silence over the events of this century, every child knows the story of the Volga. Children learn in the earliest grades that Russia was united for the first time when Ivan the Terrible conquered the Tartar cities of Kazan and Astrakhan in the sixteenth century and the whole long reach of the Volga became part of Muscovy. They all know that the army of Prince Pozharsky, which pushed back the Poles in the seventeenth century, was organized and financed by the rich merchants of the middle Volga; that the two greatest peasant revolutions in Russian history had their origins on the Volga; that the Civil War, which divided the White Guard troops of Denikin from the Red Guards of Kolchak, was decided on the Volga, that the decisive battles of that war were won by Frunze at Kazan and Samara, by Kirov at Astrakhan and by Stalin at Tsaritsyn, the city that was later to bear his name, at least for a while.

The Volga is the longest river in Europe, but that's not what binds it to Russian hearts — there are Siberian rivers that are much longer. The Volga has been central to Russian life from the time of the Huns, through the invasions of the Vikings and the Tartars, to the days of the Five-Year Plans and the Great Patriotic War of the anti-Nazi crusade. With the Volga intact, the Russians say, Russia is never conquered. The Khans (chieftains) of the Tartars knew this, and so did the Tsar who took it from them. So did Hitler — why else the fanatic drive for its shores, and the insane hurling of division after division onto the bloodstained streets of Stalingrad? All the invaders, all the rebels, everyone who tried to master Russia tried first to master the river: Ivan the Terrible, Stenka Razin, the legendary Cossack who unleashed class warfare on Russia, Tartar Khan and French emperor, the Nazi hordes, Tsarist and Revolutionary, renegade and saint, the legions of Islam and the regiments of Christians, White Guards and Red Army . . .

It isn't just Russian romanticism or pan-Slavic chauvinism to assert that the Volga rouses deep emotions among the Russians, though both of those newly resurgent movements are seeking to cash in on this wellspring of sentiment. I myself have seen Russian travelers at the rail of riverboats staring and meditating upon its placid waters, their voices filled with the emotion that rises so easily in them, to the amusement and envy of travelers from more phlegmatic nations. No, this isn't just another river. In Russian folklore, the Volga is mother and mistress, comrade and beloved,

When you come home, fatigued but safe
Then dip your hands in a Volga wave

Not that my tame journalists-with-a-boat had any of this at the back of their minds. Not at all.

What they mostly wanted was a way to travel without becoming dependent on the dubious merits of the Soviet hospitality industry, a chance to drink a little beer, do a little fishing, hang out and poke about some interesting places. They were quite content to leave Slavic romanticism to me. Like most journalists they were cynics, and thought romanticism was generally a crock.

For a Westerner going along for the ride, there'd be an added benefit. The state of the nation was changing at a dangerous (or exhilarating) pace, if you believed the press and the pronouncements of the Moscow intellectuals. And even if you didn't, the USSR seemed to be coming unraveled — ethnic dissent, a collapsing economy, political chaos, "democratic centralism" that had ground to a halt with nothing to replace it. Gorbachev and his allies had been remaking the nation — no one any longer doubted this. But now — in which direction were they moving? What were they making? Did they know? Did anyone know? Was anyone any longer in control? Was it any longer controllable? Would the Union sink back into first anarchy, then tyranny? It was easy enough to find out how the drama of perestroika was playing in the bars and meeting rooms of the Foreign Press Center on Smolenskaya Boulevard in Moscow. But how was it playing in the heartland?

What was *going on* in this heartland?

The Russian Revolution had burst upon the world in 1917 with the force of a natural cataclysm — the Ten Days That Shook the World were still shaking it three generations later. Russia's hated tyranny had produced, after years of turmoil, another hated tyranny. The Revolution, as the manual forecast, had devoured its children, resulting in famine, pogrom, genocide, the Great Terror and a dreadful silence that for decades no one dared to break. It produced a society in which no one spoke his secret thoughts, in which everyone lied, in which only informers and thugs flourished. What could emerge from this terrible history? Perestroika may or may not be able to remake the economy. Did it have a chance of remaking men's minds?

I remembered a passage from Arthur Koestler, writing in the depths of disillusion with Stalinist madness: "A moribund society creates its own morbid grave diggers . . . We see again and again how a polluted civilization pollutes its own revolutionary offspring." When we think of Bolshevik history we're apt to forget the "polluted society" from which it came; there has recently been a depressing nostalgia for Tsarist memorabilia, inside Russia as well as in the West. And now, when we cheer for perestroika and resign ourselves to what seems the inevitable eclipse of its inventor, we are just as apt to forget that three generations of "democratic centralism" have sapped the people of will and drained them of trust, so that even attempts to foist on them the Wall Street emotions of self-centered greed fall on deaf ears; Gorbachev was reduced in 1990 to lamenting the need for "psychological perestroika, first of all."

This trip would take me into the countryside, to the places where ordinary Russians lived. Gorbachev had chipped away at the stony centers of Western hostility; was he as easily able to shift the sly hearts of the Russian peasantry? The Russians I talked to seemed mostly confused, worried and depressed, in about that order. The worry and depression were easy to understand, but the confusion seemed deeper than just uncertainty over political strategies. In addition to confusion over how to order their economic and political lives, they seemed confused about who they were as a people, about what to make of their history, about how to reclaim a sense of personal and national dignity, about self-worth, about values they described with the shorthand "soul," which seemed ethical and spiritual in nature — they were all groping for some meaning in national life.

I phoned Valentin, who seemed to be the ringleader of the loose assortment of journalistic "fellow travelers," to say that I'd love to go, and when should I arrive?

A year went by.

The boat they'd acquired went mysteriously missing. They somehow got it back. They decided they didn't want to go, that they did want to go but not yet, that they would leave soon and when could I be there, that I could write about the trip but not

about them or where they "requisitioned" our transportation, and
did I have a spouse or a girlfriend because if I did some of them
thought it would be fine to bring her along and others didn't, so
maybe I should come on my own . . .

There was another hitch.

Valentin called me two days before I was to leave for Moscow.
The conversation was unsettling. The boat, he said, had been
impounded (again), "but don't worry, it's not serious, we'll be able
to get it back, it's necessary for you to bring with you a VCR, a
Sony model VCR, the best you can get, we'll be able to get it back
for that."

"Back from whom?"

"Don't worry about it, it's not serious. Just a question of a paper.
The VCR will fix that."

"I'm on a tourist visa. How can I walk through Customs with a
huge cardboard box under my arm with Sony written all over it?"

"That won't be a problem, believe me. Everyone does some
such thing. They are used to it."

This seemed to me unlikely. What would I tell the Customs officer? That I absolutely had to watch *Meatballs III* every night? That
it was a gift? Well, if so, who was it for? I said I couldn't do it.

Valentin had expected this. "Well, all right, we can get it here in
a *valyuta* [foreign currency] store, but you must bring dollars with
you to buy it." He told me exactly how much.

"This I can do."

I was developing some skepticism that the boat would ever leave
Moscow. I'd taken to thinking of it as the *Novosti Express*, since it
didn't seem to have a real name — it was always just "the boat."
Novosti (news) because the "crew" would consist entirely of journalists. The "Express" was meant ironically.

I was still unsure how many people were supposed to be traveling on it. Did any one of them know anything about boats? They
were vague. What had that earlier comment about spouses and
girlfriends meant? What did it matter whether there were women
on board? I wasn't going to Russia to practice male bonding; I
wanted to see the country, not just drink beer and swap stories;
perhaps a few women would be a good idea, get another perspective on what was happening . . . How long would it all take? They

were vague on this too, mostly, I discovered, because they hadn't any idea how fast the boat would go, or how many hours a day they'd travel, or even how far things were — they knew the Volga was long, but I seemed to know much more about it than they did.

Even if the *Novosti Express* worked as planned, which seemed dubious, at best it wouldn't reach more than a third of the Volga. I wanted to travel the full length, from source to end. But by the time I arrived in Moscow I had, by Soviet standards, very few of the arrangements actually in place. Partly this was because the *Novosti Express*, while far from a sure thing, was at least a strong promise; and partly because to achieve my goal of seeing all the river I'd have to get to places that were closed to foreigners and to cities and towns in which Intourist, the Soviet travel monopoly, had no facilities. I tried to devise a route that would do as much of this as possible if the journalists' boat fell through. As a precaution, I planned an itinerary with Intourist that would at least give me a visa for the principal cities along the Volga (Yaroslavl, Gorky, Kazan, Ulyanovsk, Saratov and Volgograd). Beyond that, I hoped that the new politics in the Soviet Union would enable me to "execute unorthodoxies," as one of the journalists put it later — to wing it, in short, once I was there.

Intourist had clearly not altogether fallen for this strategy: after a long delay in my visa, they had grudgingly agreed that I could go to Ulyanovsk and Volgograd, but Gorky was definitely closed to foreigners, and so was Saratov. They had also added Rostov-on-Don, for which I hadn't asked, and Sochi, for which I had, calculating that I'd need a little R&R in a resort town at the end. But, they'd told me in Toronto, internal travel arrangements would have to be made once I was in Moscow, once I was already safely in the hands of the Mother Corp. itself. I had an appointment with a sub-director of Intourist the day after my arrival, and this person would see what could be done. I was dubious about this. There are severe penalties in Soviet law for traveling without permission, and especially for traveling to cities officially closed to foreigners. And sub-directors, especially Soviet sub-directors, are not known for their flexibility, except perhaps on the gray market.

I did have another piece of insurance: I'd booked passage on a Soviet cruise ship that was to make the run from Moscow to

Kazan, about halfway down the Volga's length, and back to Moscow; I could always take that if the *Novosti Express* went nowhere. Armed with all this and plenty of American dollars, I figured something could be made to work. At the last minute, another problem appeared: the Soviet cruise ship venture was also in trouble. There was some problem with the passenger list. They'd see what could be done . . . I should check with them in Moscow . . .

In early June, I flew out of London into Sheremetyevo Airport and immediately plunged back into the familiar Soviet smells: badly refined gasoline, rough tobacco and the rank clothing that was the consequence of no deodorant and virtually no dry cleaning. The terminal was built in 1980 for the Olympics, and is by Russian standards efficient and modern. Russians were deplaning from what were still called the Fraternal Socialist Countries, each passenger with a Sanyo, Panasonic or Sony box bound with string. Everything had been in the passenger cabin, nothing checked — the Soviets were too canny for that, for pilfering among baggage handlers is endemic. The usual long lineups, of course: first a lineup to pay for a luggage cart, then a lineup to get the carts, which were then mysteriously not there, but at the other end of the terminal, where there was another interminable wait . . . This was all reassuringly normal.

I tried to call Valentin from the airport but didn't have any Soviet coins. The bank wouldn't give me any, only paper. I finally exchanged a dollar bill for kopecks at an Estée Lauder foreign-currency store, and called his office. He wasn't working that day. No, they wouldn't give me his home number. Damn. Why hadn't I brought it with me? There's no telephone directory in Moscow, I'd known that. No information service, either; without a number I was lost.

I took a cab to my hotel, the Izmailovo, in the northeast quadrant of Moscow. This was another part of my travel insurance. I needed a place to stay for a few days in case the cruise ship was canceled and the *Novosti Express* never got un-impounded. In order to get a visa, one has to demonstrate where one will be at all times, and since I had no idea, I resorted to risky subterfuge. I'd managed an unorthodox deal on the phone with a clerk at the Izmailovo. He'd rent me a room, yes. If I didn't need it, he'd refund half the money, he'd keep the other half, and officially I'd still be registered, if the visa people asked, while he rented the room to someone else. This was pretty brazen on his part, but I accepted. The few hundred dollars it cost seemed cheap insurance.

The Izmailovo, a massive complex consisting of four gigantic highrises, is a joint Canadian-Soviet venture, not run by Intourist. This latter feature had appealed to me at first, since that meant it was almost certainly less efficient at keeping track of foreigners, but I grew to regret it. Intourist may be a smothering bureaucracy, but its absence is worse: the Izmailovo is a hotel that's as hostile to its guests as a hotel can be and still stay in business. No other Western tourists were staying there, except one busload of Japanese, who are Western by Russian standards since their currency is convertible — the only true measure. The hotel was full of Russians and East Europeans, and endless numbers of pasty young women with hard eyes and industrial-strength makeup, traveling in packs. I never did discover who they were.

An hour after I arrived, I encountered the Soviet service industry, at Banquet Hall D of the Izmailovo Tourist Complex Corpus C.

"When does the restaurant open?" I inquired.

"Not till nine."

I returned at nine. It had opened, of course, at eight. There were no more places.

"*Nyet, nyet*, go away, it's full."

I knew enough about the Soviet service industry from past experience to ignore this injunction. I went in. About half the enormous room was empty. I went back to the doorkeeper and insisted on being assigned to a table. My insistence was reinforced with strong language in English, which proved useless, and a package of Marlboros, which was less so.

The gorgon at the door wasn't going to let me off easily, though. She sniffed. "These are not real Marlboros," she said. "These are made in Austria."

How on earth did she know? The package said nothing about country of origin, but she could apparently tell. It was possible. I'd bought them at Heathrow Airport, in London. They did the trick, however. I was seated at a table inhabited by three *muzhiks*, peasants, with an impressive array of mineral water and beer bottles in front of them, and piles of torn slices of stale bread.

I brought out another package of Marlboros. One of the *muzhiks*, in felt jacket and steel-toothed grin, reached for it, but I politely moved it out of reach. It was for the waiter, who happened by in about thirty minutes.

The waiter took the package and disappeared. Another thirty minutes went by. I surreptitiously took a bread slice from one of the *muzhiks*, and began to chew. I hadn't eaten since high over Denmark somewhere, and it tasted wonderful.

Meanwhile, the obligatory floor show was under way at the front of the room. There are always floor shows in Russian restaurants. Occasionally the "show" is just a rock band playing at high volume, but usually they're more elaborate. This one was fairly standard. First, "Russian dancers" took the floor, though this was nothing they'd recognize down on the *kolkhoz*, the collective farm: the dancers wore very short skirts and high-cut panties. This was followed by a chorus line; two of the five girls had runs in their stockings. After this an elderly couple did some demo ballroom dances (a tableful of Japanese applauded wildly at the tango). A singer followed, a chubby woman in a too-tight gown; then a juggler who performed on a unicycle and dropped things (the ceiling was too low). The chorus line performed a demure cancan, and the merciful finale was a band playing apparently unrelated notes.

At the adjoining table a group of dissolute children of the Moscow elite were annoying everyone — they were sarcastic, drunken, arrogant to the help. My waiter finally brought *zakuski*, a series of appetizers, of which cucumber and a sweet potato salad were the most prominent. He said the kitchen was now closed. He also brought a bottle of sweet red wine (I think it was actually port, but by this time was too tired to care). I went up to my room and watched an episode of *Yes, Minister* dubbed into Russian. I wondered what the Russian audience was making of the program's satirizing the manipulation of politicians by bureaucrats.

In the morning, I wrestled once more with the Izmailovo catering staff. The hotel has four enormous dining rooms, each one capable of seating three hundred or more people. I wandered into

Salon D, where I'd dined the night before; people were peacefully eating breakfast, and I made for an empty chair. Before I reached it I was intercepted and bundled from the room — fairly hustled out by two commissionaires in semi-military uniforms. "Groups only. Go away." Where to? If I wasn't a group, they didn't care. In Salon A, I successfully found a chair at a table occupied by two Russian matrons who seemed furious at something, and a dozen small children. Breakfast consisted of sweet cake with sour cream, fermented apple juice, followed by two amazingly salty wieners with sour pickled cabbage, washed down by lukewarm coffee diluted with boiled milk, a cool scum floating on the top. All in all, this was a truly disgusting breakfast. But it *was* food, and I obediently put it away.

Later, I went to the Intourist head office on Marx Prospekt to see my sub-director, as I'd been instructed in Toronto. Predictably, she'd never heard of me, and I had to patiently explain my requirements again: permission requested to visit the towns of the Volga.

Soviet bureaucrats have always been adept at finding ways to do nothing, and they've recently discovered the perfect device to help them do it — the computer. Instead of simply having to say "It's impossible," the usual first Soviet response to any request, they can now say, with an air of tired virtue, "I'll have to ask the computer . . ." This phrase translates into a shrug. It means, This is out of my control, I can do nothing, come back when the computer has answered, possibly tomorrow, possibly next week . . .

In this case, Intourist said, it would almost certainly be next week.

"But by next week I'd like to be gone. I don't want to sit around Moscow." I was thinking of the Hotel Izmailovo.

Shrug. "Come back tomorrow afternoon. We'll see."

I wandered onto the street and lunched on what passed for a hamburger from a street kiosk. Most of the lunch hour was spent dodging Gypsy beggar children.

I made another stab at finding Valentin at an information kiosk, which is how one generally finds out telephone numbers in Moscow. But in order to extract a number from the kiosk one has to know the person's name, address, place of birth and age. Officially this is because there are so many Borises and Tatianas, but everyone accepts that it's just the way Russian bureaucracy works: endless small inconveniences are built into the system, for no apparent reason. I had to guess at Valentin's birthplace — I took him for a Muscovite — but I had no idea when he was born. I gave up, and for the rest of the day reacquainted myself with Moscow, then repaired to the Izmailovo, where I spent the evening watching Boris Yeltsin, who is wonderful on television, run the conference of the Russian Federation Soviet of Deputies. On another channel Maggie Thatcher and Mikhail Gorbachev were holding a press conference at the Kremlin.

The following day, without much optimism, I went back to Intourist's Gorky Street offices, where I finally drew an operator who seemed to enjoy her work (thank you, Olga) and who admitted that it would, after all, be possible to visit at least some of the Volga cities. So even if the *Novosti Express* sank a hundred yards from its moorings, I'd be able to do most of the trip I wanted. Moreover, I was confident that once I was in the provinces, a way would be found to evade the restrictions and visit what Moscow forbade. It was *impossible*, of course, but a way can always be found. In a country where most of the economic activity happens in the gray market, there's always a way.

In the afternoon I finally reached Valentin. I wrote down his home phone number.

"We have the boat back," he said. "We managed to buy a VCR. You owe us some money."

"Don't worry, I've got it."

That evening we met for dinner. Valentin had bullied his way into a reservation at the Aragvi, a Georgian restaurant, and had somehow managed to acquire vast quantities of Georgian white wine; this was surprising, since a trainload of the wine had been hijacked on its way from Georgia a few weeks earlier, and there was supposed to be a shortage.

I tried to persuade Valentin that we should begin our journey at the very source of the river. It made better symbolism, I urged, to start where the Volga started. The river was 30 kilometers (about 20 miles) across in some places, and more than 200 feet deep. Out of what secret place did the Mother bubble?

He disagreed. "We're not interested in symbols," he said. He and his friends wanted to go downriver, they had their hearts set on it. We got out a map and argued. The Volga starts northwest of

Moscow, in the Valdai Hills about halfway to Leningrad, heads southeast for a while and then swings northeastward and curves in a great arc around Moscow a few hundred kilometers north of the city. It then wanders in a southerly and easterly direction through the heartland of Russia before swinging south and beginning its plunge to the Caspian Sea, 3,500 kilometers from its beginnings. The source of the Volga was likely to be swamp and scrub forest, Valentin pointed out. Better to go downriver, to Yaroslavl and Kostroma, Kosmodemyansk and Nizhni Novgorod, all the old towns of the Russian heartland.

And besides, he said, they weren't ready to leave just yet. Affairs, politics, were at a critical pass. A new law was about to be passed that . . . Gorbachev was said to be planning some hard-line move . . . Yeltsin was on the point of . . . Ligachev would . . . It rolled out, one reason (excuse) after another: The Moldavians were the latest to declare independence, the Party would split, the Party would never split, the Party's influence was waning, waxing . . . Gorbachev was out, was vulnerable, the country was on the verge of a serious famine, there'd be a civil war in six months . . . On behalf of the others, he whined and complained and equivocated — they were journalists, after all. I gave up. "Okay," I said, "I'll go on my own tomorrow."

I told him about my Intourist success, but he wasn't listening. "We need more money to buy some Western beer," he said. "Lowenbrau. We'll make arrangements later. Call me when you get back."

The boat, the *Novosti Express*, was moored at Moscow's Northern River Terminal, he said. By coincidence, that was the same place the cruise ship I'd booked was supposed to depart from, if it was departing at all. Its scheduled date was not for a few days, I told Valentin, "and I'll check it out when I come back from Volgoverkhovye."

"Okay," he said. "We'll meet you there. If you don't use it, maybe we can sell your ticket. What's the boat's name?"

I looked at my documents. "The *Rus*," I said.

He started to laugh. "Well, at least it's not the *Yuri Gagarin* or the *Mikhail Sholokhov* or another of our Socialist Heroes," he said.

I knew a taxi would be my best bet to reach the Volga's source. I could have rented a car from Intourist, but the license plates are marked and I didn't want to have to explain to a suspicious member of the GAI, the Soviet traffic cops, why I was wandering around the countryside without explicit permission; my purpose on this trip was to avoid arousing the curiosity of officialdom if at all possible, and it's a truism of Russian travel that anything not expressly permitted is forbidden; for foreigners deportation — at best — is the penalty for violations.

It's difficult to explain to those who have never visited the Soviet Union how hard it has always been to travel inside the country. The endemic suspicion, the lack of facilities, the need for permits and permissions, the general xenophobia inherited from the Tsars, the notion still widely held among Russians that it's dangerous to talk to foreigners, the difficulties of the language, the multiplicity of petty functionaries who apparently make up the rules as they go along, the fact that whole areas of the country are inexplicably closed to foreigners, sometimes at a moment's notice and on pain of imprisonment and severe interrogation — no wonder most visitors rely on Intourist. It's permissible to drive your own car through Russia on a vacation, though each night's stop still has to be planned and paid for in advance, and a missing tourist is still generally taken to be further evidence of foreign duplicity or, at worst, subversion.

In this case, I could have taken a train to the town of Ostashkov, which is close to the Volga's source and on the Moscow-Leningrad main line, but what then? There are no places in the countryside to rent a car or a boat, and the rural transportation system is utterly unreliable, even were I to successfully evade the functionaries who run it. From Moscow to Volgoverkhovye is a trip of about 300 kilometers, but I knew I'd be able to find a driver who'd take me there. It was just a matter of price.

I took the subway from the Izmailovo downtown to the Intourist Hotel, where cab drivers congregate like crows around a ripe carcass. There are always groups of men standing outside these major Intourist hotels; many of the foreigners who stay there assume they are somehow operatives of the KGB. Actually most are what *Izvestia* in its more puritanical days called "hooligans." They're often con artists, salesmen for overpriced schlock "art," pimps or muscle-for-hire, and I've always found them a particularly good source of gossip, since they have to be riding the political wave to stay ahead of arrest and prosecution. These hard-looking men usually have black Volga sedans, the car of choice of the Russian bureaucracy, and can be hired for the right licit or the wrong illicit purpose, if the price is right and the currency anything Western and convertible. I preferred the cab drivers, who were just as avaricious but slightly less likely to roll you when you weren't looking — I had no desire to be abandoned in a rural ditch.

Half an hour before I reached the Intourist Hotel, a street lamp in front of it had fallen off — suddenly come unstuck and plummeted straight down — and smashed through the window of a taxi parked below, giving the two American Baptists who'd just hired it a shaking fit. They thought a terrorist bomb had gone off and by the time I arrived were already blaming the KGB's anti-religious zealots, much to the amusement and scorn of the assembled crowd. I sidled among the crowd of cab drivers and made my pitch.

One of them took me aside.

"Where did you say you wanted to go?"

"Volgoverkhovye. It's near Lake Seliger," I added helpfully — Lake Seliger is a popular holiday lake about 300 kilometers from Moscow.

"How much?"

This was a trickier one.

The ruble, since it's not convertible to any other currency, has no fixed value. It's worth whatever the buyer and seller can agree it's worth. State enterprises trading with Western businesses usually just make up their own exchange rate, and if the West buys, the State Bank will grit its teeth and go along for the ride. Intourist, which in 1990 still had a monopoly on foreign travel, could get away with charging an outrageous $1.50 American per ruble to tourists. The State Bank was giving visitors 6 rubles for a dollar. I'd been getting 12 on the street and 15 was pretty common. At the time, it was still illegal for Soviet citizens to have and spend dollars, not that anyone paid any attention. A decent monthly wage was 250 rubles (less than $25 at the street price).

"A hundred dollars," I said.

"At least $150," he said.

We settled on $120, which, for a 600-kilometer round trip and an overnight stay, wasn't too bad a bargain.

"I don't want to do it myself," the driver said, "but I know someone who will. He's been wanting to go to the source of the Volga for years, and he has a little boat. Come back here at two this afternoon and he'll be here."

"How will I know him?"

He looked amused. "He'll recognize you. I'll tell him, 'Thin guy with funny glasses.' Be here."

He got into his car and gunned off into Revolution Square. I had three hours to kill. I bought a *bif gril* (steak sandwich) and a Pepsi from a kiosk, and then wandered over to the Lenin Museum, which I'd never visited in the years I lived in Moscow.

"What is your group?" the cashier asked.

"I have no group. Individual tourist."

"Only groups today," she snapped, and slid the window closed.

We got off to a bad start.

"I'm Karel," he said, thrusting out his hand. He pronounced it with the stress on the second syllable.

"Karel — that's not a very Russian name," I said tactlessly. His face darkened.

"I don't have to explain myself," he said. "Do you want to go or not?"

He was a big, burly man, dressed in the shiny suit and appalling shoes that were later to be dunked in the Volga's swampy beginnings. He had bushy eyebrows and fleshy lips, like Brezhnev, and a cross look, which I attributed to my opening remark. To mollify him, I pressed $50 American into his hand, followed by a pack of Marlboros, always the currency of choice in Moscow. Later, mollified some more, he confided that he'd been named in a mad moment after Charles, the heir to the British throne, although of course his parents hadn't told anyone, it being the time of Brezhnevian stagnation and not a good time to be romancing foreign royalty. "Ka-*rell*" was as close as they wanted to come to Charles.

We walked over to his brown Volga, parked around the corner in front of the National Hotel. Strapped to its roof was a small blue dinghy, which needed a coat of paint but looked otherwise service-able. I was reassured by the professional-looking knots in the rope holding the boat in place. On the back seat was a cardboard box, bound with string, that had once contained a Sanyo television set. It concealed no end of wonders — a change of clothing (which came in handy), a huge kolbasa cut in two, a loaf of sour rye, a cucumber and two formidable bottles of Siberian vodka. Plus a map of the Kalinin district, which proved completely useless.

The first hurdle would be the GAI post at the city limits. GAI stands for Government Auto Inspectorate, and traditionally its men were both traffic cops and population control officers under the supervision of the KGB. GAI control posts existed — and still exist — at every highway exit to every city in Russia. Years before, when I lived in Moscow and drove a Russian car, it had plates that were color-coded to signal "foreigner" to the GAI. They could then easily check to see whether its passage had been pre-cleared with the authority that dealt with foreign diplomats and reporters, called UPDK, which stood for Administration Responsible for the Diplomatic Corps. Most of us evaded the GAI on occasion by finding a pliant taxi driver, but Soviet citizens, too, could be stopped for random checks, and often were. The GAI took very seriously attempts to evade their scrutiny; they were not gener-ally people with an active sense of humor, and it was best not to irritate them.

I was curious to see to what extent matters had changed: would the GAI have more important things to worry about than the wan-derings of a few errant foreigners, or were tight restrictions still in place? Was population movement still as controlled by the bureau-cratic centralism of the Soviet state? No one I spoke to in Moscow seemed to know. We headed north on the Leningrad highway and sailed past the GAI post without slowing down. It was still there, still manned, but no one paid us the slightest attention; the incum-bent officer seemed to be reading a newspaper. I flagged this for further mulling, and settled down for the ride.

We followed the highway north, through the old town of Klin to Kalinin, where there was a bypass that swung west and north and crossed over the Volga. This was my first glimpse of the river in twenty years, and I stared down through the crumbling railing at the water below. Karel had slowed the car and, seeing my look, stopped in the middle of the bridge, somewhat too abruptly, as a swaying, creaking truck loaded with newly minted concrete lampposts was forced to scrape by, the driver cursing and hauling on the wheel as he skidded past our car, before his angry glare disappeared towards Leningrad.

The river was swollen and gray, pregnant with late spring floods, gray on gray, flowing past with barely a sound, like a mirage on the move. I tried to imagine Viking ships sailing down this same water at the dawn of Russian history, moving on past Tver, past Kazan, until they met with Arab traders at Samara, who reported their astonishment at the sight of golden hair and fierce blue eyes, and tried to barter for the women of the Golden Race to take back to Baghdad to amaze the Sultan . . . The Volga waters are rich in the nutrients that feed imagination, and it was easy to feel in the hackles on the neck the Tartar hordes of Batu, the Great Khan, and the wrath of the Terrible Ivan.

The Volga is the River Road of Russia, down which Russia's history has always moved. From the ancient days, everywhere travelers went, they went by water. Russians have always written about these travels, sometimes prosaically and sometimes romantically, like Trotsky: from his lonely Mexican exile he wrote of "a people that geography had condemned to a life of savage individualism, condemned and thinly scattered in this inhospitable place, who found their community on the great rivers." Russia, he believed, was the loneliest country on Earth, small hamlets huddled in an immense wilderness that the folk legends filled with forest demons and wild wolves. Chance meetings on the river were the occasion of orgies of good fellowship; Russians have always believed their "natural communalism," such as it is, was born on the Volga's banks.

Then Karel's taxi, brown on brown mud, its checker markings obscured by highway dust, lurched into motion at the angry blaring of another truck horn behind us and we swept over the river and lost it to sight.

Beyond Kalinin the road split, and a few kilometers further it split again. Both times we took the left fork, heading west through the dreary towns of Torzhok and Kuvshinovo to Ostashkov, the fishing and tourist village in the heart of the lake country of the Valdai Hills, where we knew the Mother River began.

They're somewhat mislabeled, these hills. They can be called "hills" only by a generous imagination, for they don't get up much beyond a thousand feet above sea level. Still, they are the highest point between the Baltic and the Urals to the east and the Caucasus to the south, and a mountain is a mountain if you call it so; and on the Baltic side, where the slope is quite steep, they do so choose, going even further in brazenness and calling it "the Lithuanian Switzerland." And why not? Might as well give it some human purpose. In truth, this is not very productive land, left over as it is from the last glacial period, moraine-covered hills, undulating or level plains and ill-drained depressions. It's swamp and sand, long since colonized by pine and birch, with an undergrowth of bilberry, cranberry, rosemary and bog whortleberry, thick beds of peat everywhere. This is hopeless country for farming, though Russian peasants have been scratching a living from it for a millennium. What it does have are many picturesque lakes nestling in the knolls — there are over fourteen hundred named lakes in the Valdai Hills. The Volga, the Dnieper and the West Dvina all rise here in pretty much the same swamps, and diverge only by a small fluky tilt in the landscape that can hardly be seen.

We knew, in theory, where the stream called the Volga rose. Finding it was another matter.

Karel stopped the car in Ostashkov, which is the closest town to the source. He asked three people and got three different answers. The "official" source is at Volgoverkhovye, whence a small creek trickles down to Lake Sterzh. An old guidebook I found in a Moscow secondhand shop (1926 edition) showed a photograph of a boardwalk leading to a small wooden hut, which was supposed to mark the spot.

I brought out the 1926 guidebook, and Karel read it to me, his finger laboriously tracing the words:

> In order to get to the upper Volga, one must travel until reaching Svapush village, situated 40 kilometers from Ostashkov. From here, by foot or driving some 18 kilometers

on a nice forest road, one can without any fatigue reach the Volga's source. After four hours of walking, the traveler will notice on the right side of the road plowed fields, structures and the churches of a monastery. Approaching the village, to the left of the road one will see a wooden chapel. Anyone who has read or heard about the upper Volga will understand that this is the river's actual source. The chapel stands on the edge of the forest, in an unstable, marshy area. This is where the "Jordan" spring, Volga's reputed beginning, is located. Here, at the altitude of 228 meters above sea level, begins the great Volga. The chapel may be approached on a boardwalk from the village located on the elevated riverbank, and a slough is cleared, out of which the Volga is flowing, a narrow stream, rather slowly making its way among the marshy banks . . .

That sounded clear enough, though I worried about those "four hours of walking," especially four hours "without fatigue."

In Ostashkov we were told, variously, that only the ruins of a chapel marked the spot, that it had long since been buried by the weir at nearby Ivankovo, and that there had never been anything marking the spot.

And where was "Svapush village"? No one seemed to have heard of it.

"The hell with this," Karel said as he pulled disgustedly away. "I've got a friend in a camp at Lake Seliger. Let's go ask him. He'll know."

Seliger, slightly to the east, is a long lake, some 45 kilometers, from which flows a tributary of the Volga. It's big enough and popular enough with holidaying Muscovites that a regular hydrofoil plies its waters, visiting tourist camps and the most popular beaches.

The place where Karel's friend was staying was no Club Med, it's safe to say. It was a shabby campground surrounded by a rickety wooden fence; at the only gate was a not very triumphant triumphal arch made of thin plywood whose plies were separating and which was nailed to poles listing seriously left and right. On the arch, picked out in capital letters, were the words "Red October Works Leisure Camp." The campground surrounded a

small cove on Lake Seliger near a neat white boathouse that doubled as a hydrofoil dock. The camp's facilities consisted of a dozen
rundown wooden cottages, a larger building that served as mess
and entertainment center, a rope between two trees draped with
bunting that passed as a volleyball net, several gaily painted blue
skiffs, a dozen or so park benches, acres of dandelions and a PA
system that seemed to play "Moscow Nights" on an endless loop.
Each hut contained a primitive kitchen and three "rooms" whose
walls were blankets.

Karel's friend Anatolii, who shared his cubicle with a sullen wife
and two joyous children, was drunk when we arrived and was
moaning about "them," who turned out to be variously the camp
directors, the plant administration, the government or all three at
once; he seemed to thoroughly enjoy being miserable. Hanging on
a string line in front of the cabin were assorted underwear, a few
socks and a dozen scrawny fish drying in the sun. After he stopped
moaning and took the time to welcome Karel with sloppy kisses
and hugs, Anatolii told us he knew *exactly* where the source of the
Volga was to be found — we were to follow a small stream that led
off from the northwest corner of Lake Sterzh, he said, and yes,
there'd be a ruin there to show us the place . . . How best to get to
a convenient launching place on Lake Sterzh? Anatolii drew confident lines on Karel's useless district map, a left here, a right there,
straight ahead here, a good beach for a boat here, all down small
unmarked roads that we later discovered did not and probably
never had existed, at least not where he put them.

Business done, we lunched. A good part of the kolbasa disappeared, as did a pickled cucumber brought out from the hut. Both
Anatolii and Karel produced bottles of vodka, and the party settled
in for a drink. The sun was warm, Anatolii's wife managed a rare
smile, and the kids bounced and bounded and pulled everyone's
hair and then went to sleep in the shy shade of a pretty young
birch. The conversation was about fishing, football, the weather,
with only a few desultory slaps at shortages "all caused by perestroika, by the looters . . ." It was one of the very few conversations
I had in the 250-million-strong politics seminar that was the USSR
in 1990 that paid so little attention to politics. Perhaps it was the
drowsy summer sun. And the fact that Anatolii's toil for the Red

October Works (I never did discover what the Works worked at) had delivered him a blessed four weeks of entirely free vacation. That must have had something to do with it.

Eventually we departed, with protestations of friendship and more hugs and kisses, and an hour or so of frustrating dead ends later, we stumbled quite by accident on Lake Sterzh and a beach to launch our little boat. By this time we were both a little unsteady from the vodka, but we got the boat safely launched and Karel rowed strongly northward.

We found the little stream that Anatolii had insisted would be the Volga, and rowed up it.

There was no ruined chapel, no little wooden hut, no boardwalk.

I went back to my guidebook, and found a passage I'd missed before.

"It doesn't say Lake Sterzh at all," I told Karel. "Your friend is dead wrong. It says here, 'Near the village of Voronova, the Volga takes in the Persyanka, its first tributary. Then it passes through two small lakes, Small and Big Verkhit. Leaving the last one, the Volga takes the form of a four-meter-wide river. Seven and a half kilometers from its source, it falls into Lake Sterzh, which is between open, rather high banks and supports about twenty settlements . . .' It doesn't start near Sterzh at all. It's already kilometers long by then. We have to find Small Verkhit Lake."

We rowed back to the car, strapped the boat on and in a grim silence took a promising-looking but rutted and unmarked road to the northwest. It was a dead end.

An hour later we finally found the twin Verkhit lakes and launched our boat again. I was weary and depressed — too much vodka, too many dead ends — but Karel, sober once more, rowed as strongly as ever. He seemed inexhaustible.

We passed what could have been the Persyanka, the Volga's tributary, a sluggish stream a few feet wide.

We couldn't find the Voronovo the guidebook mentioned.

Svapush village still didn't seem to exist.

There was still no chapel, no boardwalk. Small Verkhit had deteriorated into a swamp, and that's all we saw. Swamp.

Except . . . under the water, faintly to be seen in the muck, were old hewn boards. It *could* have been a boardwalk, once. "It *was*," said Karel, pointing a little further ahead, at something he saw in the water. He stood up. "Look, it is! It *is*! This *is* the place!" He turned around to look at me, grinning hugely, and lost his balance.

"Oh no," he said, "Oh no." And then, as he began to fall, "Shit, oh shit," and he toppled with a great splash into the swamp.

●　　●　　●

By the time we got back to the car, Karel was cheerful again, though his blue suit had gone a dull gray and he squelched water as he walked. The vodka he pulled from his cardboard box helped. He took a deep swig and skinned out of his wet clothes, hopping around mother-naked in his ankle-length socks, his pale white body as shambly as a dank Arctic bear. We'd seen it, we really had, the beginning, the very source, of the greatest river in Russia, of the River Road itself. We slapped each other on the back and drank some more, full of good fellowship. There were worse ways to start a journey to Astrakhan.

CHAPTER 2

Kilometer 235

Rzhov

W e'd stopped for the night by the side of the road not far from Ostashkov — we'd been too weary to push much further, and night was falling. Karel started the night outdoors, tying the stern of the dinghy to a tree to make a neat lean-to and spreading a blanket on the ground, but the mosquitoes drove him inside. I'd brought a vial of lethal bug-killer from Canada to fend off the famous Volga mosquitoes, the *komari*, whose reputation made them sound like small helicopters. We both smeared this stuff on and rolled up the windows, which didn't help the rank air much but did keep the ravenous mosquitoes at some remove. We slept uneasily, me in the back seat with the ruins of the garlic kolbasa, Karel in the front, lurching about, snoring and snuffling. I woke feeling thick-headed, with a sour taste in my mouth. Rubbing mint-flavored toothpaste on my teeth helped a bit, but kolbasa for breakfast didn't add to the comfort level. Karel watched the ritual with the toothpaste dubiously, but followed suit and liked it.

It wasn't much after five in the morning when we set off again. The sun was already up. The road accompanied the Volga, and we caught glimpses of the river through the trees. Once, going around a bend near the village of Hikola-Siska, situated on the high right bank near the ruins of an ancient Varangian town, a wonderful view opened of the river and the gentle slope of the left bank, soft meadows and fresh-plowed fields. The newly minted sun turned the Volga into shimmery molten gold; Karel stopped the car without being asked and we trotted to the river to see. There was a footpath on the bank, the smell of fresh dew and the water of the river looked as smooth as Spandex on a dancer's thigh. Both of us threw off our clothes and dashed into the water, yelling like schoolboys, splashing and jumping and shivering. It was clear and cold and a dark forest green, and I dipped my head and felt wonderful. The mosquitoes drove us back to the car, and we proceeded in companionable silence, feeling good about the whole venture. Karel wanted to stop for tea in the next village, Selizharovo, but from my map I saw that Eltsii, the village I had visited years before, wasn't much further, and I suggested we press on.

There are many small rapids along this part of the Volga. The folk tales say there are thirty-two altogether; the rapid called Bensk is the most famous and most dangerous, and is the subject of a local song:

> *When men fall out*
> *Out at Bensk*
> *They fall like stones*
> *Like stones they roll*
> *Volga makes them*
> *White like chalk*
> *And they're never seen*
> *Never seen again*
> *Never seen*
> *In this poor world.*

A cheerful sort of song, perfectly in keeping with the grim humor of the Russian countryside.

We saw occasional open fields, and farms, but they were poor-looking things. In this moraine country the soil, what there was of it, was still shallow and sour, and pools of water filled every depression. Flax and potatoes were said to be the main crop of the region, but all we saw were hay fields and a few scrawny cattle. There'd been considerable controversy in recent years over the massive use of chemical fertilizers on the collective farms of the region, the farmers trying to goose potato yields. Karel's friend Anatolii had told us the day before there'd been civil unrest in the area — farmers had thrown a blockade across the main Tver road, which had been overrun and demolished by armored militia vehicles. What had the farmers wanted? There was said to be a shortage of the chemicals they'd come to depend on, and now the city people, the Greens, some of the bureaucrats even, were saying too many chemicals were running into the Volga and their use would have to be curtailed. This was a typical city sort of trick, the farmers believed — complain about food shortages, but don't allow the proper tools to produce more. Most of the farmers apparently believed the ban on fertilizers was a backhand way of rationalizing critical shortages in the chemical industry. Outside the village of Lukomo we saw a huge mound in a field, a mountain of last year's potatoes left to rot because the harvesters reached them too late. Karel looked at them gloomily. "Longer lineups than usual this winter," he said.

The upper Volga, the section we were now traversing, has always been marshy and densely wooded. The middle and lower Volgas are steppe (prairie) country. The forest and steppe zones are complementary in Russian history; it's no accident that the capital lies near the junction of the two. Russian folklore ties the national character closely to the country's geography. The plains have yielded up the Cossack prototype — bold, anarchic, aggressive, anti-intellectual. The forest, which for most of Russian history held more than half the population, teaches different instincts. The peasant working with an ax must coax a living with infinite slow labor from the grudging soil. The forest teaches caution; behind every tree may lie danger. It also teaches slyness, for one might hide in its depths. The forest is a refuge and a trap.

Near the shores of the Volga this famous forest looked forlorn, consisting as it did of stunted spruce, alder, a few birch; most of the hardwoods have disappeared into the sawmills of Tver, and there are few oaks left. There's more industry here than farming, and every few kilometers a factory chimney would appear above the trees. Local propaganda says that this is a substantially industrialized region, especially since the Moscow Canal opened in the Thirties and the hydroelectric plant at Ivankovo was constructed at the Volga reservoir (1937). Most enterprises I saw were of no great size, and many of them looked quite rundown.

We reached Eltsii a little after eight.

The village is perched on the left bank where the Volga makes a sharp right turn, and from several points the river seems to be going in both directions at once, something I remembered from twenty years before. Nothing much seemed to have changed in those twenty years. There was still the same haphazard arrangement of sheds and little wooden houses. Most of the houses had television aerials, but there'd been neither building nor painting in the intervening decades. The highway was considerably more active than before — lumber trucks heading for Rzhov as well as tourist vehicles traveling between the lake country and the capital — but the village itself was no different. As we entered, a stout woman in head scarf and high boots was filling buckets from the well I remembered from before; her yoke looked to be willow, just as I remembered. The sun was already hot, and the village was dusty from the passing traffic. Then I spotted one difference: there was a small general store called Ko-op. This *was* new. "Ko-op" was the euphemism of the day for "private"; private enterprise had reached Eltsii. The store, however, was closed, so I couldn't judge its efficacy, and we walked down to the Volga landing.

A wooden platform had been built into the river, and four women were kneeling on it, rinsing their laundry in the cold water. They did the scrubbing and soaking at home, in the kitchen, and in the good weather they came down to the river with their plastic pails on a yoke and rinsed the laundry in the Volga. Two of the four were babushkas, robust grandmothers in homespun skirts above heavy varicose veins, short boots and the traditional head scarves. One was a young girl of perhaps eleven or twelve, who seemed mostly to be watching. The fourth was a young woman in a striped shift, pimply but pretty in a doe-eyed way; most of the time we were there she regarded me with open mouth, and said nothing.

Karel asked if we could persuade someone to make us tea for breakfast, and perhaps give us a little bread. I was a foreigner, he said, and we'd just been to the source of the river.

One of the babushkas struggled to her feet and fetched a cracked white jug from under the bushes. It contained cold tea and smelled sour, as if it were fermenting. "Go on, take some," she encouraged. We did. It was very strong and very sweet, tasting of raspberry jam. It was delicious.

"Did you visit the monastery?" she asked.

Karel looked puzzled.

"What monastery?"

"At the source. St. Nilus. All the foreigners go there, I hear. They all want to pray." She cackled, and spat. "Now everyone wants to pray again, but not me."

She looked at me. Staring at me from six inches, she spoke to Karel. "Why's he here? No foreigners stop here, they all go hunting and fishing at the lakes. Why here?"

"I was here twenty years ago, for a day," I said, answering her in Russian. "I passed a pleasant day here, I was in the area, I wanted to come back."

She cracked a wide grin, flashing gold and steel teeth. "It wants to come back, does it?" she said. "Well, there's not much to see here. There never was. And anyway I don't remember you. I was here twenty years ago."

Nevertheless, she invited me back to her house to get the bread, leaving Karel to flirt with the open-mouthed young woman; I could see he was taken with her bare knees and would stay all day if I let him.

The old woman's name was Maryonna. She lived in one of the small houses on the embankment overlooking the river. It was unpainted except for the window trim, which was bright blue. The doorway was sagging, and there was serious rot in the sills, but inside it was scrubbed clean and neat, the battered aluminum cooking pans hanging on nails on a wall in a cross shape. I remembered a passage from the Marquis de Custine, an acerbic French traveler who was visiting a Russian village for the first time as he journeyed from St. Petersburg to Moscow in 1839. "Here I was overwhelmed by the odor of onions, sour cabbages and old greasy leather that the Russian villagers and the villages themselves exude." He'd gone on to describe the ugliness and shabbiness of Russian women, and how they deliberately dressed themselves more poorly than their men.

Maryonna's house smelled of nothing at all. It was utterly odor free — no pleasant nor unpleasant odors. The village smelled only of dust and badly refined gasoline from passing trucks. Of course, all is now electrified, and each house has a small electric cooker; the *pech*, the traditional stove, is used only for heating. And the women? Maryonna had the pouty mouth and cheeks of the Slav, the small eyes, the broad face, filled with good humor and strong character; her smile was golden in more ways than literally.

All the men in the village were "away," she said. She didn't elaborate, and I assumed they were working on the farms or in the factories of the district. Of wider events, she would say little. Things were grim, she said, worse than they were a few years ago, before perestroika, and getting worse all the time. More troubles were ahead, a long time of troubles. I asked her about Gorbachev, and she looked contemptuous. "Tough where he should be soft, soft where he should be tough," she said. It was the first of many harsh judgments I was to hear.

She gave us half a loaf of dense black bread and a couple of green tomato pickles from a jar under the bed. With the raspberry tea, this made one of the best breakfasts I'd had for years.

We left about eleven, both of us reluctantly, and headed southeast towards Rzhov.

"What was this about a monastery at the source?" I asked Karel.

"Damned if I know."

"Are you sure we were in the right place?"

"Of course I am!" he said indignantly. "You prefer to believe an old woman?"

"Not at all," I said hastily, but in truth I had begun to wonder.

There was plenty of river traffic on this stretch of the Volga, most of it consisting of small barges and tugs. Once we saw a startling sight: a wooden barge, laden with bread and kerosene, being dragged up the river by horses, a scene from Ilya Repin's famous painting *The Volga Bargemen*, reminiscent of the past when the whole Volga resounded with the cries of the barge-haulers and horsemen.

Somewhat east of the Volga are the Ilyin Hills, and to the west a high watershed, which used to be known as Okovskiy or Volokonskiy Forest. The banks in this region are limestone laced with coal, which makes them look like candy twists. There's fireclay in the banks, too, and generations of villagers have gouged deep holes on both sides. Cold springs bubbled out of the clay, giving it a glistening polish that was quite beautiful.

Just before a village called Bakhmutovo, after a stretch where the road had diverged from the river, we stopped again. I wanted to consult my references to see what they said about Rzhov. I was under the impression it had played some interesting role in early Russian history, but there was not likely to be any real reminder of this in Rzhov itself, since Napoleon's army as well as Hitler's tanks had rolled over the town.

Rzhov was first mentioned in the twelfth century. It made a brief appearance in the Russian Chronicles as having shown "some independence" of Novgorod the Great, the city that was then the dominant political force in Russia. What this independence consisted of was not specified; very likely Rzhov flirted with the new principality of Zagorsk, to the east, or perhaps Kiev had tried to draw the Rzhov gentry into its orbit. This flirtation had in any case been fruitless: the revolt was crushed.

These Russian Chronicles were begun in the Monastery of St. George, called the Monastery of the Caves, founded by Yaroslav the Wise in 1019. The monks began their holy work in the chalk caves under the city of Kiev, setting themselves the stupendous — and presumptuous — task of "recording all events." They thought of themselves as adjutants to the Recording Angel himself. The task of Chronicling humanity's span on earth soon spread outwards from St. George to other religious institutions, some of them only nominally Christian; the chroniclers drew upon preacher and shaman, on witch and yarner, on the folk sayings and folk legends, the *bilini* of Russia, to capture their time in ever-widening circles of local narrative. The Chronicles were systematized in the twelfth century and continued for some time thereafter. Many of the doings and sayings of the wise are recorded therein, as well as the betrayals and treacheries of the powerful.

The Chronicles mention only that Rzhov had been brought to heel; they don't say by whom. There is mention of reliquaries in the city from the "elder days." I wondered how elder the elder days were, what these reliquaries could be, and whether they were still to be found.

The eldest of elder days, the dawn of recorded history in Russia, saw the invasion of the Huns.

Invasions are the pattern of Russian history, and their significance can't be overemphasized in trying to understand the national character. From time to time invaders would sweep into Russia, often from the east, crossing the Volga, riding roughshod over the people who stood in their way. The Huns swept through Russia and reached France in the fourth century, before disappearing as swiftly as a tornado; while they were there, the Chronicles say, they "struck terror into all who saw them, for they had huge heads, deep-set eyes and cruel faces; they had bow legs because they never walked. They even slept on horseback." As the Huns swept through, the Slavic tribes hid in the woods, what nascent civilization they'd been developing scattered, fragmented into small clans or single-family villages. Before they could recover and regroup, invaders struck again, this time from the northwest. These were the Varangians, or Vikings, pushing deep into the great unknown where they supposed they'd find the mythical city of Asgard, the home of the Norse gods, of Valhalla. They came by swift boat down the River Road, bringing baggage and chattel with them, and easily cowed the villagers along the Volga's banks. By the ninth century, according to the monks who wrote the Chronicles, Russians were already paying tribute to the Vikings.

The Chronicles are not always reliable on these matters, reflecting as they do tribal Slavic indignation. Ancient legend has it that the Slavs threw the Vikings out, and then, when the tribal remnants descended into quarrels and petty tyrannies, demanded them back. Three Viking brothers responded to this unusual request and came down from Scandinavia in 862 with their followers: Rurik became the prince of Novgorod, Sineus became ruler of Belo Ozero, and Truvor selected a place called Izborsk. Only Rurik survived for more than two years and in time, through conquest and treachery, gathered in his brothers' lands. His Slavic and

Viking followers, the first Russians, pushed outward and south-ward, going as far as present-day Ukraine, where they built a fort and called it Kiev. Some believe the very word "Russia" comes from Rurik's name; others believe it is an old Slavic word having no connection to the invaders.

Whether or not these brothers ever really existed, the line of Rurik had a magical hold on the Russian imagination; all Russian rulers down to the sixteenth century proclaimed that they had "the blood of Rurik" in their veins. It's this blood, diluted as it is with the thinner blood of German and Polish princelings, that still appeals to the mystical fascists who call their organization Pamyat (the name means remembrance).

We pulled into Rzhov in the early afternoon. The Volga here is compressed from its 100-meter width to less than 30 meters; the high, steep banks give the site a picturesque appearance. Nothing else, however, is picturesque: there is little in the town worth seeing.

A railway station, a crossroads, a few factories still decorated with white-on-red Party exhortations, a small, thinly populated and pathetically empty market where sweet old ladies sold flowers for a ruble a bunch, home-pickled dills for 20 kopecks and a few crafts made of cheap felt (there were more sellers than customers) — there are towns like this all over the Soviet Union. The centralized planning system has produced places that are virtually inter-changeable in their banality, in their lack of architectural merit, in their shabby subdivisions of tumbledown new highrises, in the poverty of their social amenities. Only parks are plentiful, littered with inept public statues of Lenin or some local dignitary, and flower beds that are "efficiently" watered in an industrial fashion, by the simple expedient of a fire hose aimed from a passing truck, so that most of the plants are entirely washed away by the process. I thought of a remark I'd seen attributed to Catherine the Great, who'd made an impromptu journey down the Volga towards the end of her reign, for once without Prince Potemkin as travel agent, during which she saw her towns for what they really were. She exclaimed, "Why are Russian towns so magnificently situated and so ignobly constructed?" So I guess this banality isn't new. Only when the Russian folk have been left to get on with their lives without supervision has something recognizable as a national style emerged.

Karel suggested that for another $20 we could spend an extra night on the road, following the Volga to Tver before turning south to Moscow. "We could probably stay in a hotel," he said hopefully, "rather than the car." I wasn't so sanguine. I preferred the car to provincial Russian hotels, which were always calculated to make a guest's stay as unpleasant as possible. I wasn't confident that we'd get a bathroom at a hotel in any case, though I longed for one. Maybe the Volga would have to do again.

We stopped at the post office to phone his wife in Moscow. This isn't as simple as it sounds. Interurban calls can only be made from selected phones, a few in each town. There's generally a longish wait. While Karel joined the line inside, I sat in the car outside the post office and went back to reviewing the local history.

The Huns soon disappeared. The Vikings followed. And other invaders: the Poles, the Swedes and Lithuanians, then the Khazars and the Tartars, then the Turks and Bulgars. The Russians believed that every invader was a "horde" — more than an army, conquerors and not transitory invaders, bound to fight to a finish because they'd come to colonize and not just plunder, bringing with them military bag and cultural baggage, women and children as well as soldiers. They had to be fought off with great ferocity and at terrible cost.

Byzantium came to Russia in the tenth century. The ruler of Kiev in the 960s was Sviatislav. He was a pagan, though he came under the influence of the popes and patriarchs at Constantinople. Vladimir, his son, was the last European ruler to be a pagan; in the fashion of the time he accepted baptism in return for military aid from the Byzantine emperor, and like many early converts he took to mystic Christianity with a fervor and a ferocity that are startling to modern sensibilities. In 990, when he returned to Kiev from Constantinople, he ordered his people baptized Christians and all images of their pagan gods destroyed.

Vladimir was a colorful figure even by the colorful standards of the time. It's possible he embraced Christianity for sound strategic reasons of state, but somehow the version that survives in the

Chronicles rings truer: he was ready for a monotheistic religion, but which one?

He asked the Jews of Constantinople why they'd been condemned to a diaspora, and they replied, For our sins. So he discarded Judaism. Islam, in turn, was rejected because, as Vladimir explains in the Chronicles, it's quite impossible to be happy in Russia without strong drink. Byzantine Orthodoxy, therefore, was adopted by default, and envoys sent to Constantinople returned entranced with the ritual opulence of the Orthodox service, an opulence that survives undiluted to the present day.

I looked around me, trying to wrench my mind from the echoing of this long and melancholy history. Karel waved from the post office; he was now third in line — only another half an hour or so to go. A drunk staggered by, and a young panhandler knocked on the window, demanding cigarettes. I gave him three Marlboros and he ambled off.

A leaning wooden building across the way bore a sign: Gorkom (Gorod Komitet, or "city committee," the local soviet or council). I tried to reconcile the work of the latter-day Party with the fractious heroes of the past. Revisionist historians now assert that the ancient Russian towns, including this one, were democratic at heart; they are trying to counteract both the Western canard about Russian "Oriental despotism" and the newer proto-fascist cry for strong leaders. It's true that power was concentrated in the city assembly, which in theory had unlimited authority. But was this in any real sense a democracy? In theory . . . sort of. The local prince was free to raise questions in this assembly, but not to resolve them. The assembly was convened whenever needed. It could be summoned by anyone on any pretext, simply by ringing the town bell. No one supposes, however, that this was a working system. In practice, a special Council of Masters with a permanent staff prepared all proposals for the assembly; unsurprisingly, this council was made up of the prince, the archbishop and members of the ruling families.

Karel emerged from the steps.

"She gave me shit," he said ruefully, speaking of his wife. "She's laid on a big meal for tonight, queued for hours to get some fresh vegetables, she's got champagne . . . She'll drink it herself now. She was celebrating the dollars," he amplified. "But it's okay. She'll get over it. I told her we'll be back tomorrow, with more dollars than ever."

He plunged into a small store nearby and fifteen minutes later emerged with a large chrome-plated tray, a gift for his angry spouse. "She'll like that," he said with satisfaction. "Lucky. You can't get things like this in the city any more." I looked at it more closely. It was crudely plated, with etched patterns. The words "Made in Tula" could be seen on the back, and the price: 7 rubles. Tula steel was once greatly prized — Catherine the Great valued it so much she kept objects made from it locked in her vaults, along with the black pearls and golden vessels of the Queen's Treasure — but judging from the workmanship of this tray, Tula had fallen on hard times. "I wanted to get tea glasses to go with it, but they don't have them here. We'll try in Kalinin" — the old name for Tver.

We returned to the car just as a small procession pulled up in the square. A bride emerged from the second car. She was a little tipsy and swayed a bit, and was being supported by a young man, who was presumably the groom. He asked me to take their picture, and I did. He was tall and thin and blond almost to the point of invisibility; she was toothy and a little plump and had obviously had a wonderful time. They stared solemnly into the lens; when I finished they beamed and kissed each other. I wished them well, and we departed.

CHAPTER 3

Kilometer 460

Tver

Nineteen kilometers from Rzhov, at Zubtzov, the Vazuza River joins the main Volga stream. The little Vazuza is only 150 kilometers long, but it affects Mother Volga by perceptibly deflecting its flow to the north. Naturally enough, this has generated a legend of an ancient quarrel between Mother and Daughter, in which Daughter torments Mother but Mother always wins. Curiously, there's some geological evidence for this folk quarrel, since the channels of the upper Volga are older than the river itself — the Volga has indeed been shifted.

Some 50 kilometers from Zubtzov we crossed over to the south side of the Volga at a place called Staritsa, a small industrial town utterly without character, located on steep banks on both sides of the river. We were carrying two hitchhikers, both going to Tver. We'd picked them up at a rural bus stop. One was a farm woman carrying a pail of radishes, and the other an industrial worker from Tver who'd been visiting family in the country. He was carrying a small folding fishing rod he'd made himself; the ferrule at the butt end was made from tin cans, pinned and soldered, and chased with a small awl into intricate floral patterns. It was quite beautiful, and

I told him so; his only response was a toothy grin. Otherwise he said nothing the whole trip.

"Let's cross the Volga," Karel said as the car passed over the rusting bridge.

I thought I'd misheard him. "We just did, didn't we?"

"No, I mean by boat. We should cross the river by boat, our own boat, to say we were on the Volga herself."

I thought this a grand, if peculiar, idea. We made a U-turn and trundled back across the bridge to the north side. There, on mud flats that had dried into big ridges churned up by tractor tires, we unstrapped the boat and its oars from the roof, and slipped it into the water. Karel told the nameless hitchhiker with the fishing rod to drive back across the Volga to the south side, where he should wait for us. I was dubious about this. All my gear — all my clothes, my camera, my Marlboros, all my maps and books, were in the trunk. What if he simply kept on going? But I said nothing. By making a fuss I would have lost anyway, and might have put ideas into his head. The notion never seemed to occur to Karel. The car disappeared, we clambered into the boat, and pushed off.

The pale brown water was moving strongly, making small sucking sounds at the bridge pylons, but Karel was a strong rower and had no difficulty making a direct crossing. The traffic thundered past overhead; the underside of the bridge was made of crumbling concrete and rusting iron, as bridges always seem to be, and everything smelled dank, like a disused latrine. The water of the Volga looked turbid and dirty. All in all, this wasn't the most romantic spot for a crossing. As he rowed Karel started to laugh, a delighted, joyous laugh, and tried a rendition of "Volga Boatmen."

> *Go down to the Volga*
> *That great Russian river*
> *Over whose waters*
> *A-groaning doth go*
>
> *The burlaki are hauling*
> *With a sigh and a shiver*
> *Towing and tugging*
> *And chanting heave-ho!*

He stopped the boat at a pylon, hauled in the oars and tried to stand up. I told him not to be an idiot. I can't row worth a damn, and I didn't want to try fishing him out of the river while keeping the boat steady. He subsided, but he was grinning like a madman. "Come on," he said, "let's sing the whole thing . . ."

"I don't know the words," I said.

"Well, make a noise then, and sing the chorus," he said. "I've always wanted to do this." He lowered his voice to a parody of a grumbling baritone and, still clinging to the bridge pylon, the truck traffic still thundering by overhead, in the middle of the murky flow, he began to sing:

> *Yo heave-ho!*
> *Yo heave-ho!*
> *All together once again*
> *Yo heave-ho!*
> *Yo heave-ho!*
> *Once again and yet again*
> *Haul the barge, brothers, haul*
> *Bend your shoulders to the line*
> *Ai da da-ai da*
> *Ai da da-ai da*
> *Bend your shoulders to the line*
> *Haul the barge, brothers, haul*
> *Yo heave-ho*
> *Yo heave-ho . . .*

By this time I had the hang of the Yo heave-ho's and joined in, somewhat timidly. My voice sounded hollow in the echo chamber of the crumbling superstructure above:

> *Once again and yet again*
> *As along the shore we run*
> *Sing our chorus in the sun*
> *Ai da da-ai da*
> *Ai da da-ai da* .
> *Sing our chorus in the sun*

> *Volga, Mother River, dear*
> *Sing our chorus in the sun*
> *Yo heave-ho!*
> *Yo heave-ho!*

Now Karel was hardly a *burlak*, an old-time Volga boatman; the *burlaki* were roustabouts and tramps, they were runaway serfs, or free peasants with an anarchic streak; they slept on their rafts and barges and stopped at villages to buy or steal food; they were legendary tale-tellers, and villagers often provided for them in exchange for strange tales of faraway places. Karel was just a Moscow cab driver, portly and middle-aged, a man used to the lies and small illegalities that are survival skills in the great capital. He was back in his blue polyester suit, and it was shinier than ever; he was impossible to think of as a figure of legend. But there was a wellspring of joy in him as he sang these famous words, a sense of connection with the past that I envied. After we finished we just sat there, the brown water sliding by beneath, grinning madly at each other.

The car was waiting for us at the assigned spot on the far side, and we strapped the boat back on the roof without saying a further word.

We reached the city of Tver a little after nine at night. (It was still called Kalinin — it wasn't to lose the name it acquired in 1931 until later that summer.) This small industrial city, at the junction of the Volga and the Tvertsa Rivers, lies on the Moscow-Leningrad railroad and is traversed by several main highways; it's the terminus of regular commercial navigation on the Volga. There are several hotels in Tver, but I was uncertain whether to try them, since officially I wasn't here. The Central Hotel, run by Intourist, was located opposite a pretty little park containing a small palace used as a way-station by Catherine the Great on her frequent trips from St. Petersburg to Moscow. I decided to avoid it. Intourist hotels are usually full, at least to those without some gray-market pull, and they always demand passport and visa. The other hotels, outside Intourist's orbit, I could probably persuade my way into through the liberal use of *valyuta*, but I'd experienced hotels like them before, and I'd pay to stay away from them. Another solution presented itself as we drove into the city; we passed signs pointing to "Motel Camping Tver." This campground proved well suited to our purpose. We rented a small cabin, and there was an outdoor shower, which consisted of a hose clamped to a tree branch, more or less surrounded by canvas screens. The "drain" was the good earth, not so good after years of cheap Soviet soap. But the weather was sticky hot, and we enjoyed the cold Volga water pouring over our bodies.

I stayed in the cabin to make notes, while Karel disappeared to find food.

After a while I went out to explore. The other campers were mostly Russians, though there was a young couple from New Zealand who'd made their way overland from Burma, of all places, and a group of "Christian musicians" (their own phrase for themselves) from England, who were traveling across the European part of the Soviet Union in a small bus, giving concerts and attempting conversions. With what luck?

"Oh, tremendous," said a scrubbed young woman. "There's tremendous receptivity to the Gospel message here, especially among young people."

"Are you Orthodox?" I asked.

"No, we're Wesleyans," she said. "But what we are doesn't matter. It's the message that counts."

I declined an invitation to join them in the morning for a breakfast concert and prayer meeting, and returned to Karel in our cabin. He'd purchased several cucumbers, a tin of sprats, a pickle jar of beer and a fresh loaf of dense white bread, almost as heavy as wood. He also brought back with him several tea glasses and an umbrella, though it hadn't rained for days. Why the umbrella? "They were there," he said, reflecting the Soviet shoppers' credo — get 'em while you can, because you can never tell when they'll return. The umbrella's packaging had been ripped off in the store. The clerk opened it for Karel's inspection, as was customary: no Soviet shopper ever leaves a store with his purchase unless he's first made sure it works. Really skeptical shoppers have been known to search for the date of manufacture stamped on the merchandise, hoping that it wouldn't be the end of the month, when factories are struggling to meet their quota without sufficient raw materials, or the beginning, when the workers haven't yet worked off their hangovers from celebrating the previous quota.

After supper we drove downtown and parked on the embankment on the left side, opposite the city proper. Every Volga town has its river terminal and its embankment, where young couples stroll up and down eating ice cream, thinking young couples' thoughts. We sat for a while under a 25-foot bronze statue of the explorer Afanasi Nikitin, who — thirty years before the Portuguese explorer Vasco da Gama rounded the Cape of Good Hope and made it to the Indies — outfitted an expedition via the Volga, the Caspian Sea and the central Asian deserts, returning with a great fortune, several tall tales and permanent favorite-son status. The statue is near the juncture of the Volga and the Tvertsa Rivers, where the Tver fortress had once stood.

The fortress has gone now, not a wall left standing.

The German tanks rolled through Tver on their way to the heartland, and when they were done the Russian tanks rolled back, and when *they* were done three-quarters of the city's buildings were gone and the rest were in ruins, the inhabitants picking over the rubble to salvage what they could. The Tver fortress, built on the left bank of the Volga to guard the old trade routes, had been considered impregnable and had stood for centuries imperturbable and impassive, but it was no match for the evil technology of modern warfare. The city was rebuilt, of course, to conform with Stalin's manic determination for industry and for defensibility, and in that atmosphere, aesthetics got short shrift.

So much history, so many centuries, reduced to shards, to fragments of legend, by army after army, by the Huns and the Poles and the Tartars and the Nazis, leaving behind only the sour taste of patriotic bile . . . Standing beside some of the last remaining ancient stones, the Church of the White Trinity of Ivan the Terrible, I could feel the blood seeping from the mortar and the dead weight of the years, and I got a sudden chill, a sense of foreboding, as if Tver were not finished with history, just yet.

The sense of foreboding was justified. The next day, just before lunch on a sunny summer morning, in the square surrounding the

Obelisk of Victory, I ran headlong into a screaming mob carrying placards and waving banners, cordoned off from a crowd by surly militiamen. Many of them were wearing black shirts, in a sinister echo from the European past. Most had patriotic symbols pinned to their chests, and military medals. This was a "demonstration" by Pamyat, the proto-fascist, pan-Slavist, anti-Semitic, anti-Western zealots of the fringe right.

Who are these people? Glasnost had liberated thought in Russia; but among the thousand flowers that bloomed were deadly variants, hothouse mutants rooted in the humus of perceived inferiority. The zealots of Pamyat are trying to come to terms with their terrible history, and as they've so often done before, they are blaming outsiders, "cosmopolitans" (a euphemism for those who indulge in the corrupting power of free thinking) and Jews. Only a few months before, there'd been an uproar at a meeting of the Union of Writers when the executive refused to do Pamyat's bidding in "officially approving" anti-Semitism; some writers were beaten by thugs in the union hall. The previous year Pamyat had called for a pogrom just after May Day. This pogrom never took place, but Pamyat's summons accelerated the lineups of Jews for exit visas.

In its modern variant, the Slavophile movement dates back to the early 1830s, to the aftermath of the Napoleonic invasion of the Motherland. The debate had been precipitated by a letter by Petr Khadayev, published in 1836 in a short lived oppositionist journal. This letter drew a merciless picture of Russia's intellectual and moral poverty — a picture of a country with no past worth the name, no present, no future; a country where the people were invisible; a country of despots with secondhand ideas. "We are not of the West or of the East, and we have the traditions of neither . . . With us, new ideas sweep away the old because they do not spring out of them."

This letter set off a great debate between the Westernizers and the Slavophiles. The Slavophiles sought a meaning for Russian history. They also turned away from "the miserable want of content" of bureaucratic Russia of the time, turned away from the West in patriotic contempt and resentment, and sought out instead those elements that had inspired Christian brotherhood, among which they counted the village community of the Slavic countryside, with its clannish interdependence.

All the foreigners who came to the country — and they needed foreigners because Russia was still so backward — were freer, better paid and better educated than the natives, and this stirred more patriotic resentment. The Slavonic scholar Yuri Krizhanich wrote of them, "They lead us by the nose, sit on our backs and ride on us, calling us pigs and hounds, think that they are like gods and we like fools." He wished to implant in the Russians a sense of self-worth; he felt they were too easygoing, too easily fooled, had no pride or spirit. The Slavophile propagandists imagined a sacred and unique mission for a Russia cut off from Europe, and maintained the spiritual superiority of Mother Russia over other nations.

One branch of the modern movement looks to the peasants for salvation, as did the *narodniki*, the nineteenth-century rural populists. In this sense, Solzhenitsyn is a Slavophile: Russia cannot be saved except by turning back to the moral force of the rural peasantry, using it to counteract the dissolution caused by urbanism and foreign influences. There's also a more sinister variant, one that harks back to the "pure bloodline" of Rurik the Viking, and whose political ideas can be traced directly to Ivan the Terrible, Peter the Great and Stalin the Monster. Later I was to see, in one of the many Motherland Clubs where the Slavophiles gather, a reprint from one of Stalin's speeches from the 1930s. I kept a copy. Wrote the tyrant:

> It's sometimes asked whether it's possible to slow down a bit in tempo, to retard the movement [to socialism and modernity]. No, comrades, this is impossible! It's impossible to reduce the tempo! On the contrary, it's necessary to accelerate it! To slacken the tempo means to fall behind. And the backward are always beaten. But we do not want to be beaten. No, we do not want this! The history of Old Russia is the history of defeats due to backwardness.
> She was beaten by the Mongol Khans.
> She was beaten by the Turkish beys.
> She was beaten by the Swedish feudal barons.
> She was beaten by the Polish-Lithuanian squires.

She was beaten by the Anglo-French capitalists.
She was beaten by the Japanese warlords.
All beat her for her backwardness — for military backwardness, for governmental backwardness, for industrial
backwardness. She was beaten because to beat her was prof-
itable and could be done with impunity . . . Such is the law of
capitalism — to beat the backward and the weak.

My journalist friends in Moscow had warned me about Pamyat.
Short of perestroika simply withering away, disappearing from lack
of achievement and general apathy, a coup could happen in only
two ways in this country, they'd said — by a revolution from below,
or by a strike from the right. "There is, after all, a yearning for the
despotic simplicities of Stalin. It is always a horrible temptation for
the men of Center," which is what everyone calls Moscow. Even
the zealots admit there was terror and hardship under Stalin, but
they believe there was also idealism, a belief that the hardship was
endured for a purpose, that it was leading somewhere. Pamyat
looks back to the days when workers put in a full day's work and
accomplished genuinely heroic feats, and compares the single-
minded purpose of those days with the sloth, drunkenness and
corruption of the present. And when they speak of shops stocked
with goods, even caviar, goods that people could afford, they tap a
rich vein of discontent. The primary purpose of Stalin's cruel
wrenching of society, the Pamyat line says, was not terror for its
own sake, or even for the sake of national discipline, but the
"desire to escape backwardness, to lift the country by the bootstraps, to protect it against invasion, to become invulnerable."
Not surprisingly, the nostalgia of the right is for the pre-
Revolutionary days, the simple days that exist only in romantic
imagination — visions of happy families sitting in a meadow drinking
tea from the family samovar . . . Pamyat wants Russia to rediscover
its Russian past, and in the confusion caused by the sclerosis of
Marxist thought and the bewildered rediscovery of Communist corruption, they have few real opponents. Their opponents, after all,
lack a coherent vision of their own — liberty is altogether too diffuse
an idea to serve as a political program, and the "market economy,"
while worthy, is not an idea to lift the national spirit.

Perhaps the ultra-nationalists will triumph; there are certainly Russians who believe in the possibility. But even in the summer of 1990, as the country seemed to be coming unraveled — as Gorbachev seemed, in the words of one of my journalist friends, to "be acting like a king who has not yet realized he has given away the kingdom" — it seemed to me unlikely. Despite Pamyat's many spreading branches, despite the many zealots of the right, the majority of the Soviet people have become more porous to dissenting ideas than at any previous time. For Russia once again to bend to a bully is no longer inevitable. Possible, yes. Russians have failed their history before, and the failures brought, in John le Carré's phrase, "another ice age of terrified monotony," and it could happen again. But inevitable? No. Or at least so it seemed to me, there in the Russian heartland.

The zealots surrounded the Victory obelisk, screaming obscenities at the restraining militia. I caught a slogan on a placard as it was twitched by, a sickening reminder of Pamyat's real business: "Down With the Rootless Cosmopolites!" it said, a reference to the Jews from Stalin's dire days. The banner contained a pictograph of Saint George the dragon-slayer, historically a symbol of both Russian courage and the pogrom. This demonstration was "permitted." Why? No one really knows; the Moscow intellectuals believed Pamyat has high backing in the Party, not so much because the bureaucracy likes their ideas as because it wants to use the zealots as a threat, a warning of what will happen if perestroika is taken too far too fast . . . Pamyat, they believed, was being held over the reformers' heads like a club. I didn't subscribe to this theory. It seemed to me more likely that Pamyat and disillusionment had a symbiotic attachment — one grew as the other did, and both would shrink if the country's problems diminished.

One of the demonstrators broke away from the crowd, through the militia line. He was shrieking. In the middle of the road he smashed his placard on the ground, stamped on it. "Blood and water!" he was yelling. "Blood and water!" He picked up a broken brick and hurled it as far as he could into the Volga. He fell to the ground, weeping, beating his head with what remained of his placard.

"What did he mean," I asked a bystander, "with this stuff about blood and water?"

"How the hell should I know? They're all crazy."

"He means the Volga," another person said. "They think we should fill our veins with the Volga's water, to give Russians courage."

"That's crazy!"

"Yes, of course. But that's how they think. Better we should pour *their* blood into the Volga, get rid of them."

Karel wouldn't talk about the demonstration. He just shook his head. "They shouldn't allow such things," he said. "This is not right. It only makes things worse." But he wouldn't go on.

We walked back to the motel for lunch. No one there seemed interested either. They refused to discuss it. They didn't want to think about Pamyat. They wanted to talk about the new "law of emigration" that was expected soon — the opening of the Russian borders. Did they themselves want to leave the country? No, not really. "But we should let foreigners come in and see for themselves we aren't bad people," said one man, a welder from Orel. "We like foreigners. The more the better. As long as they bring their beer with them . . ."

That afternoon I bought a book about the Kalinin district at a kiosk in the inevitable Lenin Square (there's one in every town). It was cheap, in full color, lots of nice pictures and empty of any real information. I wondered who it was for. Tourists could learn little from it, and local people didn't need it. Of course, in the "command economy," as centralized planning has come to be called, things are not necessarily "for" anyone. There's a plan to be fulfilled — so many books, so much paper, so many people doing so many days of work. There's no shortage of photographers willing to spend a month or two on the road on assignment, and if the price is to include a few snaps of local bigwigs, who'll argue? So there are inevitably pictures of the local brass inspecting some benighted factory, or sitting in their offices receiving Important Guests.

And the text? The text is almost always boilerplate from the canons of Socialist Realist "writing," phrases that, in George Orwell's wonderful expression, are "tacked together like sections of a prefabricated henhouse." Then the thing is printed and distributed. No one buys it. Why should they? They are saving their money for the bootlegged copies of works of real writers being sold at little folding tables in pedestrian underpasses.

There's still nothing more dispiriting than a visit to a Soviet bookstore — even now that popular writers have been uncensored, and exiled writers are coming home to tumultuous welcomes. There are shelves after shelves of massive tomes no one wants to read, including the assembled speeches of the current leaders — the collected *pensées* of Mikhail Gorbachev. Brezhnev's assembled orations have long been pulped, but others have come to replace them on the shelves, big, heavy, boring, turgid, replete with the all-or-nothing imagery of Leninism, unreadable and unread. Why do they print this stuff, when there's a paper shortage? So the leaders can say, "I have so many million copies in print"? Surely they know no one reads them. Aren't they embarrassed? Self-importance accounts for much of it, of course. But part of the answer, surely, is fear — fear of the future, fear of the angry masses, fear of retribution for betrayal . . . For decades Soviet leaders have diverted criticism by invoking the hypnotic effect of the Great Dream, and as the promised future slipped into the past, they needed to keep alive the people's trust in delayed benefits. Thus, from the 1930s on, Soviet writers were ordered to treat the present as though it did not exist and the glorious future as if it had already arrived; this literary and artistic device became known as Socialist Realism.

At the other end of the bookstore are the textbooks — approved works on chemical engineering and *The Biology of Aquatic Species of Russian Lakes in the Post-glacial Moraine* . . . Not very lively stuff, but necessary enough. I don't know how good these texts are. There's been severe criticism of many of them in the Soviet press as being out of date, written by hacks appointed by privilege, misleading and ideologically driven.

Textbooks have always been a problem for Soviet academics. In the Stalin years, free-thinkers got shot, and Khrushchev, for instance, was prone to believing in crackpot theories (and in the world of democratic centralism, what the Leader believes, everyone perforce must believe). For many years sociology was a null discipline in the Soviet Union, since scientific Marxism made it redundant. As late as the mid-Seventies I had a friend who toiled away in the American Canadian Institute in Moscow because he couldn't put his real training to use. He was a criminologist — but of course there was no crime in the Soviet Union, except that committed by the remnants of the bourgeois classes, so his specialty didn't officially exist except in documents internally circulated in "police circles." The police of course had no illusions, but in public they did what their masters told them. Perhaps those simple-minded days are over, but it wouldn't do to count on it.

What else can be found in the bookshops? The approved heroes, to be sure, Mikhail Sholokhov (*Quiet Flows the Don*) and others. A few Western writers. Hemingway and Faulkner are not uncommon. The classics: Tolstoy, Turgenev, Pushkin. A few popular modern writers, but their books don't last long in the stores; they're printed in small editions and never reissued, despite the obvious demand; consumer wishes have nothing to do with it. There are also picture books and maps, which is where we came in.

Entirely lacking is the notion of a popular literature, of reading for entertainment. This is not because, as many Western writers naively believe, Russians take their writers more seriously than we do. (If they did so at one point, it was because the Russian people had no other mirror in which to scrutinize themselves, and learned for a while to rely utterly on their writers; but those days are gone). Yevtushenko has a marvelous image for this secret life of Russian literature: "The lines of verse fluttered like butterflies trapped in a bellows. But as soon as the pressure eased for an instant, the butterflies, which had seemed dead, flew up into the air." Now, however, the bookstores are necropolises, where only dead ideas are to be found.

If there's no popular literature in the Western sense, what do people actually read? Newspapers and magazines play a much larger role in Russia than they do in the West: how many times have I seen a young person in a park or on the subway or buses reading *Novy Mir* (New World) or one of the other literary magazines, because they publish writing that deals with real things that people really want to know? The people read magazines, and devour newspapers and borrowed copies of hard-to-find books.

We set off to return to Moscow, rejoining the Leningrad highway. I looked back at Tver, and saw an endless series of dumpy white apartment buildings and, in the distance, a small golden dome of a church left mysteriously whole after centuries of destruction.

I remembered that Adam Olearius, the German traveler who passed through Russia on his way to Baghdad, crossed the Volga at Tver. Olearius was secretary and adviser to the Grand Duke of Holstein, and traveled with the Duke's ambassadors. He first published his reminiscences in English in 1662 (*The Voyages and Travels of the Ambassadors from the Duke of Holstein to the Great Duke of Muscovy and the King of Persia*). He passed through "in March, very cold, we traveled easily on the ice." In town, Olearius attended a wedding of an eleven-year-old girl and reported that marriages of children were very common: "Often widows marry young orphans, so they can keep their property." He reported that he passed "many monasteries, also a surprising number of taverns along the way, after which islands and even towns have been named."

Tver was always a restless city, with an anarchic streak. In 1327 Chol-Khan, a cousin of the ruling family, came with the usual Tartar arrogance and violence to collect tribute in Tver. The Tverians rebelled and killed him, along with all his followers. The Slavic leader and Tartar toady Ivan I of Moscow (known to history as Ivan Moneybags) enlisted fifty thousand Tartars and put the city to the torch; Alexander, Tver's ruler, was murdered. In disgust at their city's ineptitude, many of the local noblemen considered Tver a lost cause and joined Moscow.

The anarchy persisted through the centuries. In 1862 Tver became a hotbed of "liberal" thought, and demanded responsible finance, independent law courts and a national assembly. No one paid any attention then, and, essentially, no one has yet.

And now? The air of Tver is thick with rancor. There are strikes, petty revolts, work-to-rule campaigns . . . So many troubles. Ivan I, Chol-Khan, the black-shirted fanatics of Pamyat, centuries of anger and turmoil . . . I looked at Karel, who was whistling cheerfully to himself, on his way home to his wife and the feast she had prepared. I shook my head. The history was taking hold of my heart.

I turned away from the past and looked to the days ahead. Tonight, Karel would be at home, and I would endure another grim stay at the Izmailovo before heading tomorrow for the Northern River Terminal to join the crew of the *Novosti*. I was looking forward to meeting them. The group had settled down to five, girlfriends not included, Valentin had told me in Moscow. The plan was for the *Novosti Express* to head off without me to the town of Uglich, 70 kilometers or so away at the other end of the Moscow-Volga Canal. Our voyage would formally begin there. Why? There was less chance of a fuss with the authorities about travel documents in a small port, he said. I found this prudence somewhat reassuring. But . . . how was I to get to Uglich?

"Take the *Rus*, of course."

"And then just not show up for the *Rus*'s second day of sailing? Won't they . . . miss me?"

"Don't worry so much," Valentin said impatiently.

I was mulling over this cavalier attitude to my own safety when we reached the suburbs of Moscow.

Leningrad

Novgorod

Volgoverkhovye

Kalinin
(Tver)

Uglich

Yaroslavl

Dubna

VOLGA

Rzhov

MOSCOW-VOLGA
CANAL

MOSCOW

CHAPTER 4

Kilometer 594

Dubna
(The Moscow-Volga Canal)

T he Northern River Terminal was built in the grandiose Stalin style but is elegant for all that. It's an imposing building with an impressive spire, but inside there's nothing much. There's an information device from which a disembodied voice issues. There's a café that is permanently closed, a post office that's never open and signs pointing to offices that are always locked. The port itself is busy with passenger boats of all kinds, small excursion boats, larger cruise liners, sleek hydrofoils called Raketas that are used almost as commuter boats by the people who live by the river: Raketa stops are located every 10 kilometers or so, and it's theoretically possible, by using short hops, to travel to the end of the river, 3,000 kilometers away. It would take a while, of course — the Raketas average 40 kilometers an hour — but it could be done. Outside the terminal building, there's an excursion board giving the departure times for various cities. Where specific boats were moored, no one seemed to know.

The taxi I took from the Izmailovo decanted me at the main terminal building. There was no sign of the *Rus* or the *Novosti*. I asked the disembodied voice of the squawkbox where it was, and it answered something incomprehensible. My Russian depends heavily on gesture and expression, and it was disconcerting to be talking to a box. I wasn't alone in my frustration; no one else seemed to be able to understand it either. A Russian woman standing in the line wanted to know when the boat for Gorky left, and got in response a tirade from the tinny loudspeaker. We both gave up. I began to worry. What if Valentin didn't show? If the *Rus*'s voyage had, after all, been canceled? I'd be stuck without papers, without a place to stay, without a way of getting downriver . . . Shouldering my bag, I wandered back outside, where I spotted what looked like a sailor getting out of a battered Moskvich car, and asked him if he knew where the *Rus* was berthed. He didn't, but asked a knot of young men standing at the entrance. Pier 16, one of them said, about a kilometer down the quay. Greatly relieved, I trudged off, my cumbersome bags over my shoulder.

I checked into the *Rus*, which turned out to be a pleasant, well-run ship, almost fanatically tidy, and staffed by people who wanted to be helpful. I found my assigned cabin and dumped my bag, then wandered back onto the dockside. Someone was supposed to meet me there.

Valentin was waiting a short distance away, by a news kiosk.

"It's all set," he said. He shuffled his feet a little, and paused. "I should tell you that . . . well, I'm not actually going along."

"What! This whole thing was your idea!"

He shuffled uncomfortably. "I know, but I just can't, not now. Listen, there's too much going on here, I've got a stack of assignments, I'm a reporter, after all, there's too much work to do." Maggie Thatcher was in town, the Supreme Soviet was debating a bill on freedom of the press. All in all, he just couldn't bring himself to leave town now. He suggested that the enthusiasm of the others was also disappearing rapidly — Boris Yeltsin's compelling harangues before the delegates of the Russian Federation, and his attempts to wrench Russians to his will, were much more absorbing than the notion of a quiet few weeks on the Volga; the Volga would still be there next year. Rumors were floating around town that Gorbachev would quit or be forced out, there were rumors of a new party — there were rumors everywhere. He tried to be reassuring: "The boat will proceed all right; there are enough who want to go."

The rest of the "crew" came down the quay. Even before the introductions, it was clear that they were annoyed with Valentin. Indeed, the whole thing had been his idea — it was he who had got them interested in the first place. Valentin introduced them. Anton, in Valentin's absence, was to become something close to our leader. He was a tall, fair-haired, amiable man who worked as a cultural reporter for one of Moscow's more liberal newspapers. Volya, the taciturn one, kept us going; he was the only one who knew anything about boats and motors. He said little, listened a lot and sang songs when he was drunk, which fortunately wasn't very often. His beat was industry. Vladimir looked like a worker — a broken face deeply pocked, black hair slicked back, even a tattoo, badly done and smudged, of a Soviet navy emblem. He had a desk job at one of the bigger papers. George (not Georgii — "my mother was an Anglophile") was fey, very quick and sarcastic. He had pale sandy hair. Vasilii, the last of the crew, was a poet and litterateur who possessed a deep baritone, talked boomingly loud, was considerably overweight, ate exceedingly well (or at least hugely), had an intelligent opinion on everything and reminded me somewhat of a poet I know in Canada. George and Vasilii were also on the culture beat.

All five were people with strong opinions, as I discovered during our voyage. Politically, they were reformers to a man, referring to themselves as democrats, or "part of the democratic opposition." From their talk, I assumed they were Yeltsinites; they were skeptical of Gorbachev's reformist bona fides and analyzed his every speech for ideological backsliding. They all shared the one fault the Russian intelligentsia seem to have universally in common: they had plenty of theories about rural life, most of them wrong. None of them knew what life on a farm was like, but they all *knew* how it should be fixed. What they thought of me was unclear. I was optimistic. I thought we could get on.

Anton had his girlfriend, Viktoria, on the dockside with him. She was a lean blonde with too much makeup, as fast-moving as a minnow, quick with a quip. She was still trying to wheedle herself on board, but the others had vetoed it.

For the moment, we left unsolved the problem of what to do about the *Rus* — since I was supposed to go to Uglich on the *Rus*,

I repeated my suspicion that its crew would become alarmed if one of their passengers abruptly disappeared after one day on board. Again I was told: Don't worry, we'll work it out.

The boat, about which they'd been so mysterious and vague for so long, was moored half a kilometer down the quay, and we walked down in the brilliant sunshine to take a look. The first sight was a bad shock. It looked something like a small gunboat, or at least an official naval or militia boat of some kind.

"Not so surprising," Valentin said. "That's what it was — a militia boat."

"Was?"

"Now retired," he said blandly.

I inquired no further. How the boat was "rescued" from its internment, I didn't know. It was about 50 feet long and seemed to have no markings except a white number painted on the hull near the bow, white on gunmetal gray, which was its basic color. The only relief from the gray was the decks, painted a nice Communist red, and the life preservers, similarly. There was a serious-looking searchlight mounted on the bridge, and what looked suspiciously like a harpoon on the foredeck. No one seemed to know what this was. The tires hanging over the side as fenders were Pirellis, which was odd since you can't buy Pirellis in the Soviet Union.

Who was in charge? Anton, as I'd thought? No one seemed to know that either. Volya was something of an amateur mechanic and had been down in the hold, tinkering with the motor. It was he who had "obtained" the fuel for the boat, and who had arranged for a further supply downriver. We elected him captain while he was downstairs. All the Russians spoke good English, and after an hour or so, while we tested our relative fluency, we developed a pattern: they'd talk in Russian until I asked for a clarification, in which case they'd give it in English. I'd generally talk in English until they asked for an explanation.

There was a radio blaring down in the hold, tuned to Radio Moscow's International Service, in English. Alannah Myles finished her song and the DJ yelled, "It's party time in Moscow!" I started to laugh, wondering what Leonid Brezhnev would have made of *that*, or the puritans in the Ideological Office of the Central Committee of the Communist Party, who of course had more important matters to worry about now, like, Whither Communism? All this was rather too complicated to explain. Volya turned the thing off while we looked around.

Inside, the boat was more reassuring. Ten bunks in three compartments, a comfortable lounge and a well-stocked bar. The galley looked efficient, even if most of the food was in tins. My contribution to all this, they had already explained, was to show up with several crates of Western beer, which I could get from a *valyuta* store in town. As discussed, Lowenbrau was to be preferred, thank you. Offer the cab driver a couple of cans, they said. Better than a fare any day (I did this later, and he insisted on drinking them en route). Most of the business end of the boat seemed to be up front; at the stern, two large holds, empty, with wooden racks on the bulkheads that smelled faintly of gasoline. Viktoria was still making her pitch to Anton on the deck as I examined the interior, and by the time I rejoined them she was looking surly. "They won't let me go," she said. "I wouldn't be in the way, but they won't let me. Russian men are all the same, they're all babies, they're all afraid women will spoil their fun. We're all so behind the times in this country." She looked to me for support. I said nothing. It didn't seem a fruitful time to argue.

They were to leave within a few hours up-canal to the town of Uglich. From Uglich, the plan was, we'd journey by easy stages to Kazan, stopping wherever and whenever we felt like it. At Kazan, they were all going to fly home to Moscow, and I'd either join them or go on to Ulyanovsk, another hundred or so kilometers further downriver, since that was what my visa allowed me to do. What was to happen to the boat in Kazan? They were vague, and I had the feeling they really didn't know. How would I find them in Uglich? Someone would find me, don't worry. And we'll fix it with the *Rus* so no one worries about you. Don't worry.

But I did worry. And it was just as well. None of this worked out the way anyone planned.

The *Novosti Express* departed before the *Rus*. I took my leave of the others, formally shaking hands all round, and went back to the *Rus*, leaning on the impeccable railing to watch them chug up the reservoir towards the entrance to the canal proper. To my surprise, Valentin and Viktoria were sitting on a hatch near the bow.

One of the others waved, and I waved back. The boat sounded reassuringly throaty, as if the motor would get where it wanted to go. It rode low in the water, pushing instead of cutting through; it was a boat without grace, but it looked quite functional. I was looking forward to joining the others.

The weather on the day the *Rus* departed from Moscow was wonderful. There was a summer warmth to the sun, with a cool breeze. It had been raining and cold for three days; now the sun was out, and the vegetation along the banks of the reservoir that made up the Moscow terminal was lush, with the fresh greens of early summer. The terminal, in Stalin's grand style, is set in a large unkempt park, surrounded by a fence with the symbol of the Soviet Union set into the wrought iron at intervals. The park itself stretched for several kilometers along the right bank of the canal ("right" if you're heading north to the Volga, as we were). Further south, about a kilometer from the terminal, was the lock that both created this reservoir and gave access to the Moscow River itself. The terminal basin was about 500 meters across and was crowded with powerboats of all kinds — no yachts or sailing vessels. I knew yacht clubs existed in Moscow, but there were no sailboats to be seen.

On the far shore of the basin was an apparently endless array of fifteen- to twenty-floor apartment buildings, each one massive in scale, the Soviet response to the housing crunch. I had spent an hour or two poking about this neighborhood in a taxi. The buildings were set a hundred yards or so apart, and separated by what was presumably supposed to be park but was generally a tangle of weeds and scrub bushes, pleasant enough in summer but bleak in winter. Each massive building had one or at most two large stores on the ground floor, either a department store that had virtually nothing in it, or a *gastronom* (food store), ditto, or a hairdresser's (there seemed to be no end of those). Every few buildings there was a post office, a pharmacy and fruit shops, whose shelves were bare except for canned apple juice. In every fourth or fifth complex there was a meat and fish shop, or a housewares shop stocking a bizarre and apparently random selection of goods, from fish steamers to pliers.

Shopping in the Soviet Union, even in the capital, is in any case a dispiriting experience, with the economy in chaos, the lineups getting longer and the shortages more pervasive. This kind of urban planning only made it worse. North American planners have been critical of the shopping mall solution to urban organization, but at least the mall is efficient; to shop in Moscow takes endless amounts of time — just to get from the bread shop to the butcher can take half an hour of trudging across acres of unprotected open space. Like so much Soviet planning, it seemed almost perverse in its imposed difficulty.

The water of the reservoir was placid, brown with silt, with no discernible current. The surrounding landscape was attractive in a slow-moving, bucolic way; the banks of the canal were gently sloped, and where there were no buildings birch forests stretched to the horizon. We reached true countryside only a few minutes after leaving Moscow; the *Rus* was a quiet vessel, its motors a gentle hum, and as I leaned on the railing near the prow I could clearly hear songbirds in the woods. Every few kilometers there was a sandy beach, crowded with bathers on this Sunday after-noon. Most of the people were sunning themselves; few were actually swimming.

The *Rus* is part of an organization called Rechflot (River Fleet), a muscular bureaucracy that seems to be in good working order — as good as, or better than, its Western equivalents. It runs freight and passenger ships on the Volga, the Neva and its canals, the Dnieper, the Oka, the Black and Caspian Seas, and all the way to Murmansk on the White Sea, and includes such oddities as the hydrofoil on the northern Karelian lakes, which goes to the museum island of Kizhi from Petrozavodsk. Rechflot is trying to update itself in the era of perestroika; it has taken to leasing ships directly to foreign tourist organizations, thus evading Intourist, which is reduced to subcontracting minor functions, such as pro-viding tour guides in the various ports of call, translation services on board and troubleshooting for foreigners who naively thought things worked here just as they did in the West.

Rechflot operates tourist traffic on a massive scale, but river tourism itself dates back to pre-Revolutionary days. I have a copy

of the busy 1910 schedules, listing regular tours on the Volga and
the Don. My 1926 Volga region guidebook describes tours ranging
from two days to a month, all the way down to Astrakhan. In 1990
Rechflot carried nearly six million Russians on cruises and holidays, most of them arranged by enterprises or unions as a reward,
in the Leninist cliché, for "contributions to Socialist Construction."
(Though this phrase has now vanished from Rechflot's lexicon; the
words "aerobics" and "bingo" are now more commonly heard on
board, if truth be told.)

A German tourist, Otto Keller, who in 1914 published a book in
English called *A Guide to St. Petersburg and Other Chief Towns of
Russia*, had this advice for foreign visitors:

> To see pictures of pure rural Russia one cannot do better
> than to make a tour on the largest river in Europe, Mother
> Volga . . . Very quaint is the view of some towns from the
> steamer. Their center uses [*sic*] to consist of red-brick build-
> ings surrounded by wooden houses. High white churches
> with green or gilded roofs are ever dotted over these cities,
> and the wide main streets fall precipitously to the water's
> edge, looking from distance [*sic*] more like streams than
> roads. The inhabitants, belonging to different races of the
> Ural-Altai tribes which live promiscuously, offer much of
> interest. The river is covered with busy life. Tugs are slowly
> hauling whole fleets of barges upstream, and most pic-
> turesque are the immense barges of timber drifting down
> from the north; these are as big as little villages and on the
> top of them are the cottages in which the crews live on the
> long quiet voyages. Every few hours we meet another
> steamer like our own. At the many halting places there is
> much life. Mountains of merchandises are charged and dis-
> charged, masses of peasants with their belongings in great
> bundles, shout and push up and down the landing bridge.

I was curious to see how much of this description still held.
Certainly the "mountains of merchandise" sounded unlikely in this
era of shortages and rationing, but I was conscious of the endless
stream of barges and commercial boats steaming past the *Rus*.

Gorky worked as a roustabout on the river fleet. Chekhov took a Volga cruise for his honeymoon with Olga Knipper, the actress for whom he wrote *The Cherry Orchard*. Part of his regime on board was to take a *kumiss* cure — *kumiss* is fermented camel's or mare's milk, the staple of the nomad tribes of the lower Volga, and a cure for practically everything; Chekhov was already suffering from consumption. *Kumiss* sanatoriums still exist on the Volga shores, near the Samara Bend beyond Ulyanovsk.

The *Rus*, when full, carries about 350 passengers and almost 200 crew, so it's a boat of some heft. There are dozens like it plying Russia's rivers. At the river terminal I'd seen six or seven boats the same size picking up and discharging passengers. Most of these were, indeed, named after our Socialist Heroes: the *Maxim Gorky*, the *Lenin*, the *Yuri Gagarin* and others. Almost all the passengers were Soviet citizens.

A few berths away from the *Rus* an old paddlewheeler had been moored, the *Spartak*, the last of the pre-Revolutionary paddle-wheelers still plying the Volga, more than ninety years after it was built. Before we departed I went on board to check it out and took a few photographs of the pseudo-Empire dining salon, unchanged from the days when the boat was first commissioned. While I was peeking about the public rooms, one of the passengers, Yuri, from Ryazan, hauled me off to his cabin for a drink. He'd spotted me for a foreigner and wanted to show off a little. He toured me through the little cabin he shared with his wife, and the cabin next door where their three children slept. The cabins had no plumbing — communal showers and toilets were located on each deck. The cabins had intricately inlaid wooden cabinets, old-fashioned wooden shutters and ceiling fans for ventilation. I could happily have spent my time on the Volga cruising in such a boat.

Yuri had everything neatly set out, and he brought out a bottle and a couple of glasses and poured a stiff tumbler of Siberian vodka for each of us. With a penknife he cut a chunk of strongly garlicky kolbasa, and we chewed as we drank, becoming more and more sentimental about each other and our respective countries with each swig. I offered him cigarettes, but he was one of the few Russians I met who didn't smoke, and we settled on an exchange of souvenirs instead; I gave him an American quarter and he gave

me a lapel pin, a red hammer and sickle on a red star, the whole
set on a white-and-gold background; I'd seen something like it on
army officers, and he sheepishly admitted he'd acquired it from a
black marketeer back from Afghanistan.

Of the 350 available spots in the Rus, only about twenty were filled
by foreigners, mostly Americans. The rest of the passengers were
Russians, about a hundred of them — the boat was far from full.
Many of these Russians were in their late twenties or early thirties.

That evening in the bar of the ship there was another floor show,
very much like the one in the Hotel Izmailovo in Moscow, differing
only in details — the "girls" in this case, three peroxided blondes,
did a tawdry pseudo-lesbian number that simply embarrassed
everyone, though this was counterbalanced by an interesting
Russian bluegrass group, whose musicians wore shades and T-shirts
that said "BDA Blues Defense Initiative" in English on the back.
The performers at these shows are often surrounded by an assortment of hangers-on: the musicians and their entourages, of course,
and also bimbos in leather, fringe inhabitants of the entertainment
world. Where does the ship (the restaurant, the club) find these
people? I asked Boris, the American-Russian entrepreneur who
had chartered the *Rus* from Rechflot, and he shrugged. "There are
many of them," he said. "They're not hard to find. This is all free-
economy stuff, you understand. They all have jobs during the day,
but this is what they do for fun and profit." Later I was told that
many of the performers are graduates of the Central Circus School
in Moscow who'd failed the demanding acrobatic requirements
there, or who simply "preferred nightclubs to horseshit," as my
informant blandly put it. I bought the "girls" and the bluegrass
musicians a bottle of vodka in the ship's *valyuta* bar. I tried to find
out something about their lives, but they weren't much interested
in being questioned. They wanted to know how things worked in
the West — how much do bar bands get paid? Who writes their
music? Can anyone sing anything they please, or is the material
copyright? Since I know nothing of these matters they soon lost
interest and made a direct assault on a group of hard-drinking
Russians in the corner, who'd crashed the *valyuta* bar by the simple
expedient of bringing their own vodka with them from their cabins.

In the lounge afterward a group of young people were drinking silently in a corner, by a window overlooking the reservoir. Many of them were beefy young men. As the evening progressed they got noisier, in the way groups in bars do, and occasionally women joined them, wives and girlfriends. The men drank many toasts, but clinked glasses only half-heartedly with the women; they grew emotional, and touched one another in the way men do when they want to express emotion but don't know how and don't want to appear gay. They'd rub each other's shoulders, or pat each other's backs. I finally asked someone who they were.

"Oh," he said, looking over at them affectionately, in a proprietary way. "They're firefighters from Chernobyl."

The cruise ship was not full, and Boris, as a gesture, had padded the lists with Chernobyl veterans. Some of the men on board had been in the first wave, the village firemen sent in a few minutes after the explosion to put out the fire in the containment building; one young man, the one in the corner with brooding eyes, had been the third person in the building, forty minutes after the explosion.

"And he survived?" I asked, incredulous.

"There he is, Sergei, ask him."

Later, I did, and Sergei gave me a small pennant as a souvenir. On the triangular silk are printed pictures of six of his colleagues who died a few days after the event, and the words "For Their Heroism and Sacrifice." I found talking to the Chernobyl people awkward; my questions all seemed obvious and intrusive, but they didn't seem to mind. They were practiced in their responses and in the story they told about the disaster and their role in it — not in a venal propaganda way, but just because they'd been asked the same banal questions so many times: What was it *like*? What were you *feeling*? The anecdotes about radiation counters, about the heroism of their fellow workers, of the ones who died, of sickness and death, the careful descriptions of government silence and neglect and then, when the government finally admitted what had happened, of being swept up in the massive wave of national guilt and care that came too late. But beyond the practiced anecdotes there was still a deep uneasiness, which showed mostly in their restlessness, in the hopeless way their wives looked at them, in the

way they shied away from the one area they did not want to contemplate: the gnawing at their vitals by the deadly isotopes they
didn't want to name.

Only once in a long night of drinking did one of them let any of
this escape him. Just as the "girls" were finishing their second set,
their bare breasts jiggling as they bounced off the stage, he yelled
at me, "It's no good telling you anything! This is going to be with us
even after we are dead!" He gulped another glass of vodka and
turned away, and his wife leaned over, and a fellow firefighter put
an arm around his shoulder and shook him, and after a while he
was all right and rejoined the crowd. Later I spoke to the doctor
who was traveling with them; she told me more about what they'd
done, and the local bureaucrats' despicable attempt to blame the
disaster on "worker neglect" (instead, it had become clear later, the
engineers in charge had conducted unauthorized and unsafe
experiments), and how they'd put together a Chernobyl victims
group to press for more and better medical care — for more long-
term care, for better chemotherapy treatments — anything. What
had he meant by "after we are dead"?

The doctor was impatient. "It should be obvious," she said. "No
one knows what the radiation has done to them. Maybe nothing.
Or to their future children, or to their children's children. It's not
just them, you see," she said. "It's possible that it has tampered
with their genetic makeup, no one knows. No one knows anything
yet. It's possible it'll be with their descendants forever, if indeed
they have descendants any more."

"They look fine now," I said. "They still have their hair, they look
tanned and more or less fit."

"They are young, and strong," she said, "but they'll all die of
cancer. They know that."

She told me she had been present when the authorities were
forced to exhume the bodies of some of their colleagues. They had
to be reburied in lead-lined coffins: radiation was seeping from the
ground, a deadly frost.

A few days later, at a get-to-know-everyone meeting on the *Rus*,
she came back to this theme, and she read aloud a poem she'd
written, a very bad poem about peace and Jesus and the salvation
of the world, and she began to cry, and it was the turn of the young

men to comfort her. It's one of the interesting cultural sidelights that in the extremes of emotion Russians still often resort to poetry to express themselves. As Joseph Conrad once said, Russians love words "but don't hoard them up . . . they are always ready to pour them out. " I was thinking of this as she cried, and was slightly ashamed of my detachment.

Between Tver and the mouth of the Moscow-Volga Canal, the banks are low, the remnants of pre-glacial streams, and the land is marshy, in some parts covered by thick peat beds. The overall impression is one of weariness; this is a land that has been wrung of its nutrients and leeched of its potential, and that is now just tired, waiting for man to go away and leave it alone. But there are villages here too, and weedy pastures, and in the evenings, in the dying afterglow of a summer day, the white bell towers of ruined churches can be seen, and the flickering lights in the windows of lonely cottages, and the jingling bells of cattle can be heard across the water. Once, in an eerie echo of ancient times, we heard a shepherd's flute from the far bank, a brave and lonely sound from the Russian darkness.

Some 30 kilometers from Tver there are more burial mounds, hidden by a pine plantation. On the right bank nearby is the old city of Otrokivichi, once described as "the cradle of Russian cooperative cheese-making." There have recently been milk shortages in the region, and long lineups for butter, and cheese production has been curtailed. The town is now famous mostly because the first capitalist-style layoffs in Soviet history occurred here, precipitating an ineffectual regional protest, to which Moscow paid no attention whatever.

The Shosha River, the border between the Tver and Moscow districts, joins the Volga on the right some 40 kilometers from Tver. There's an ancient fortification at the Shosha's mouth, but it can now really be seen only in imagination.

A little further, near the town of Korchev, is a small village with a large monument to A.I. Gertzen, the Bolshevik hero, who was born here, at Novoselie. To the right, the Dubna River once entered the Volga, near the site of an old Stone Age encampment. Now there's only the canal, and a showpiece state farm, called

Pekunov. The site is very rich in Stone Age tools, and there's a bitter local joke that the state farm system is still using them, since "they're much more useful than Soviet tractors."

In the 1932 edition of the Volga region guidebook, published in Moscow, there's a small hand-drawn map titled, "Routes of Two Variants of the Volga-Moscow Canal." Neither of the two variants, it turned out, was to be built. One veered sharply west about 60 kilometers north of Moscow and entered the Volga at Rzhov; its advantages, clearly, were ease of building (it followed not only existing streambeds but earlier Tsarist attempts at canal building). Its disadvantage was its length, almost twice as long as the second variant, which was much closer to the one Stalin would push through a year or so later — a slightly sinuous curve west and then east, generally keeping to a northward line; it followed the course of the Yakhroma River and entered the Volga just west of the little town of Dubna, 121 kilometers north of the Moscow river terminal. The canal as actually built is more Stalinist in its execution, paying no attention to the course of other rivers, streams or the lay of the land — it bullies its way north, pushing the little Dubna River out of the way, until it reaches Mother Volga, then stops.

The canal is placid now, calm and unhurried, and it's easy to lose sight of how it was built: by Stalin, in great haste, with absolute disregard for the lives and health of the prisoners who dug it out, shovelful by shovelful. Just as Leningrad is said to be constructed on the bones of Russian peasants, so the *Rus* glides passively on water prepared for it by the bones of those who inhabited Stalin's gulag. Stalin always was a man in a hurry, and the industrialization of Russia was a task he was prepared to pursue at whatever cost to the lives of his comrade-subjects. That these comrade-subjects perished in their thousands, millions, in this frantic effort to modernize Russia no one any longer doubts. It's sometimes forgotten, as we look back now on the dictator's final paroxysms of paranoia, and now that central command economies and five-year plans have become fit subjects for ridicule even in their homeland, what stupendous achievements the first and second five-year plans recorded. What stupendous achievements, and at what stupendous cost!

Stalin, being Stalin, was not content with one canal. He turned Moscow into a Port of Five Seas: the Volga Canal that connected Moscow to the Caspian via Astrakhan; the Volga-Don Canal first attempted by Peter the Great, to connect Moscow to the Sea of Azov and the Black Sea and through the Bosphorus into the Mediterranean itself; the Volga-Neva Canal, which gave Moscow shipping access to the Baltic through what is now Leningrad; the White Sea Canal, which connected the capital to the White Sea ports and the Arctic.

I was thinking of the cost of all this labor as I leaned on the railing in the dawn's early light, of the cost in lives wasted, of men ground down by forced labor, of the gulag in which millions perished. I was up very early, so I'd see us leave the canal and enter the Mother Volga herself; it was four-thirty, the summer sun already rising, the early rays catching the outstretched arm of the statue of Lenin placed watchfully at the canal's terminus, and I heard a melancholy sound coming from the bow of the ship, a song of lament and sorrow. I crept forward to see who it was. One of the Chernobyl wives, bundled up against the morning freshness, her blonde hair pulled tight into a bun, her eyes squeezed shut, was keening into the wind.

> *Our way lies through the steppe, through*
> *sadness without bound*
> *Your sadness, Rus, your tears,*
> *The haze of light, the haze of the beyond*
> *I do not fear*
> *The sunset and the heart astream with blood*
> *No calm, not anywhere*
> *Weep heart! Weep loud! Past field, past wood*
> *Gallops the steppeland mare . . .*

This was a poem by Alexandr Blok, she told me later. But the music was her own. To sing softly of the sunset in the Volga's early light was inexpressibly sad, and I left her there to her solitude, singing of her pain.

CHAPTER 5

Kilometer 739

Uglich

W e passed Kimri, a gloomy industrial city sprawled on both sides of the Volga. My 1926 guidebook, in its chatty way, said of Kimri that "in 1919 it became a city. It was first mentioned in 1549. Even then it was a trading village, attracting a lot of folks. Presently it's a prominent shoe center." It still contained "a lot of folks" but I couldn't see how it would attract them; factories on either side were pumping a yellow smoke into the morning air, and the ranks of shabby highrises for the workers seemed to be directly downwind from the chimneys. A little further the air cleared, and we stopped for a picnic on the left bank opposite a town called Belyie Gorodok.

We moored in a small cove at the north end of an island that was covered with pine forest; a number of campers had set up their tents in the woods, and there were barbecue sites and stacks of neatly piled firewood and logging roads through the damp woods. The old Malishkovo estate, one of the grandest of Tsarist Russia, is nearby. Belyie Gorodok is just a village now, but it was a city until it was sacked by the troops of Dmitri Donskoy, prince of Moscow, in 1376. Ancient burial sites can be found nearby, and signs of a former monastery. A little to the north, from the left, is the Medveditza River, which for centuries was the border between the domains of Tver and Novgorod the Great. It was the main route to the Volga for the people of Novgorod, and at its mouth was a massive fortress, now in ruins.

Nearly 300 kilometers from Tver, and 266 from Moscow via the Moscow-Volga Canal, is the town of Uglich.

In a poem by Pasternak the name Uglich is used as a kind of incantation; it has the twin poetic virtues of a name that in Russian is pure compone, and a history that is steeped in drama, not to say melodrama, which makes it doubly Russian. I got to know it quite well, as I departed from it twice, to my irritation, and passed it by a third time. Its name — Uglich — comes from the word *ugol* (corner) and was bestowed for the sensible reason that the town lies in a crook of the river about a hundred kilometers from the northern end of the Moscow-Volga Canal. It's a small, pleasant, rather shabby place in a bay on the Volga's right bank, a bay that sweeps in a wide and gentle arc, with the town set well back from the stream of the river. To the right, on a bank with a commanding view of the approaches, is a complex of ecclesiastical buildings — several churches, the remains of a monastery and, at closer inspection, the foundation walls of a thirteenth-century kremlin, or citadel. The surrounding countryside is flat and heavily wooded; the riverbank is about 30 feet high at this point, and the road that parallels it is dominated by an old mansion, now a factory, and the Chaika watch factory. The town square is between the loading dock and the church complex.

When the *Rus* pulled up to Uglich's small pier, the ship's band marking the occasion with a rousing if dysphonic rendering of a marching song, there was no sign of the *Novosti Express* — I searched in vain for the dull gray hull, and I could see most of the small harbor. My heart sank. The damn thing had been impounded again, probably. Or the crew had fallen to fighting. Or, more likely, had simply failed to agree on when they should get here, or whether they should get here at all . . . Maybe they'd all said the hell with it and gone home, having put away my Lowenbrau in a great orgy of consumption.

I got a little giddy thinking of this. These things have a long history here, after all, for this is a country that embraced its religion because of a fondness for strong drink. It isn't well remembered now, but the immediate aftermath of the Bolshevik triumph in 1917 was a monumental binge, a week-long national drunken orgy of licence and licentiousness, so bad that even the Red Guards sent to clean it up disappeared into the cellars of the Winter Palace, not to emerge till they had drunk the place dry.

I wondered what to do. I'd been skeptical from the start about this notion of switching ships, of transferring from the *Rus* to the *Novosti* in mid-cruise. Wouldn't someone *notice*? Most of the tourists on the *Rus*, including the crowd from Chernobyl, were debarking to visit the town, which has a melodramatic history tied into the Time of Troubles that led directly to the coronation of the first Romanov. Should I go along?

But how? I wasn't thinking of the Time of Troubles. I was thinking about what to do with my baggage. It would surely arouse suspicion to leave the boat for an hour's excursion burdened down by a massive suitcase? Could I get it written off to Western paranoia? Valentin had put forward what I took to be a truly harebrained scheme — the notion of substituting another passenger for the balance of the trip. What the crew would think (not to mention the other passengers, whom I'd already gotten to know) when a Russian masquerading as a Canadian showed up on board I couldn't imagine. That's how he thought it would work: I'd travel the first night to Uglich, occupy the cabin, establish its occupancy, then someone else would travel the rest of the way. As he said triumphantly when he broached this idea, I'd get my way and be freed from the more rigid schedules of a ship with a timetable, and one of his friends (or he himself) would get a free holiday (since I'd paid for passage on the *Rus*). He thought it was brilliant. In the warm sunlight of an Uglich morning, it seemed even more idiotic.

When the others failed to show, I thought that perhaps the problem had gone away. Only to raise another problem: I was confronted with trying to get a feel for the country from the deck of a cruise ship, difficult even if it was filled with Ukrainians and Russians.

I left my bags on board and wandered down to the complex of

churches with the others from the *Rus*. There seemed nothing much else to do.

The first of the churches, a pretty red-and-white building with six delicate domes in blue and gold, was built on the spot where Boris Godunov had the royal heir murdered in order to clear his own way to the throne. On a bench behind it, sitting in the sun, was a grinning Anton, still pressed tight against Viktoria, who as before said barely a word. She seemed to be wearing a kind of black fishnet, and not much else. Anton was wearing tight — very tight — Soviet jeans. I was surprised he could sit down.

"There's been a hitch," he said.

I was supposed to be surprised?

The boat, he explained, was moored about a kilometer away, just out of sight of the town, at an old pumping station. They couldn't move it right now.

"Why not?"

"Well," he said sheepishly, "it turns out the fuel we were expecting hasn't arrived yet. It's coming. Still coming."

I took this news with mixed feelings. It was hardly a surprise that a shipment hadn't shown up. Nothing else seems to work in the Soviet Union — why should this? Still, without this boat everything became much more difficult. I could go on the *Rus* cruise, of course, but after that? I'd have to make arrangements on the fly, trusting to quick movement and the American dollar to keep ahead of officious Uniforms demanding Permissions. It would be exhausting. I'd have nowhere sure to sleep in the evenings. Where would I put my baggage when I was shopping for food?

It's hard for Westerners to understand how complicated moving around in the Soviet Union can be. Facilities for storing baggage — such as lockers — don't exist. There are few public washrooms. We'd stayed in a motel outside Tver, but they're scarce, and there are no flophouses, no expensive hotels either that are available to the casual traveler. It's virtually impossible to rent a car. You can't just walk up to a bus or train counter and buy a ticket. To get an intercity ticket you need to show a document granting permission, usually an internal passport if you're a Soviet citizen. Foreigners need to have the destination city stamped in their visa before a ticket can be issued. Same with hotels. And restaurants . . . well, more on restaurants later. The banquet halls at the Izmailovo had been only the beginning . . .

On the other hand, there's always a way.

I followed Anton and Viktoria down the embankment towards the *Novosti*. They walked so close together they looked as if they were in a three-legged race. The embankment was crowded with townsfolk. People were sitting on benches overlooking the bay, packs of children everywhere, young couples strolling, eating ice cream and sunflower seeds. The town had a holiday air to it, though it was a working day. It was early June, and the birch trees and lindens were in lush spring leaf. After a while we left the town behind, and the embankment faded to a narrow footpath. About a kilometer further, at a crumbling concrete pumping station, the *Novosti* was moored. It looked even shabbier than it had in Moscow, but ever so much more desirable. The "crew" were lounging around on the deck, drinking bottled Zhiguli beer and cans of Lowenbrau. They all looked thoroughly disreputable, more like a small band of petty hooligans bent on trouble than representatives of the newly liberated Fourth Estate.

They welcomed me amiably enough and I opened a Zhiguli.

"When will you get fuel?" I asked Volya, who still seemed to be more or less in charge. He shrugged.

"Maybe a week," he said. "Ten days at the outside."

"I can't sit here for ten days!"

He shrugged again.

Valentin wasn't here. He'd gone back to Moscow.

I looked at my watch.

The *Rus* would be leaving in about an hour. My baggage was still on it. I'd have to hustle.

I calculated. I had time on my schedule. The *Rus* was to make Kazan and back in about ten days. I could take the trip, get a fast overview of the Volga (the *Rus* was scheduled to stop in Yaroslavl, Kostroma, Gorky and a few other places) and get back to Uglich in time to take the *Novosti Express* . . . And do it all again, only this time more thoroughly. That would still leave time, I believed, to travel the rest of the river below Kazan — the Volga of the Tartars, the Chuvash and the Kazakhs.

I pictured the Volga in my mind. It rose northwest of Moscow, ambled in a flattish semicircle around the capital, passed by Gorky, which was almost due east of Moscow, wandered in a southeasterly direction to Kazan, and then dropped south to Volgograd, where it turned southeast again to enter the Caspian. The part from the source to the mouth of the Moscow-Volga Canal I had already done with Karel. Now I would take the *Rus* to Kazan and back to Moscow, then the *Novosti* would retrace my steps, either to Kazan again or only as far as Gorky. And then? I could fly to Ulyanovsk, which is not very far downriver from Kazan, and trust to short hops in Raketas, hired cab drivers and sheer luck to take me the rest of the way . . . This was something like traveling from Boston to Miami by heading for New York, traveling from there to Charleston, South Carolina, back to New York, back to Charleston and only then beyond, down the coast to Miami. But it would have to do.

I explained this as quickly as I could, and they agreed it seemed like the sensible course. We arranged to meet at this same spot in another ten days. I felt like synchronizing our watches.

It won't be so bad, I thought. I'd have a quick look at some of the places along the way, get the sightseeing done. I'd noticed on the schedule posted on the *Rus* that there was a political lecturer on board, whose job was presumably . . . what? In the old days he'd have been there as an agent of orthodoxy. Now he might be interesting.

I took another bottle of Zhiguli beer and made my way back to the ship, just as the atrocious band was limbering up for a farewell-to-Uglich serenade.

•   •   •

When I returned to Uglich for the second time (post-*Rus*, pre-*Novosti*) I spent a morning poking about before going in search of the *Novosti* and its crew, and had a beer in the park near the crumbling statue of Karl Marx, where an old lady sat selling home remedies for arthritis and constipation. (Could one have made up a more appropriate political epitaph for the old gent, especially here?) There's not very much left of Uglich's kremlin — a few rubble walls are all that the invading Lithuanian army left when they swept through in the seventeenth century.

Uglich is the oldest town on the upper Volga; it was founded in

937 by a tax collector, son of a Kievian prince who'd been sent up-country in search of tribute; the first reference to the town in the Russian Chronicles was in 1148. For a brief period Uglich was the capital of a principality independent of any authority, but in 1329 it was joined to Moscow. After Prince Andrei the Grand ruled here in the fifteenth century the town slowly faded into obscurity, its sleepy provincial life undisturbed by Moscow's furious armed squabbles with Tver, or even by the Tartar invasions.

The modern town, despite its pleasant setting, is dispiriting, consisting of largely empty stores, crumbling apartment buildings, some of them brand-new, poorly dressed people, more "souvenir" shops than is sane, *kvass* trucks crusted with grime (*kvass* is a sort of light beer), and not much else. I did come across a modest nineteenth-century house in which "the famous inventor V. Kalashnikov" spent his early days, but I was unable to establish if this was the inventor of the machine gun of the same name. All that anyone knew was that he was "a famous inventor" and the builder of Volga steamers. Krupskaya, Lenin's wife, lived in Uglich briefly during her childhood. I peeked into the Uglich hotel, which isn't on Intourist's recommended list, and shuddered: it reminded me of a similar establishment I'd stayed in some years before in the town of Bug, on the Polish border: horsehair mattresses, damp sheets, disgusting public toilets and no amenities whatever.

I strolled back to the complex of churches on the river. There were four main buildings: the Cathedral of the Transfiguration, white with green domes, which is being lovingly restored by Uglich students; a squat little church in cream and peach called the Church of the Nativity; an intricately carved building that is the only surviving fragment of the Palace of the Independent Princes, now a museum of local artifacts; and the Church of Dmitri on the Blood.

It was here, on the ground where this little church stands, that the tragedy of Boris Godunov had its melodramatic beginning in 1591. Inside the church, fresco painters have recounted the tale with grim satisfaction and in great detail: here are the swarthy assassins striking down the defenseless Tsarevich Dmitri (the Tsar's son), his nurse cowering away from the blows; here are the outraged citizens lynching the assassins to the crowd's evident enjoyment; here are the minions of Boris dragging the little corpse on a sled through the streets of the town; here are Boris's thugs taking their reprisals on the townsfolk who objected . . . Some historians think Boris was given a bum rap on this one; the countervailing tale is that the young boy slipped and fell onto a knife in the course of an epileptic fit.

Outside in the sunshine I photographed an old man hobbling along with the help of a cane, and we parked ourselves on a bench and fell into conversation. I asked him what he knew of the events that historians call the Time of Troubles.

He laughed, without humor. "Not at all like our time, were they!" he said. "Oh no, we're rebuilding it all now. Reconstructing, aren't we? Reconstructing everything? And to what end? We —"

I cut this off, since it threatened to develop into a tirade. "But," I prompted, "Dmitri? Weren't there false Dmitris? Several of them?" The storyline of the opera *Boris Godunov* was dim in my memory. The first of the Romanovs, Michael, had come to power in 1613 in a time of chaos, bloodshed and confusion comparable to his successors' exit — what a sorry history! Blood and murder at the beginning, tyranny and oppression throughout, and an end in debacle. Only Peter the Great, the monomaniac, stood out in this sad tale of incompetence and maniacal tyranny (though the upstart German princess who came to be the fat and tyrannical Empress Catherine was almost his match in statecraft and surely his match in guile). The rest were dim and ineffectual, and postured on the European stage, building their foreign alliances on the stubborn and bent backs of the serfs they called their people.

The old man had stopped laughing, and with an effort he reached back and told me what he could remember of the story.

It started, as a drama should, with Ivan the Terrible, and his howling madness and solitary death in 1584. Having murdered his legitimate heir, Ivan left behind his second son, Fedor the Feeble-Minded, and Fedor's half-brother, the infant Dmitri, the son of the fifth of Ivan's six wives. The other players were the Shuisky family, who'd been regents during Ivan's own minority; and Boris Godunov, a Tartar who'd been one of Ivan's agents during his latter and most terrifying years, and whose claim to the succession was tenuous — his sister Irina had been married off to the feeble Fedor.

Boris struck first, and awarded himself the ringing title of Familiar Grand Boyar and Viceroy of the Realms of Kazan and Astrakhan. He immediately began acting as if he were Tsar, exchanging munificent presents with other monarchs, most notably Elizabeth of England, for whom he developed an infatuation.

It was in 1591 that young Dmitri was murdered. Afterwards, the Patriarch led a religious procession to the monastery where Tsaritsa Maria, Ivan's widow, had retired, followed by an immense crowd that knelt down in the square and moaned its requests that Boris should be Tsar. Since those who did not moan loudly enough were struck repeatedly until they did, this moaning was effective, and Boris, "giving in to the overwhelming demands of his people," graciously accepted the throne.

From 1601 to 1604 famines occurred all over Russia, and great bands of robbers formed in the middle Volga and Dnieper regions, sometimes carrying their raids almost to Moscow. Boris, though troubled by these events, had a more serious problem — "Dmitri" was back. This first of the false Dmitris was probably Yuri Ostrepyev, a member of the Russian gentry who'd frequented the house of the Romanovs before becoming a monk and taking the name Grigory. Subsequently he'd taken refuge in Poland, and claimed to be the real Tsarevich, miraculously not murdered after all. Soon he was raising an army and marching on Moscow. In the discontent of the time, the angry masses seized his cause as their own, and he took city after city without opposition. In the heat of the battle, Boris suddenly died, and in 1605 "Dmitri" entered Moscow. There he met the nun Maria, the mother of the murdered Tsarevich, and to the fury of Boris's former supporters, she confirmed him as her long-lost son, though he resembled him not at all. He made a surprisingly good ruler for a few years, and married a Polish girl, Marina Mniszek.

The Shuisky family, who thought one of them should succeed Boris, soon regrouped and stormed the Kremlin with a loyalist assault force. False Dmitri leapt from a window to escape, broke his leg, was caught and killed. His body was exhibited in Red Square, then burned and the ashes indignantly fired from a cannon in the direction of Poland, whence he'd come.

Prince Shuisky had himself declared Tsar. But the troubles of the realm were far from over. In the lower Volga another pretender appeared, this time a false Peter instead of a false Dmitri. That there'd never been a real Peter didn't stop anyone; the convenient legend arose that Theodosia, the infant daughter of Tsar Fedor, had been a boy all along. At the same time, in August 1607, a second Dmitri appeared, again miraculously escaped from his fate. The now aging Maria identified this one as her son too, and when the nobles brought in Marina, the wife of the first false Dmitri, she promptly claimed him as her husband, though he looked as little like the first false Dmitri as he did like the real one, and she bore him a son. Shuisky, desperate to lay these multiplying ghosts, had the body of the real Dmitri exhumed, and he himself dragged it through the streets of Moscow and had it buried in the Kremlin, where miracles were soon reported. Since only the dead can perform miracles, this was a shrewd stroke. The sled on which the little corpse had been dragged from Uglich has been recovered and is now in the town museum.

There were revolts everywhere; government was at a standstill and the countryside was seething with intrigue and revolution. The first false Dmitri's wife, Marina, had meanwhile identified yet another Dmitri — the third? the fourth? the fifth? — as her "real" husband, and soon she bore this one a son too. In the chaos, Vasilii Shuisky, the putative Tsar, was deposed. The throne was now empty. Armies stood outside Moscow; among them the Swedes, the Cossacks and the Lithuanians; the leaderless garrison, defending they knew not whom against they knew not what, resorted to eating dead bodies to stave off starvation, before the Cossacks' loyalties were turned, and they drove off the foreigners to end the siege.

Clearly, the country could not survive without a ruler. Intrigue was everywhere; everyone was looking for a candidate untouched by the scandals of the Time of Troubles. Finally the Cossacks proposed a name already put forward by some of the nobles: young Michael Romanov. What settled the matter was his connection by marriage with his great-uncle, Ivan the Terrible — when in doubt, look to the old lineages.

The Romanovs were to rule from 1613 until the Revolution of 1917, and for part of their rule Russia had never seemed greater. This greatness was largely illusion; disguised from view by the pomp, splendor and excess of the royal court was the desperate poverty and cultural backwardness of the nation. In truth, the Time of Troubles never really ended, it was only suppressed; the Russian people went underground, invisible, unheard. Several times in the next centuries peasant revolts erupted, their anger bubbling like hot rock to the placid surface of the immense Russian pond; the universal despair was seldom seen, except as periodic and savage reprisals against the land-owning classes. Foreign commentators in the centuries to follow were to remark on the bovine placidity of the Russian peasant, and always seemed surprised when this placidity erupted into savagery, as it inevitably did.

The old man on the bench in Uglich spat. "Not at all like the present, is it?" he asked slyly, implying that it was, in all its chaos and confusion.

"In fact, no," I replied. "One thing you now have is mechanisms for dissent, ways for people to express themselves, no matter how primitive. That's one thing Gorbachev accomplished . . ."

"I meant the cynicism," the old man said. "Just like those days, no one believes in anything any more, no one has any trust, or faith. We have to find a national culture again. And I for one don't want the Romanovs back."

After lunch I shouldered my bags and trudged down the bank to the old pumphouse where the *Novosti* had been moored before. There, indeed, it was, which was just as well, for I would have been stuck without it: I'd made my way to Uglich by hydrofoil, and this time I had all my baggage with me, nowhere to stay and no *Rus* to fall back on. On the boat's foredeck were several rusty barrels that hadn't been there before; presumably our fuel had arrived. There was no one on board except Volya, who was snoozing in a bunk below. I helped myself to a Zhiguli beer and waited — someone had placed a few ragged pillows on a hatch cover to serve as a chair. I was wearing a *Toronto Life* T-shirt and a baseball-style cap that said "CCCP" in bold letters; passing fishermen were cordial but wary — the boat did look like a decommissioned military vessel. A few barges and tugs grumbled by, but no one paid our boat any attention.

The rest of the crew straggled back during the afternoon, and at about six, on a calm and sunny summer evening, we set off in a northerly direction, downriver, heading for our next port of call, the town of Yaroslavl. As Volya opened the throttle, I heard the same reassuringly throaty sound I'd noticed in Moscow. We pulled out of Uglich Bay into the river, dodging a Raketa hydrofoil and passing by a couple of cruise ships somewhat similar to the *Rus*. There was another four hours of daylight at least before darkness fell, and there seemed no reason why we wouldn't make good time.

It wasn't to be so simple. Of course not.

After only half an hour a small blue boat with a powerful motor pulled into sight behind us.

It was, alas, the real militia.

Shit, I thought, we've only come a few kilometers and here they are already. Isn't this why we didn't leave from Moscow?

"Shit," said one of the others. And to me, "Better go below."

"Why?" I asked. "What's the use? They won't fall for that."

"Go below anyway. Wait in the toilet."

I was skeptical. Would any cop still fall for that old trick? But I went anyway. I tried not to show it, but I was really worried. For all my bravado about "winging it" in the era of glasnost, I was aware that Soviet habits of authoritarianism die hard, and I was suddenly forced to contemplate a stay in a grim Soviet prison. I felt cold as I waited.

The militia boat pulled alongside. I couldn't hear very much, only scraping sounds, a few shouts and footsteps overhead. The militiaman was demanding papers. How many people on board? Five, someone said (there were six). Why are you here? Where's your permission? Who's in charge? Whose boat is this?

He did not, however, come on board, so I guess the footsteps were ours. Either Anton's papers were okay, or the cop hadn't seen the same old movies I'd seen — the refugee huddled in the train's toilet as the Gestapo tramps on by . . . In any case, this wasn't the Gestapo, and he departed with a cordial admonition to make sure the running lights were on and to stay out of the way of commercial traffic. He apparently waved cheerfully as he roared back upriver, presumably to Uglich.

I went upstairs to the deck. The others were lounging about, looking smug. Volya offered me a beer, then wiped the non-existent sweat from his brow.

"Close," he said.

I patted my pocket where my passport was stored — the passport that didn't entitle me to be here — and nodded, trying to be casual.

"No problem," he said, opening the throttle a little more, and we surged downriver.

One of the more enduring images of daily life in Russian cities is the graying, greasy feel of official paper, and the perpetual sight of Russians clutching a torn, worn piece of paper that permits them to be doing whatever they're doing. Often these scraps are being pushed through tiny grilles, behind which sit cashiers, information persons, permission givers, ticket sellers, and the dozens of other petty functionaries that make life go — sort of — round. The system turns Russians into wheedlers and whiners. They find themselves wheedling even as they hate doing it, because there is no other way to get anything done; they are apparently there to service the service industry, to keep the petty functionaries in jobs.

A Russian needs a piece of paper for everything: buying a train ticket, staying in a hotel, going to a library. Some of these documents are pure holdovers from serfdom: Russians need a passport to travel, even within the borders of the USSR, a residence permit to live where they live, a work permit and, when they're applying to change houses, jobs or towns, a *kharakteristika*, or character reference, from the security authorities. A permit is also necessary to die and be buried. I know. I have one, for years ago when I was negotiating the purchase of an intricately chased iron cross at a cemetery office in Moscow, the recalcitrant official in charge insisted that "only the deceased may have a cross." For a small consideration, I was officially declared deceased, and was able to depart in peace with my purchase.

And then there's the special-purpose *spravka*: in our case, permit for the boat, permit for the diesel fuel, permit to be on the river . . . Each of the crew members had a fistful of documents ready to show anyone who asked; they were relatively cynical, fast-moving, streetwise and mediawise, but they were still beholden to the Russian passion for documents and had to pull them out on demand. Even in my case, the hotels were obliged to look at my visa to see whether I was "legal" in their city; no stamp in the visa, no hotel room. In theory. In practice matters have been . . . looser since the Brezhnev days, at least to those with convertible foreign currency, and now they're looser than ever.

My fellow travelers all had permission to live and work in Moscow. This is the most coveted piece of paper in the Soviet Union, except for permission to travel abroad. A *propiska* (residential permit) for Moscow — as well as for many other cities — is hard to come by, since the authorities have attempted to freeze the population of the major centers. That this isn't working has been obvious for twenty-five years, as the villages empty and the cities fill up. One of the little-looked-for after-effects of perestroika has been the acceleration of the process. Whatever else Gorbachev has done, he has brought one revolutionary concept front and center: he insisted on changing from commands to incentives as a basic way of running Soviet society. As a result, of course, no one was paying any attention to the rules any more, and the militia are busy deporting thousands back to the empty villages, from which they promptly start off again. It reminded me strongly of South Africa's futile efforts to keep black South Africans in remote rural areas.

I asked Anton, "What did you tell the militia about the boat?"

"I simply showed him the *spravka*," he said.

"I thought the boat was . . . not authorized . . . ?"

It cost us, sure, he said, reminding me of the VCR I had been asked to bring. The Sony that liberated the boat also made it official . . .

"Is this likely to happen again? Must I be constantly on the watch for the militia?"

"Who knows?"

In fact, it happened only one other time, long after the *Novosti Express* had been abandoned and its crew back at their desks. By a happy fluke, it was in Ulyanovsk, a city that was stamped in my visa. If it had happened in, say, Yaroslavl, I would have been arrested and possibly deported. Unless of course the militiaman wanted a Sony VCR . . . I never felt nervous about this again.

There's always a way.

The next morning, after a pleasant and uneventful night on board, we chugged steadily downriver on a stunningly beautiful day. The water was placid, the river broad; on the banks birch forests were succeeded by the occasional large farm. All down the river people were fishing, lazing on the riverbanks, kids were swimming. After an hour or two we came to what looked like a village: a dozen neat houses, a few larger buildings, a barn or two, a boat house. There was a grove of willows where a brook entered the Volga, and a couple of kids swinging from a rope, shrieking.

"Can we stop here?" I asked. I wanted to see a *kolkhoz* (collective farm), if that's what this was, or a state farm. I told the others I was curious about how these places work, what their lives are like, whether anything had changed since I last saw one like it.

"They're farmers. They farm. What's to know?"

"Maybe we can get some supplies here," I said.

Someone, George, sneered. "There's no *valyuta* store here," he said.

I insisted. Only partly because I wanted to see the farm; but I wanted to establish a pattern early, a pattern of frequent excursions ashore. Otherwise all we'd do is laze about the river for a couple of weeks, fishing and drinking beer. A pleasant way to kill time, though not very productive. I'd seen many *kolkhozes* from the decks of the *Rus*, but I needed something more accurate than guesswork about their lives. I wanted to talk to them.

We pulled over to the shore. The kids raced down to the water's edge, but shyness overcame them as we neared. There were two girls and a boy, dressed in universal kid gear: cheap plastic sneakers, shorts, cotton T-shirts. The boy was wearing a shirt that said, somewhat mysteriously, "Nu-Nu!" We wandered through a forest of dandelions to the front door of the nearest house, which was leaning a bit and badly in need of a coat of paint. Peeping inside, I saw a small room that seemed to be kitchen, living room and bedroom in one. There was a threadbare rug on the floor, a rudimentary table and chairs and scattered other furniture. Two small beds were tucked into a corner. There was no one there. The first adult we saw was outside in the yard. He'd come up behind us, silently, and was, at first, hostile and suspicious. Volya set to work in rapid-fire Russian heavily laced, deliberately, with regional vulgarisms, and, at least to the Muscovite ear, hayseed pronunciations. I thought he was overdoing it a bit (surely the *kolkhoznik* would see he was being condescended to?), but it seemed to work, for he took us back to his house. There, I had a better look around. There was a black-and-white television perched on top of the fridge. An imitation Bukhara rug hung on one wall; there was linoleum under the rug on the floor. The other walls were bare except for a crescent of pictures from fashion magazines. One end of the room was dominated by a large, overly ornate wardrobe. A white bed in the corner had a pillow and a few toys neatly ranged on it. The stove was tilted at an angle (the floor wasn't level), and the aluminum cooking pots were neat and shiny.

Our host thawed quickly. Much later, after his third or fourth vodka, he put his hand on my arm, leaned over and said, "You're my first foreigner. The first one I ever met." His eyes teared. We drank again. The children stood by the door, fascinated. He pressed my arm and I squeezed his shoulder.

Later, we visited the ruined church on a small promontory at the edge of the village. "Oh," he said, "we could probably get it back to use as a church if we wanted it. The local soviet is quite sympathetic. But they have no money, and no one here wants to fix it up. Few of us pray in any case, and the religious ones don't seem to care whether they pray in a church or not."

This was an old village, this village that was now a *kolkhoz*, but the seigneur's house was still in reasonable shape; it had become the home to four families. All the farmers talked freely, in the glasnost way, about what they thought was going on at Center. Most of them seemed fearful of change. Over and over I heard the lines: "It's all very well for city people." "*They* can get to the authorities. We're too far. We do what we have to." "There are people here who remember the famines." And someone said: "Even now when the cities want milk they care only what we *should* produce, not what we *can* produce, and then they make us give all ours away. That's what they want. Of course, we keep some back. They never know it. Now there are some people in this district who are saying, Don't send them any milk until they send us new workers, new machinery, money, something in return . . . Why should we work for them, and not for us? I don't know . . . No one knows what's going to happen to us."

Everyone in the room nodded. "Now the Party comes around and says, We'll lend you money and you can buy things, a tractor for yourself, and some farmland for yourself, and you can become rich, a *kulak* [the upper class of peasantry] . . . But we know what will happen. We know who'll get rich. The Party bosses, that's who. If we accept this offer, if we do this, we'll work hard for five years and then they'll come and take it away again. We don't want to get rich." Here the others nodded. "We want more rooms, more houses, better houses, proper things, we want what they have in the cities, we want to have a nice life, and no bosses, we don't want to be rich . . ." He wound down, somewhat taken aback at his own vehemence.

Someone else said: "Damn it, farming is goddamn hard work. Why should we work all our lives?"

I asked: "How much time do you put into the private plots?"

Our host looked puzzled. "Oh!" he said. "Individual husbandry!" I'd noticed this before: the "market" may be in, but "private" is still a taboo word. He responded obliquely: their monthly wage, 170 rubles, wasn't enough to get by on, and it didn't change no matter how much — or how little — they produced. The rest of their income came from growing vegetables on the private plots; they marketed their produce in Yaroslavl. Most of them at least doubled their incomes.

"Well," I asked, "what happens if the private plots get to be the whole farm? I mean, if you owned everything? If the whole thing was yours? Isn't that what they are suggesting now?"

"Yes," he said, "but we can't possibly cultivate a thousand hectares of vegetables — and even if we could, we couldn't sell that many."

"But you don't have to grow vegetables, you can go on growing lucerne. Isn't that what the farm grows now?"

He looked puzzled again. "Lucerne is what a *kolkhoz* grows. Private plots grow vegetables and fruit."

I didn't understand. "Why can't you grow lucerne *and* vegeta-bles privately? In the same proportions you grow them now? Only they're all yours? Surely the same people will buy it?"

This hadn't occurred to him. Private husbandry, by definition, was for luxuries; big state or collective farms for staples. That private people could grow staples was a new thought.

"You could still grow vegetables on one of the hectares for Yaroslavl," I said.

He brightened. He liked this idea of an ace in the hole. But I'd begun to see the difficulties Center faced, with, as *Izvestia* had put it euphemistically a week earlier, "the intractable matter of the human element." Center's reformers not only had to persuade the *apparat* — the huge, sluggish bureaucracy — of the need for reform, they also had to persuade its mulish customers that change was both possible and acceptable. Center wanted to re-create in a few months what three generations had had drummed out of them; yet Center itself still hadn't accepted the notion that it was legitimate for private people to hire other people: being a "boss" was still anathema. All this at a time when farming in developed countries was moving the other way — away from private farming to agribusiness; in the West, family farmers were rapidly growing broke without massive government subsidies, and yet here the family farm was being reintroduced as the solution to all modern ills. I was depressed at the difficulties facing the planners.

Before we left, our host took us to the swine shed, where we saw dozens of piglets still suckling. His family didn't eat pork, he said. We poked about the back, where the butchering was done with two-bladed axes, in the traditional manner. I departed with much to think of, declining invitations to stay and watch the USSR play soccer on the television set in the *kolkhoz* office.

It occurred to me that television was a two-bladed ax of its own in this context: it could be used for information and for propaganda — for message sending (Yeltsin was brilliant at this) — but it could also breed discontent. Television certainly aggravated black resent-ment in South Africa, where the Cosby show was a revolutionary force, and I remembered that many years earlier the Soviet Union had tried to show a disintegrating America on television (black ghettos in flames, yes, but crowds with placards everywhere) and had succeeded only in showing the Soviet people that citizens of other countries were taking their destiny into their own hands. Television has changed the way politics works in the USSR. From the Revolution until the early Eighties, political messages reached the people through approved texts in the papers, through political pamphlets and through the intervention of the *apparat*. Now politicians like Yeltsin can bypass the *apparat* altogether and reach the people directly in their homes. It's made the Yeltsin phenomenon possible. It's made populism possible. And demagoguery too.

"Goddamn peasants," Anton said as we went back on board. "I told you you wouldn't get anything there. Stupid farmers. None of them can work worth a damn." He put his head down on a pillow and went to sleep, and I started to laugh.

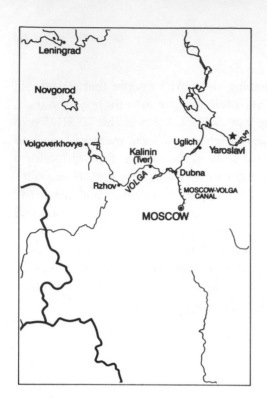

CHAPTER 6

Kilometer 948

Yaroslavl

By a lucky fluke, the boat was at dockside at the little town of Tutaev, built by the Yaroslavl prince Romanov Vasilyevich, when the motor stopped. I thought Volya had simply switched it off, but after a while he came upstairs, looking sheepish.

"We ran out of fuel," he said. "We didn't put enough in at Uglich. We have to fill up."

"You have the fuel?"

"Oh yes, it's right there," he said, pointing to the barrels lashed to the deck.

But it turned out not to be so simple. The men who'd delivered the fuel had taken their pump and hose with them when they departed. How were we going to pour diesel fuel from a 40-gallon drum into a small stopcock? Three of us together could barely lift the thing.

"We'll have to siphon it," I said. "But with what? Is there a hose on board?"

There wasn't. George was volunteered to go into town to get one, and I went along with him. Tutaev was an agreeable small town on the left bank, tilted towards the Volga. There were pleasant gardens near the river. Someone must have a hose. How else to water the gardens?

At the Tutaev general store they had a few shovels, some green wooden stakes for climbing plants and one wheelbarrow. That was the entire gardening department. There were no hoses. The store was otherwise the usual Soviet mix of useful and useless in an insane jumble. Most of the shelves were simply bare, and store clerks were standing around doing nothing. Outside the women's clothing department, a milling crowd was getting restless; they'd heard that a shipment of bras had arrived. I asked one of the clerks if things had always been this bad.

"No," she said, "they're getting worse. In Center they make speeches, here they get worse. People are getting more angry. Do you think I like being yelled at all the time? Listen . . ." She was warming to her theme, becoming agitated at her own recitation, when George dragged me away.

We tried another store, with similar luck. One of the clerks offered me a watering can, and I tried to imagine filling a 300-liter tank with a one-liter watering can. We tried several houses, to see if we could borrow a hose. There were apparently no hoses in town; everyone used watering cans, or waited for the rain to fall, or sometimes used big stewpots from their kitchens.

Eventually we stole three lengths of electrical conduit from a construction site, bound them together with strips torn from an umbrella, and siphoned the fuel in that way. It was another interesting lesson in Soviet consumerism.

Custine, who hated most of the things he saw in Russia, was almost effusive as he described the Volga city of Yaroslavl. "The painted and gilded bell-towers, almost as numerous as the houses in Yaroslavl, shine from a distance like those of Moscow . . . The nearer one gets to this city the more one is struck by the beauty of the people, and the villages are rich and well built." I came to agree with him; Yaroslavl would be a pleasant place to spend a few days' vacation, simply wandering around the old monuments, exploring its parks and talking to the people, who seemed approachable and well informed.

My first view of the city was less impressive. We spent that night moored by what looked like an abandoned cement factory. In the morning, after I'd walked about the city and breakfasted on pirogis and apple juice, I went back to the boat. I'd seen a placard tacked to a wall announcing a meeting of the Yaroslavl Communist Party that evening, to discuss "certain laws and actions of the perestroika era," and I told the others I'd like to go and would surely appreciate some informed commentary. I got the usual grumbles about boring life in the provinces, but this time the grumbles were half-hearted; Yaroslavl's Party was "progressive" and self-confident in its interpretation of Center rules — it was dominated by what was essentially a pro-democracy faction — and the Moscow journalists were as curious as I was to see how things would go. The Communist Party was in turmoil everywhere. Gorbachev had stripped away the notion of the "leading role" of the Party that had been inserted into the constitution by Brezhnev, and the Party wasn't sure what its role was any longer. There was in any case no longer one Party but many, ranging in the ideological spectrum all the way from deep red through royal purple to trendy green. Yaroslavl had a reputation for being "democratic" and, at least in part, Green — because of the dismal record of the local authorities in pollution control — though Kostroma, not very far downriver, was hard-line.

As in Leningrad and other cities, Yaroslavl's voters, given their head by new election rules, had thrown the hard-liners from office. Anton had that morning been explaining how the ballot worked, and it seemed to me in some ways more flexible and democratic than the two-party American system, where voters were presented with a choice of candidates selected as much by party machinery and the exercise of money as by "registered" voters. In the American system, you voted for your candidate, provided there was one you liked. In the new Russian system you could vote against people as well as for them. It must be satisfying, I thought, to systematically cross off a list of time-servers and hacks. In order to win, a Soviet candidate had to score a certain percentage of the popular vote, so it was theoretically possible for everyone to lose if no one caught the popular imagination. And indeed, it was more than theory — in some elections the voters simply rejected the whole slate.

The meeting hall was packed with working men and women — no sign of the "bosses" here. Many were carrying placards, as if they had recently come in from a street demo. "Democracy Immediately Please!" one said, a nice mix of pleading and imperative. Many supported Yeltsin, though hardly any used his last name: Boris Nikolaievich was usually enough. The speaker of the evening, a thin man with thick glasses and an indignant expression, was making an impassioned speech as we entered, and no one paid us any mind. Early on in his harangue, I actually recognized a passage: "Comrades," he said, "we must fear the present. Something terribly important is about to begin, but is unable to begin, is trying to begin, cannot begin . . . It's like a plane taxiing along a runway forever, unable to take off . . . Eventually, the end of the runway comes, and there is either lift-off or catastrophe. This is where our country is now. Comrades, this is a very dangerous time for us all . . ." His audience seemed to like the runway metaphor, but it wasn't original: I'd read the same thing a few days before in *Moskovskiye Novosti* (Moscow News), in an interview with the writer Georgii Vladimov.

The impassioned speaker amplified the theme: "We can't just let it stop here. We must get the job done . . ."

"Yes," someone yelled from the back of the hall, as the crowd craned to see. "But get what done? If we have to get out of economic life as a Party, as Moscow tells us we must, if we have to get out of economic life as Party people, if we can't help direct the economic life of the people, what's there left for us to do? It's naive to think you can separate politics and economics."

The speaker, his spectacles gleaming intelligently, was up to the challenge. "Economics is a mess in our country," he said, "a shambles. And why is it a shambles?"

"Because Brezhnev was a horse's ass!" someone yelled.

"Because Gorbachev is a horse's ass!" someone else yelled.

"No! Because economics has been suborned to politics!" the speaker yelled. "Because no one cared what was *really* going on. Only what they thought should be going on!"

Trotsky, writing on the organization of the Communist Party, believed the Party should "express the leadership's organized distrust of the members, a distrust manifesting itself in vigilant control from above over the Party." This was of course to become the hallmark of Bolshevism and Leninism. That is, the party would substitute itself for the masses and act in proxy on their behalf. Here we have it going the other way, the inevitable legacy of this mistrust: here we have the ingrained mistrust of the members for their own Party.

The tone of the meeting was indignation. Indignation that this Party, to which they'd dedicated their working lives (they weren't all cynical), was falling apart. They were appalled to find themselves looked on by their fellow citizens with contempt, no longer mixed with respectful fear. Meetings like this were taking place all over Russia; as I've observed before, I often got the feeling the whole country was one 250-million-strong politics seminar.

When *Vremya* (the evening television news; the name means time) came on at nine, the meeting stopped for a while to see what was happening in other parts of the country. I'd been told that much of life in the Soviet Union stopped at nine each weeknight; attendance at movies and theaters was down because of it; everyone wanted to watch the news, wanted to watch the political debates that last until the early hours of the morning. People were coming to work bleary-eyed not from alcohol but from an overdose of politics. The whole country was on a politics binge, endlessly jabbering, endlessly arguing, endlessly practicing the kind of democratic politics that hadn't been seen since the meetings and rallies that preceded the October Revolution . . . When they're not watching TV they're at meetings like this one themselves, quarreling, debating, setting up committees to fight a new factory, or earnestly debating the big issues of the day.

The Communist Party was worried and ill, but all its members still seemed to feel that the most important things happening in the world were happening right here. People were not only asking at the meeting: Are we seeing the end of the Communist system? They were asking: Was there ever a Communist system?

As one speaker said, "We go into the city and glasnost has given us new eyes: we see the holes in the roads, the dirty buses, the shops with nothing in them, the lineups, the anxious faces, the fear, the stories once more coming out about Jews, we see all this now and we realize for the first time that we're poor. After three generations of sacrifice, after seventy years of privation, we realize we're poor! Look at this shirt!" he shouted. "It's criminal! No one should have shirts like this!" He pulled at his collar as if it were choking him. "Soviet power is a fraud. We're a poor people and the West is laughing at us . . . We must learn from our mistakes." He was shouted down (the line about Jews was greeted with hisses — this crowd would tolerate no anti-Semitic innuendo, though the speaker had meant none) and the discussion moved on to the ability or inability to make decisions, to the political process itself, but I could see they all agreed: *We don't want to be poor in our own country any more.* In their imagination, the growling of the masses could be heard far beyond the hall. When we left four hours later, exhausted, they were still arguing. We went back to the boat, having bought a few Zhelezni beers on the way (the Lowenbrau was being rationed), and on the boat the discussions continued long after I'd fallen asleep.

The following day, at lunch, we fell into conversation with a Soviet judge. We were the perfect group for this: the Soviet journalists were cynical about their judicial system (as well they might be: the rule of law wasn't a concept high on anyone's must-do list in the Soviet hierarchy), and I, as a foreigner, was the foil to enable them to ask the naive but necessary questions. The judge herself we found by accident: she'd been taking pictures in the Yaroslavl cathedral. She was a student of icons and, without prompting, began to lecture me on the relative merits of the Yaroslavl and Andrei Rublov schools of icon painting. I have only a limited interest in icons; they're okay, in their way, as historical artifacts, but their technique is in my view a subject fit only for pedants. Still, I listened as well as I could, and afterwards we found a café that wasn't too jammed and not too filthy, and discussed, as usual, politics and the doings at Center. One of our group, George, was unkind enough to remind her of the Russian proverb (there's *always* a Russian proverb to fit the occasion) that went, "Offer a candle to God and a purse to the judge," but she paid him no heed.

I was produced as Exhibit A and made to explain that I was, alas, a defendant in a lawsuit myself, and I attempted an explanation of the laws of libel and the process that surrounds it. The judge was interested in the concept of judicial impartiality: she was mostly interested in the reality versus the theory. Was it really true? The Soviet Union had plenty of high-minded rules too, she said, though they are not always observed.

At this "not always" the others in the group snorted. They wanted to know whether the "leading role of the Party," which was no longer the leading role in theory, had changed what she did and how she made her decisions, and whether there was gossip in judges' chambers about what they were now encouraged to do. Is there any psychological perestroika going on among judges (using one of Gorbachev's favorite phrases of the day)? We all knew that the "leading role" was the code word for bureaucratic interference in judicial decisions, and she hesitated. Glasnost won out even here, and she said that, well, yes, it was true, but she "no longer received as many calls from the Secretary" as she used to. That was the way it had been: decisions were made on the basis of political expediency that had been called political principle. "We could always justify this, even to ourselves," she said. "It was our function to help bring about a changed society, a transformed society. A particular injustice can easily be rationalized in this cause. On the other hand, we sometimes knew why decisions were *really* made."

She paused, and fixed us with an indignant stare. "We were all like this," she said, suddenly angry at the questioning. "You must know that — you're old enough. You journalists — look at the newspapers of only a few years ago. And some of them even now, *Pravda*" —giving the Russian word for truth an ironic emphasis. "It was all rubbish. Worse, everyone *knew* it was rubbish. You knew it was rubbish even as you wrote it. So why did you write it? You're no better than we were. You'd go to a meeting, or to a trial, and you'd hear all the rhetoric, all the bullshit, you should excuse me, and you'd go home and you'd report it. You wouldn't report that it was bullshit, or that the people saying the bullshit knew very well that that's what it was — "

She was nearly shouting by now, and suddenly caught herself. She fell silent. The others had also fallen silent. Then she said, very low, "I remember that earlier self of mine, and I'm surprised and depressed, actually, at the kind of person I was. Are you?"

To this, she got no answer.

She began to weep quietly, and I was struck again by the sentimentality of the Russians, a sentimentality, alas, so often mixed in the past with cruelty. The others were not in the least embarrassed by this display, and waited her out. "Now," she said, drying her tears, "we in the judiciary are trying at least to establish new norms in Soviet law, just as you are. These norms are simple, actually. They're the same norms as those for journalists. The laws must be more than fiction. They must say what they mean. The people must be told the truth. But in fact these are very hard norms to bring about."

"Soviet law"! It was an oxymoron to all of them, a phrase of ridicule, one more of the many perversions they now had to face. The norms of Soviet law! There was an urgent need for such norms. To most people, perestroika has become a licence for everyone to steal, instead of just the bosses; and this is supposed to be an advance! I remembered back to the early Seventies when I lived in Moscow; I'd spent many days in court, trying to understand the Soviet system, and had passed an interesting Saturday in an apartment building in the north end of the city, at a Comrades' Court. These Comrades' Courts fascinated Western reporters and jurists: they were the usual combination of a naive theorist's attempt to introduce communalism and a cynical attempt at social control. The idea was that petty offenses would be tried by a lay court composed of the "offender's" immediate neighbors and comrades; the notion being that a healthy community would therefore police itself without recourse to any outside authority. What happened in practice, particularly in a shortage economy, was that the courts became the opportunity for personal vendettas, small acts of petty revenge, snitching and tale-bearing; justice almost always gave way to conformity. Of course, I was seeing the system in its post-Stalinist incarnation, but nothing I heard led me to believe it had worked any better when first introduced.

Despite its naiveté, it was at least a brave attempt to repatriate justice from the tyranny of Center (of the Tsar, originally, and then the Party's central authorities) and place it in the hands of the people. Through the centuries the law had been whatever the Tsar said it was; until the nineteenth century Russian laws had never even been codified and printed, and those charged with enforcing them had no idea what they were doing. The equation of the tyrant with the law persisted; Nicholas II, the Reformer, only succeeded in imposing between himself and his long-suffering people a dense layer of bureaucrats, until the administration of the law, as of the country, almost disappeared under a massive tide of paper. At one point, ten wagons of paper being carted from St. Petersburg to Moscow for one small trial were hijacked, and simply vanished, and the trial was delayed a decade so the papers could be reproduced.

As we left the bar, the judge pressed into my hand a card with her telephone number scribbled on it and said sadly, "If you ever come back and have a lawyer with you, give me a call. The more we learn the quicker we'll put our past behind us." I promised, one of those promises one makes with no intention of keeping, and wished her well.

That night we joined a group of workers in a bar, about half of them Party members. We'd just finished watching *Vremya* (the Soviet Union had lost in soccer again, and there'd been another huge demonstration in Armenia) and we were all slightly drunk, and someone suddenly said, "I think I've become an optimist," as if this was news we'd been waiting for. He went on, "We now have hope where there was no hope before, things are possible now where they weren't before, we have here the law on emigration coming and it can all go wrong, but we're developing a new way based on human values instead of the 'inevitable currents of history,' and we can believe cooperation is essential to the survival of us all . . ." It deteriorated, as these things do, into maudlin toasts, yet it was a spirit that I caught over and over: people are anxious, and angry. Yet they're perceiving pathways to the future that weren't there before. They're allowing themselves some timid hope. "At least the goddamn plane is moving," someone said when I laboriously explained the notion of the endless runway.

The following day my journalist colleagues remained on the boat, and I went to the Intourist office in the Yaroslavl Hotel to see if I could arrange a quick tour of the town's highlights. They provided me with Svetlana, a young woman who seemed not to have heard of glasnost or the busy doings at Center, and was intent on showing off industrial enterprises, which she described in the frightful clichés of Socialist Realist writing. She displayed not the slightest sign of a sense of humor about anything. I knew there was an active ecological movement in the city — the local paper had carried a lengthy report of one of its meetings that morning; apparently massive chemical factories in the region are turning the air into a poisonous stew. My guide would have none of this: chemical factories were a real part of Soviet Power and of Socialist Construction, and she wasn't about to be diverted. Still, despite the guide, I liked the city. It was in the best repair of any I'd visited so far. There are wonderful architectural monuments everywhere, and they were crumbling less, and falling down less, and were showing more signs of restoration work, than any other place I'd seen. I actually saw workers working, where elsewhere I'd seen only scaffolding. Svetlana showed me the Recreation House of the Tire Workers Union, which she said was evidence that Soviet workers had amenities beyond measure. When I pointed out the poster for the movie *Superman* on a board outside the recreation center, she gave me a frosty look.

Yaroslavl is very well laid out, with monuments (usually churches) at the ends of radiating vistas, and generally a population that seems more secure, more confident and less harassed than the Muscovites. There are many boulevards and parks, particularly around the place where the two rivers meet. Once again, the weather was wonderful.

I dropped off my guide at the hotel — she was still talking up the virtues of Socialist Construction — and wandered off into the city.

There was a vodka store nearby, with bottles ranging from 7 to 20 rubles; and the cashier, Tamara Bogomolova, told me she'd already sold "by 8:15 in the morning, at least 40 liters." On the embankment by the Volga a group of men who'd filled up big pickle jars with beer from a kiosk were settling in for a serious bout of drinking. I joined them and took a glass. The one who seemed to be the ringleader gave me his name readily — Mikhail Belusov. "I can't work today," he said with a grin, "I'm really ill." The others laughed. "We're all ill," another man said. "Must be something in the air here in Yaroslavl. We seem to be ill a lot." In the main squares and streets outdoor cafés had been set up, kiosk style.

There were tennis courts in a former moat, in good repair; men were painting the perimeter.

In a quiet backwater near Sovietskii Square, just off Kirov Street, posters on a hoarding were attracting a lot of attention. There was also shouting and scuffling. By the time I got there it had subsided; I was just in time to see two men being hustled into a militia van and driven off as the rest of the crowd scattered. The posters that remained advertised a meeting of the People's Front, which I knew to be a loose federation of generally oppositionist groups, though it does include Communists.

"So what was this fuss about?" I asked a young woman, who was looking about eagerly for someone to talk to. "They were arguing about the composition and flavor of the CP of the Russian Federation," she said. "There were pro-Yeltsin and anti-Yeltsin forces."

"Who's anti-Yeltsin?" I asked.

"They're people who hate both perestroika and Boris Nikolaievich," she said. "Men of the old way, the old world. Mostly men, did you see?" And then, with a ferocious smile, she drew a hand across her throat and said (mixing up her anatomy some), "We'll cut them off at the knees, you can be sure."

Seeing my puzzlement, she instructed me further: "The Communist Party of Russia is new. There hasn't been one since Lenin's day, only an All-Union Party, a party of the Soviet Union, and it's just a ploy by the old guard to undercut reform. Yeltsin is the main countervailing force."

"Where does Gorbachev fit in?"

"Gorbachev's view is at this point unknown," she said, somewhat delicately.

In the kiosks and stalls of the "private" street market, fruit and vegetables were for sale without, for once, lineups in front of them. There were strawberries, and piles of tomatoes in varying states of disrepair, and the salespeople were letting the customers pick through them — usually in Soviet stores you take what you get, whether it's ripe, rotten, or in between. Nailed to a wall near the market were a series of informational bulletin boards to which were pinned scraps of paper from people looking to rent or swap apartments. The boards were being studied in a desultory way by a small crowd.

There's still a desperate shortage of apartments in Yaroslavl; by official statistics up to a hundred thousand people out of a population of half a million are looking to upgrade their homes, and I would have expected a denser crowd. A typical ad: "I have 3 rooms 3rd floor in older building — what am I offered?" There were other notices, most of them from industrial and state enterprises seeking workers — a kind of Employment Wanted bureau in the open air. One was an appeal from a state farm director: "We need specialists! We need an agronomist! We need seed people, and vets! Livestock specialists! People! The keys to your new flat are lying on my desk! All our houses have gas, we have an excellent House of Culture, a kindergarten, a daycare!" Another appealed for miners: "We need people not only with knowledge, but with initiative, energetic, brave, good organizers . . . Our mine is the largest in the Kuznetsk Basin . . ." And there was one signed by one V.V. Filipenko, director of a timber station at Vyazma: "We need rate-fixers, foremen, technicians, a chef . . . Do not think that we live in a God-forsaken hole — each settlement has its school, kindergarten, daycare, medical aid station . . . We're connected to town by our own narrow-gauge railway . . . We have good hostels with TV sets . . ."

I sat for a while in the park near the cathedral to make notes, where I was shamelessly hustled by two young women. I don't have the Russian vocabulary for this, but they did — their gestures were admirably explicit, and so were their intentions to do it only for dollars. They were young, tough, overly made-up but pretty, wearing denim skirts cut very short and, as one proceeded to show me, no bras — an incongruous display under the old linden trees, with the green onion domes of the Church of Elijah the Prophet peeping through the leaves. They took my decline philosophically: I believe their middle-of-the-day approach was as unexpected to them as it was to me — apparently tourism was way down in Yaroslavl that summer. Generally girls hung around the Intourist hotels and in the bars, "hard-currency hookers" as they're called by resident diplomats, but these two seemed more like schoolgirls out for a lark.

As the Soviet cinema will attest, attitudes towards morality are changing fast, if possible even faster than attitudes towards politics.

The generation of women who would angrily criticize younger women in the street for showing too much calf are now silent; bodily display is tolerated, if not encouraged.

Of course, it was thus at the beginning of the failed experiment called Communism. After the Revolution there was a time of sexual license, just as there was a new freedom in art; and for years afterward in the foreign press there was horror expressed at the freewheeling attitude of Soviet people — especially women — to sex. (There was also the reverse canard, put about by anti-Communist zealots, mostly in America, that the Soviet Union had perpetrated what they called "the nationalization of women.") The only Soviet women most foreigners came to know were precisely these hard-currency hookers, widely referred to as *shpana* (spawn), hard cases who hung around the foreign ghettos.

The early sexual license ended as quickly as tolerance in politics or experimentation in art. Lenin denounced promiscuity as "drinking from a muddy puddle," and he said angrily that Soviet youth was "stupefying itself with sex orgies." Leninism was, in a way, puritanism pruned of the notion of sin, but it was still puritanism, and it had little to do with the way men and women actually lived, or with what they actually did. Official attitudes towards sex became, therefore, simply one more destructive aspect of the divorce between theory and practice in Soviet history, and led quickly and inevitably to cynicism.

Later, I found in my notes a scrap from a book by the American journalist Dorothy Thompson, called *From the New Russia*, published in 1929. In the aftermath of the Civil War, "even prostitution has been degraded," she wrote, and she went on to describe:

A community of girls, diseased, despondent, yet clinging to life with a wild and a terrible tenacity, keep open house for all who come — NEPmen [the entrepreneurs of the New Economic Policy, of which more later] and chauffeurs, workmen and students — in the ruins of an ancient palace where the clients creep in through holes in broken-down brick walls, where the light above the roofless walls is the moon, where the beds are the weed-grown earth; a brothel in a rabbit warren of bricks, stucco and crumbling stone.

That was a long way in tone and mood from these two young beauties in a Yaroslavl park.

But the same thing happened a few minutes later in the Yaroslavl city history museum, which was located near the Volga embankment. Or so I thought at first, for she was also young, also in denim, also made-up and pretty in a hard way, and she looked about fifteen, though she was probably older. I was wrong, though, for all she wanted was to practice her English and the new-found freedom to talk to foreigners.

"This freedom is not much use unless we can find some," she said artlessly. "We get a lot of German and French tourists here, but not too many English, and the Americans are always in a bus, you can never find one on the street."

What did she think of what was going on around her? In her country? Had she heard about the People's Front demo? She didn't want to talk about that. Did I have any English books? Only a guidebook to the city, I said, and I need that. I gave her a *Toronto Life* pen and she blushed and said she had nothing to give me. I said yes you do, and she looked alarmed; so I said give me your company for half an hour, and we went and had an apple juice at an outdoor café. It's still unusual to be able to do that in the USSR — find a café that isn't already jammed, I mean — and I gave Yaroslavl another positive mark. She blushed most of the time I was with her, mostly at her own daring, and when the half-hour was up she fled prettily.

What did we talk about? How people her age live in the West. How many people lived in her flat (too many). How she and her friends live. Like virtually all the young people I met, she interpreted perestroika as the chance to go abroad. To the young, the politics of the moment are interesting only in an oblique way: when will "they" do this or that, allow this or that. The young now take it for granted that it *will* be allowed, *will* be done; they see no reason to fear otherwise. Indeed, in them fear seems wholly absent. In this indirect way my journalist friends are right when they say that we in the West do not understand the depth of the transformation that has gone on here: it's not just that old orthodoxies are under siege, but that the old ideas have given way entirely and the questions are only: How to change? How to control change? How to avoid chaos and fiasco? What to change to? Communism seems to exist only in the slogans and the *apparat*, and even there not very much.

There were strawberries in the private market, but eggs and milk are only to be bought with new ration coupons — there are severe shortages in many commodities. And this is July! When the July sun is shining and the fishing tackle shop is doing great business selling line and hooks to eager anglers, it's hard to believe in the growling masses and their pre-Revolutionary anger. But then one sees the lineups, and the resigned faces outside the shops, and people fighting for their coupons, which are doled out sullenly by the petty tyrants who "administer" apartment buildings . . .

These ration coupons are now being used for the basic necessities of life, for butter, meat, eggs, sometimes milk, sometimes even sugar. They represent the equivalent of a base ration for all individuals. One suggestion being floated in the country is that in the short term these coupons *become* the currency for basic items, and that prices beyond them be allowed to float in a true market economy. Anton argues strongly for this process: prices will rise sharply as the rich (and there are many rich) compete for scarce goods, but will eventually fall as supply increases and competition sets in, at which point the currency currency and the coupon currency can merge . . . That's the theory. Is this a plausible policy? Does anyone know? Will the people allow it? Does anyone here understand a "market" and how it's regulated?

If you ask the question skeptically about understanding the market you get only evasive answers. "We'll worry about regulating monopolists only when we've got some wealth for them to accumulate."

Later, back on the boat, the journalists were depressed by the day's news. Not just by the founding of the Russian Party, but by the strident right-wing rhetoric that accompanied it. The Russian Party was solidly in the grip of the *apparat*, they feared. They were suddenly much less sure than they had been of the inevitability and rightness of recent history. They discovered that in the provinces the doings of Center were less important than they seemed in Moscow. Gorby this and Gorby that — no one here seemed to care. The masses only stared sullenly at the empty shops, and wouldn't miss Gorby when he was gone. This has put the wind up the journalists considerably, because they're all Gorby men, I discovered. I'd thought they were really Yeltsin people, but their hearts were with Gorby all the time. They worried at the day's news: What could Gorby do now but compromise with the *apparat*, or yield to Yeltsin? Could he bring himself to do either of those things? Would he be forced to transform himself yet again, this time into a hard-liner? What would there be left for the Party to do? Would Yeltsin care? Was it all coming unraveled? The night ended in deep gloom. George suggested going into town to find a bar, but no one was interested. Let's find girls, he said, but hardly anyone even listened, and no one bothered to reply.

CHAPTER 7

Kilometer 1,029

Kostroma

From Yaroslavl the Volga winds lazily eastward. For the next two or three hundred kilometers the landscape that flowed past the boat was gentle, undramatic, a landscape with the same quiet tone one would expect from the sunshine sketches of Russian writers; it was easy to imagine Tolstoy setting here the pastorales of his placid years, or Turgenev his hunting tales, or Chekhov placing in these broad sweeps his inturned, remote, softly decadent estates (with their slow, strange, poisoned conversations), estates set down among village folk whose lives have proceeded without interruption or change, apparently for centuries. It is a landscape of wide horizons, whose drama is contained only in its size, a landscape perfectly fashioned for Russia.

The right bank is thickly wooded with birch and alder, and slopes steeply up 75 or 100 feet to the hay fields above. From the top of the bank remote villages can be seen, and gently rolling hills, rolling and unfolding, hills that crest southward for hundreds of kilometers, until they flatten into the steppe country of southern Ukraine. The left or northerly bank is lower, and in the old days had been vulnerable to floods. It is covered with scrawny wild cherry and swamp alder, with new-growth birch pushing through in places. Much of the original forest has been floated down the Volga to the sawmills of Tsaritsyn; but Russia is so immense that only a hundred or so kilometers to the north the forests resume, and march on endlessly northward, to the limit of the treeline, as grand and as ungraspable as the steppe to the south.

Not far from Yaroslavl, at the terminus of a tiny, pitted road, is the village of Dievo-Gorodishe, which has a rudimentary pier on the left bank. It's a pilgrimage spot for city people; an easy seven-kilometer hike away is the old family estate where the poet Nekrasov grew up, "a spokesman for the sorrows of the people," as the local phrase has it; there's a sweet little bust of the poet, looking resolutely poetic, in the village square. Further down, at what used to be called Bolshiye Soli and is now Nekrasovskoe, is a thirteenth-century monastery, closed to the faithful and now serving the possibly more useful purpose of a cattle research center.

It helped that the weather was cooperating. The spring had been damp and chilly in Russia, but the early summer was more than making up for it. Each day dawned cloudless, and though some high cumulus clouds appeared after noon, we had no rain. It was warm, balmy — the breeze caused by the boat's movement was just enough to soothe. There were no mosquitoes.

It was only 80 kilometers from Yaroslavl to Kostroma, our next port of call, and we took our time. We stopped frequently at farms and villages, sometimes to check out the availability of food (meager) but mostly just for the pleasure of meeting new people. We hardly ever saw anyone working; whenever our boat arrived, the farm population would drift down to the water to stare. They wouldn't say very much, but no one wanted to miss the arrival of strangers.

As we traveled, Anton trailed out over the stern a line with a peculiar metallic lure at the end of it, which he said was based on ancient Russian tradition, though it somewhat resembled the double helix of a DNA model. Whatever it was, it worked. He caught more fish than we could possibly eat. Not that we ate them — none of us knew enough about the ecology of the river to judge whether they were safe, and we found conflicting evidence along the way. Some villages seemed to subsist largely on fish, and their inhabitants looked healthy enough. In others the local people were convinced that Volga fish were toxic. We tried to get some official position on this, but it varied from town to town. We compromised by eating one meal of fish about every third day. None of us knew what kind of fish these were. Like many urbanites, I generally buy fish in a market where they are clearly labeled; otherwise I buy the few I can recognize. The Russians, on the other hand, shopped the Russian way — if there was fish, they bought fish, and neither seller nor purchaser knew or cared what it was. Usually, in any case, it came in a tangled, bruised, frozen mass, and the fishmonger sold it by the kilo, breaking off chunks with a mason's hammer.

Kostroma is 173 kilometers from Rybinsk, according to the Rechflot map. It lies on a high bank where the Kostroma River joins the Volga. The Kostroma itself rises in the marshy forests of the Soligalitzkii region and winds its way slowly through a placid valley. We arrived in mid-morning, chugging up to the pier and throwing the rope over the stanchion like pros. The MV *Lenin*, one of the Rechflot cruise ships, was already in port, and we tucked ourselves into the back of the landing dock. The *Rus* had just departed for Kazan again.

Kostroma was founded sometime in the twelfth century — no one knew exactly when — and like most upper and middle Volga towns had lived through its moment of political glory. In Kostroma's case this was very early, when one of the sons of Yaroslav the Wise, the founder of Kiev, governed there in the eleventh century, and set up a power center in opposition to the regional stronghold at Rostov. Kostroma's Convent of Ipatiev, founded in 1330, had been important; "there the Boyar Mikhail Fedorovich Romanov, later Tsar, lived hidden while persecuted by the Poles." The monument to Susanin, a local hero who saved the Tsar from his enemies, has long gone, but the monastery remains, now a museum to local art and architecture, and Michael Romanov's apartments are still visited by the curious.

I liked Kostroma. It escaped the Nazi invasion relatively unscathed, and although not grand in the Yaroslavl manner it preserved much of the flavor of an older Russian town. It was typically shabby — dandelions standing in for gardens, buildings with scaffolding but no workmen, masonry crumbling everywhere.

Still, many wooden houses in the old style survive, and a few larger brick houses, their vernacular ornament intact. In the center of town there was a handsome quadrangular building that had originally housed a bazaar; its arched arcades now contained a private market. Kostromites are proud of this seventeenth-century marketplace.

I'd been told that the local soviet was renowned for its conservatism; and in Kostroma I saw more posters and slogans and billboards pushing hard-line Leninism than I'd seen anywhere else. In other cities the more banal and blatant propaganda had been abandoned; a mix of embarrassment and citizens' hostility had persuaded the local authorities to follow Gorbachev's lead at Center and do away with crude sloganeering. In Kostroma there were wall posters redolent of the great years of Communist exhortation: "Glory to the Russian People!" said one gigantic billboard in white letters on a flame-red background, with an immense tractor driver and dairymaid striding purposefully into the future. "Glory to the Communist Party of the Soviet Union and Its Inevitable Triumph!" said another, tacked securely to a building housing the city soviet. The local *apparat* has engaged in a slanging match with Yaroslavl, a feud generated only partly by political differences. It contains elements of historical rivalry as well as commercial jealousy, and is being conducted in the local press at a fever pitch of indignation.

In June, the city looked fresh and pretty despite its shabbiness. There were trees, there was plenty of green, and many of the houses had small gardens — overgrown with dandelions, but also with wild flowers and fruit bushes. Productive gardens are an unusual sight in Russia. There's no Russian tradition of the urban garden — to an essentially peasant culture, gardening for pleasure must have appeared a very foreign notion, and only people soft in the head would spend precious time troweling up weeds. Few city dwellers have flower gardens, and the communal gardens that surround the massive apartment complexes are usually a pathetic sight, with a few meager flowers struggling against brambles and weeds.

Gardening has always been regarded with suspicion by Russians, as can clearly be seen on a tour of the Russian museum of Leningrad; the landscape and cityscape painters showed the typical Russian yard to be untidy and unkempt, with few straight lines or predictable blocks of color. Russians have rejected the maniacal French desire for orderliness in nature; even the English garden, which looks anarchic to the French, smacks to the Russian of excessive restraint. A Russian garden allows nature to take its course; wild grasses and wild flowers are infinitely to be preferred to the monocultured lawns of America. I confess to some admiration for this notion.

However, the scarcity of fruit and vegetables is changing a lot of minds. Gardening may never achieve status as a hobby, but as a way of putting food on the table? And as a way of making a little money on the side? I began to understand why the gardening departments of the provincial stores seemed better stocked than most other sections, our experience in Tutaev notwithstanding. Gardening books were appearing in the bookstores, and bootleg copies of Western fruit and vegetable gardening how-to's were a hot item on the black market — the Rodale Press is a big name in Soviet underground publishing. In Kostroma vegetable seed vendors were to be found on many street corners, the virtues of their products scrawled on scraps of paper — the same exaggerated claims of flavor and appearance that seed catalogues make in the West, only with less colorful printing.

We went to the market to see what we could do about supplies.

Outside, under one of the arches, there was a long line of women. The front of the line disappeared into a milk and butter store. Eggs were rationed — we were unable to buy any. There was hardly any butter. Milk was in very short supply.

"You see what we've come to!" Anton said as we walked away. "Did you know there's a breed of Russian cows called Kostroma? And yet in Kostroma there's no milk!"

I'd frequently seen herds of black-and-white cows on the Volga's banks. They were similar to the breed the Dutch call Frieslands and the Americans Herefords.

"What happens to the milk?"

Anton shrugged. "Who knows? Maybe they pour it into the Volga from anger. Maybe someone steals it. Maybe Moscow grabs it. Who knows?"

What happens to the milk is this: Moscow requisitions it, and the people of Kostroma are forced to travel the many kilometers to Moscow to buy it, thereby depleting the Moscow stores and angering the Muscovites. Like so much else in the command economy, it seems wilfully perverse.

We picked up a couple of loaves of bread — of that, at least, there was no shortage. Inside the quadrangle long trestle tables were set out under canopies for farmers to sell their wares. Three-quarters of the tables were empty. I remembered the old Russian saying, from the famine years: *Shchi i kasha, Pishcha nasha* — which means "Cabbage soup and groats sustain us," and I wondered if they'd have even those by the time winter came. I stopped to chat with three grandmotherly women selling cut flowers and other produce. One had bundles of chervil and basil wrapped in newspaper, another garlic and green onions. I took a picture of the three babushkas. They were cheerful and clapped when I photographed them. One of them asked me to send her a copy, and wrote her name clearly and strongly on a piece of paper, a hand that was steady and idiosyncratic — quite unlike the unsteady scrawl I'd unconsciously and unfairly expected: *Natalya Krivonogova, Kolkhoz Kalinin, Kostroma* . . . I sent her a copy later, and I hope she got it.

Cherries and lingonberries were piled on other tables, and a number of people had green tomatoes; on the far side of the market fatty pork was for sale at 3.60 rubles a kilo; this was butchered in the usual ax-murderer style, straight through with a double-bladed ax, without attention to cut or grain or bone. Other *kolkhozniks* were selling a wide variety of pickles and flowers and some fruit, including sour cloudberries, which were so tart I believed their vendor's exaggerated claims for their healthful properties. There was pathetically little variety, but it was healthful enough — no starvation, only boredom. Then I remembered that this was the middle of summer. If the choice was this meager now, what would the winter be like?

After the others went back to the boat, I returned to visit some of the monuments I'd seen when I passed by on the *Rus* a few weeks earlier, including the pleasant old monastery where Michael Romanov lived for a while. Inside the cloister are a couple of wooden churches in the northern style, steep and tall, their spruce shingles a silvery gray; the cloister itself was strongly fortified when it was built and was well preserved, with a fresh coat of whitewash. Michael's house is an ornate double-storied affair with garish geometric designs surrounding the upper windows. I bought a dill pickle for 40 kopecks from a woman standing patiently next to the souvenir kiosk outside the main gate; next to her was an amiable, somewhat simple young man with a cluster of flowers he'd made from birch bark, which he was now offering diffidently for sale.

Back of the monastery was a neighborhood untouched by modernity, with a quaintness (as well as a primitiveness) that was very appealing. I stood on a log to take a photograph over someone's fence; the picture shows a jumble of small sheds and sloping roofs; in the foreground is an overgrown garden, a few tomato plants under plastic, and fruit trees in full leaf; in the background are the six small onion domes of another wooden church, this one used as a barn by its neighbors. The streets were unpaved, and the sidewalks bare earth or boards, the houses small and neat, with window and door trim in contrasting colors — white trim on a bright blue house, white and pale green on a bright green house, blue and white trim on a maroon house. Some of the entranceways could hardly be seen for the profusion of alder and cherry; the walkways were rich in yellow dandelion.

Nearer the center of town, I visited Kostroma's one working church, which was locked, by the simple expedient of giving the priest in charge a few rubles and crossing myself in the approved way, a gentle fib that seemed to please the priest and his shabby, bearded young acolyte. I'd heard there was a thirteenth-century icon in the church that had once been the personal property of Alexandr Nevskii, and I wanted to see it — my interest in Nevskii was somewhat higher than my interest in icons — and indeed there it was, so blackened with ancient grime that it was virtually invisible. It was hanging in the place where bridal couples stand during the wedding ceremony. The young acolyte showed it to me with great pride.

I asked the priest whether young people used the church much for weddings. He looked smug.

"Almost as many come here as don't," he said. "More and more every year. The young are coming back to the Church, and our time is come again."

No worshipers were in the church, but I believed him: religion was in the air. It was common to see young people with crosses around their necks. Some wear the cross as a signal of political opposition, but most wear it from simple piety — the Russian church did seem to be renewing its hold on the new generation of adults.

I wandered up the hill to check on the local hotel, the Volga. From a distance it looked attractive, showing unusual architectural flair, but up close it was gloomy and unpleasant. In the lobby were a busload of French tourists, many of them complaining loudly that everyone spoke English to them instead of French, and tsk-tsking about everything in sight and out, Russian or not. A local Intourist rep, Abel, tried to sell me a couple of lacquer boxes at inflated prices, and some amber jewelry, though to my surprise he refused to take dollars. I had a coffee in the hotel's espresso bar with him and his girlfriend, Tanya, an ice-cool and disdainful blonde, before he lost interest in me as a prospect and returned to the whining French.

The previous time I'd passed through Kostroma, as a passenger on the *Rus*, I'd arranged to skip the boat to the next stop, Plyoss, 60 kilometers downriver, and took a cab instead. It proved to be a good way to see the countryside, but it was too rushed, and we hadn't had the time to stop, or even pause. I wanted to repeat the trip in a more leisurely way — the *Novosti Express* would wait in Plyoss until I arrived, not having a schedule to keep. There was no difficulty in finding another cab driver; the first one I asked said he'd be happy to take me wherever I wished. The fare? Ten dollars.

He was a taciturn man who said hardly a word during the drive, but he was good-natured enough and agreed to stop when I wanted to, and patiently waited while I saw what I wanted to see. His driving skills were rudimentary, unfortunately. He had a tendency to pass trucks at the most inopportune moments, and for about 10 kilometers, he tailgated a GAI police vehicle at high speed, which I thought tactically inept as well as potentially suicidal. He got away with it, however — the cop didn't seem to mind.

A few kilometers outside the city a dozen motorcycles, some with sidecars, were drawn up in a line on the shoulder of the road. At my request, the cab driver feigned repairs, and while he fiddled under the hood and the motor hiccupped convincingly I chatted with the Kostroma Hell's Angels (yes, they really were called that). The Hell's Angels' reputation seemed to have been transmuted considerably from the California prototype; in Kostroma, it appeared, to be an Angel was to be a member of a "picnic club," and the club's social hellraising consisted of finding an agreeable spot in the countryside to eat and smoke (tobacco) and drink a little beer. Each cyclist had a saddlebag with kolbasa and cucumber and hunks of bread carefully wrapped in newspaper. One offered me a heavy chunk of sausage. Later I learned that this Angelic image was somewhat misleading. In the large provincial cities there are other motorcycle gangs more Californian in temperament — they are renowned for their ethnically based clannishness and their propensity for random violence, usually administered with clubs.

Along the highway were small wooden cottages, the dachas of the city folk, constructed from wood and sheathed with planking in a neat herringbone pattern that was reminiscent of some of the traditional architecture of Old Russia. There seemed to be hundreds of them. City folk might not have gardens, but they loved the countryside, and that love was best expressed, in Russia as in the West, by owning a tiny patch of land with a cottage on it.

It's hard to quantify the dacha-owning proportion of the population. If the Friday-evening traffic jams leaving the major cities are any indication, a great many citizens have a country refuge. In Leningrad the previous year I'd been told with great assurance that as many as 40 percent of the people had dachas, albeit very small, or at least a garden plot somewhere. Tanya, the ice-cool blonde, had told me blandly that her family owned a summer house, a much grander sort of dacha, in a village somewhere south of Ryazan. The family actually lives in Moscow, and the village is, she said, unfortunately too far to go for weekends.

"We spend our summer holidays there," she said. "It's wonderful. The air is so cool, so clean after Moscow, we can buy fresh things from the local people, everyone knows us there . . ."

How did they get this treasure? Her grandmother grew up in a neighboring village, which had lately been deserted.

"The whole village? Empty?"

"Yes, no one left, all gone. Left for the city."

They can't keep the young people in the villages or in the small towns any more, despite the *propiska* system, the housing shortages in the towns and the official displeasure at drifting about. Many houses, and whole villages, are simply being abandoned.

"And the village your family is in — abandoned too?"

"No, a few houses left, a few families. We bought our house from the family that lived in it."

"Is this legal?"

"Not exactly, and not exactly not, but who's there to argue? The family was moving to the city, and they needed money. The other villagers, the few who were left, were just as happy to have someone in the house occasionally. It's not as if we were like absentee landlords," she said, with a slight grimace, since the word "landlord" was one of the few dirty words left in the Soviet Union. "We are local people, we live there when we can, we help everyone and they help us. The family's still important, in the villages, you know . . ."

"Your family?"

"No," she said impatiently, "it's the idea of the family that's important."

The money Tanya's family paid for the house helped the vendors "acquire" ("not exactly to buy") a flat in flat-short Moscow.

"And your family?" I asked. "They have a place in Moscow as well as a summer house?"

"A bourgeois family, exactly!" she said, with a rare grin.

The notion of real estate ownership has been changing for the last dozen years or so. "Ownership" has become "virtually legal," in Tanya's phrase. There have always been ways around the country house or dacha ownership problem, even when all private land ownership was expressly forbidden. Through the Brezhnev years, enterprises or unions would acquire the property, then sell shares to their members, one share corresponding exactly to a particular dacha. These shares were even heritable, and could be bought and sold, though the price was always fixed.

More recently, a flourishing real estate trade had grown up, performed mostly through newspaper classifieds, although the notion of a real estate broker is still unknown. Once a week in most cities there's a newspaper or a supplement consisting entirely of classified ads for real estate, mostly dachas. I scribbled a few typical ads in my notebook: "For sale, winterized cottage, terraced lot, running water and electricity, no phone, call Anatolii." "For sale, small house with garden, 20 kilometers from city, near railway." "Family wishes to buy small cottage or share of cottage in country." "House for sale, small garden, on main road." Prices are steady. For about 1,000 rubles you can buy a minute house and about a third of an acre of land. For 5,000 rubles you'd get a small winterized cottage on about half an acre, perhaps near a forest. For 10,000 you can buy a two-story house on a secluded, substantial lot. The taboo against speculators is so strong that no one person is supposed to accumulate more than one property, or to rent it to others. Nor is "flipping" allowed.

What do people do with the money they get from selling real property? One way for the society to cope with the traffic and its consequences would be to build bigger and better co-op apartments for the new rich and raise the prices for them dramatically . . . but then you'd get a class of rich people. All this is agonizing to a good Soviet Marxist, and even to a newly minted Soviet democrat: should one encourage the people to want to be rich? The American theory, now hotly debated in the provincial Soviet papers (Milton Friedman's economics are alive in the Soviet heartland, even if dead in D.C.), is that enriching the entrepreneur raises everyone's standard of living. The Soviets are now contemplating and debating Friedman's grim theorem: either accept a society with huge disparities in wealth, or maintain a level of gray mediocrity. Meanwhile Tanya's summer home is empty eleven months of the year, looked after, for a fee, by local villagers.

I was mulling on these matters as the cab pushed eastward to Plyoss. The notion current among city dwellers and dacha owners that part-time farmers — not Tanya's family, but dacha owners multiplied a millionfold — could feed the country through small farms is agrarian romanticism. Smallholders can help diversify Soviet agriculture, but the only way a massive city can be fed is through massive farming, through agribusiness, highly capitalized, with hired hands — just like farming in America, where the family farm is similarly a romantic anachronism. The most efficient system should be, in fact, just like the state farm in post-Stalin Russia, just like the *kolkhoz* I'd visited outside Uglich. Except, as I'd seen, it was state policy to go the other way, to make the farmers once again masters of the land — if they could persuade the reluctant farmers to take them up on it.

Our cab passed by several massive *kolkhozes*. One had built a highrise apartment building to house its workers, an odd sight — an apartment tower standing all alone in the middle of a field. This highrise seemed one of the more bizarre consequences of the edicts of administrative centralism: workers, already alienated from their toil by a prohibition on personal property, further alienated from the very soil they were supposed to till by a device cities were using to overcome overcrowding — a city solution mindlessly extended to the country.

We passed by orchards, hundreds of acres in extent, with thousands of trees, most of them bent and untrimmed, the fields unfenced, cropped at random by goats and cows from the private plots. One farm was irrigated by massive, 3,000-foot-long sprinklers, many of which were so sited as to entirely miss the crops. Human activity at three-thirty in the afternoon was minimal: a few hefty women were hoeing threadbare private plots, and a knot of workers gathered around a machine shed, siphoning gasoline from one vehicle to another. Still, the fields were in generally good repair, the lucerne crop a little late for this time of the summer but not critically so, and the irrigation schemes were, at least in general, actually irrigating. The herds of cows looked fit and healthy. The soil itself, what I could finger of it, wasn't first grade, unlike the black earth to the south and west, but it looked adequate.

There were no rotting piles of potatoes in the fields in this region. In Kostroma I'd been told that the real problem with agriculture wasn't the farming itself, but the distribution network. I'd read in Moscow that the previous year the Soviet Union had actually produced enough food to export, though the country had been forced to import instead. Why? The amount imported was equivalent to the amount that rotted (or was stolen) between farmer and consumer. It was as much a distribution problem as a farming problem. Maybe they should privatize trucking first.

In any case, it's not as if the Bolsheviks had invented the ruination of farming in the Volga lands. For centuries the story of the Volga region has been a story of recurring famines, of droughts and desperation, of critical shortages following years of excessive production.

The Russian Chronicles had first mentioned a bad famine in 1024. Another in 1215 was described by the monks in the Chronicle of Novgorod: "O brothers, then was the trouble; they gave their children into slavery. They dug a public grave and filled it full. O, there was trouble! Corpses in the market place, corpses in the street, corpses in the fields; even the dogs could not eat up the men . . ." Other famines occurred in 1601-1603, during the reign of Boris Godunov. And again in 1873, 1891-92, 1921-22. Again and again and again. Tolstoy in 1873 appealed for aid in the *Moscow Gazette* for famine victims along the Volga, where he owned property.

Famines were commonly caused by droughts, followed by bitterly cold winters. Even near the Volga the water supply was erratic. In the Kuibyshev district, which lies in the fertile black soil zone, more than half the peasants went hungry even in the good years. Throughout Russia's history, most people lived in the country and most lived in poverty, and the emancipation of the serfs barely affected this most rooted tradition. Nor did the Revolution. In the Civil War that followed, fully a quarter of arable land was removed from cultivation. And what followed that? Stalin's cataclysmic forced collectivization. Followed in turn by decades of apathy. Little wonder farming is in trouble. Some surprise, in fact, that it works as well as it does.

After the Revolution, hard on the heels of the armies, came the looters — gangs of men and women desperate for food, bent on revenge and plunder. The most notorious was Antonov, who looted the unfortunate (but relatively prosperous) Volga German communities.

And after the looters came disease. In 1921 there was typhoid.

Even where crops were planted, there was no transportation — the roads were in disrepair and the trucks in ruins, as were the trains. Hunger turned to starvation, and starvation soon turned to famine: along the Volga, even in the farm villages, the peasants were reduced to mixing grain with straw and bark in a desperate attempt to fill their bellies. In the cities, it was even grimmer.

The new Bolshevik government, which knew nothing about farming or farmers, apparently believed the shortages were caused by counterrevolutionaries, and not by despair. They insisted that the peasants yield up more food. When the peasants refused — for they had none — teams of official confiscators seized whatever they could find, even seed grain. Search parties moved from village to village, house to house, cellar to cellar, weed pile to weed pile, taking whatever they found. Even discarded junk was examined. Nothing was left. And then drought came.

I found a passage from Arthur Koestler: "I saw the ravages of the famine of 1932-33 . . . Hordes of families in rags begging at the railway stations, the women lifting up to the compartment windows the starving brats which, with drumstick limbs, big cadaverous heads and puffed bellies, looked like embryos out of alcohol bottles; the old men with frost bitten toes sticking out of torn slippers. I was told that these were kulaks who'd resisted the collectivization of the land."

It's important to keep perspective. The dire reporting on contemporary Soviet agriculture — all the stories of shortages and rationing and grotesque inefficiencies — is solidly grounded in fact, but the Volga no longer dries up in the bad years and floods in the good; agriculture is chaotic but no one is hungry, and famine no longer fills people's minds in these parts.

Which is not to say it won't again.

Just outside Plyoss, in a small no-name village, we went into a no-name store, the "Ko-op" store. I'd seen one in Eltsii, but it had been closed. These co-ops are a visible sign of perestroika, a small capitalist bud on the barren branches of centralist planning. They are essentially privately owned. Most of them are little better than the state stores they replace, and their prices are generally higher; but the staff are friendly and helpful, and here outside Plyoss the person behind the counter was quite prepared to sell you something herself, if she had it. My cab driver and I bought each other a pleasant capitalist ice cream.

CHAPTER 8

Kilometer 1,088

Plyoss

I'd traveled overland from Kostroma to Plyoss, and I turned to the guidebooks to see what I'd missed on this small stretch of the Volga.

Rechflot's annotated map wasn't very forthcoming. It mentioned only one village, Krasnoe-na-Volge, which it described as a "picturesque village in the Kostroma style, a center of jewelry-making from the seventeenth century." A sixteenth-century church was listed as the prime attraction, along with a jewelry and folk art museum.

The 1926 guidebook was somewhat more informative. Before Krasnoe, on the opposite bank quite close to Yaroslavl, was the "prosperous Chernopenye village, the home for generations of Volga transportation workers, pilots and skippers. Out of this environment came the sharp-eyed, smart and long-bearded pilots with a first-rate knowledge of the Volga, directing with able hands steamers in shallow areas and around shoals in the dry summer months and on dark nights or in the foggy mornings of the fall." Presumably these pilots now live elsewhere. Still, I was sorry to have missed a pilgrimage to Chernopenye; all early travelers on the river made much of the Volga's treacherous shoals and of the skill of the pilots in knowing which channels were safe and which impassable. I imagined that Rechflot's pilots learned their trade at some remote naval academy, and so it proved: the skipper of the *Rus* was educated in the Baltic ports. River traffic demanded some special skills, he told me, though not the same set as the old pilots had needed: dredging and the series of locks have eliminated the worst hazards of shallow water.

Then, without exaggerating, the old guidebook described Plyoss thus: "The Volga crosses a range, lying between Galich and Kostroma; on its lower and upper terraces is the picturesquely located Plyoss, which was founded in 1410 and is famous for its amazing location."

The cab driver dropped me on the Volga embankment right in the middle of the aforesaid amazing location, but he didn't drive away. He rummaged in the trunk and emerged with a box, which he set down on one of many benches along the kilometer or so of Plyoss riverfront. It was just before eleven in the morning, and he began with great energy and obvious relish to devour an enormous late breakfast of bread and cucumber and fatty cold pork and kolbasa and several swigs directly from the vodka bottle. It's curious that Russians seem to be able to eat almost anything at almost any time of the day. Perhaps this is a result of a shortage economy. Still, sometimes when I saw parties of people, early in the morning, tucking into huge meals, I wondered whether it was the other way around, whether the shortage economy existed because of the appetites of the people — consume when you can, don't delay, do it now because there may be nothing left in an hour, and do it at great speed, with great energy and in great quantities. Stories of great Russian repasts are as common as stories of prodigious feats of endurance and toil. In wartime, Allied soldiers noticed with some awe that Russian soldiers seemed to be able to go for three days without sleep but then, when sleep came, they wouldn't wake up even if a Stuka divebomber was thundering past directly overhead. I accepted a piece of bread and a slice of kolbasa from the cab driver, and we sat in companionable silence, watching the river traffic go by — substantial commercial barges, a tug towing lumber, two Raketas, a number of small powerboats and, from a cove set into the bank just downriver from us, a flotilla of pleasure boats.

Of all the towns and villages I saw in Russia, Plyoss was the most beautifully sited, the most attractive, the least spoiled by modernity — this must be what the Russia of pre-Revolutionary history was like. The town is perched on a steep hill, burrowing into the slope, its little wooden houses, many of them hundreds of years old, sheltered under the birches and poplars, hidden and protected by the forest. The streets are precipitous, many of them cobbled. The town surrounds a deep cove in the right bank of the Volga, and there's a pleasant walk along the embankment. A splendid Orthodox church has been converted into a museum of Russian folk art; it's set on a bank above the harmonious town square, where the Party headquarters are to be found, and a few stores, a *kvass* truck, a bazaar. The latter contains the usual depressing range of consumer goods, but the building itself is unusual, Tartar in its origins. In the square is a statue to the Moscow prince Vasilii I, son of Dmitri Donskoy, erected in 1910 to mark the 500th anniversary of the founding of Plyoss.

As I poked about the streets, peering over intricately carved fences into backyards that were untidy, lush with vegetation, I thought it no wonder that Russian painters loved to come to Plyoss — which they did in their dozens, for the museums of Moscow and Leningrad are full of landscapes that slowly seeped back into memory as I crested a hill here, opened a vista there. Levitan, Baksheev and Prorokov lived in Plyoss; the great Ilya Repin visited, as did Vereshagin, Makovskii, Shalyagin and a host of other greater or lesser figures. Even if they were not primarily landscape painters, they came to Plyoss to live or for the summer, painting portraits of each other, of the townsfolk, of themselves, of the village, of the birch trees, of the Volga, of the Volga through the birch trees, of the Volga from the summit of the hill, of the Volga at dawn, at night, in storms, in the peaceful spring sunshine — what a grand place it must have been to work!

Russians believe that Levitan is the most essentially Russian of all the great landscape artists, the painter who most deeply understands their emotional attachment to the countryside; he's important to them in the same romantic way Pushkin is. I was introduced to his work years before in Moscow by a Russian friend, Alla, who was gently insistent that I learn to understand him if I wanted to know something of her country: he speaks, she said, for a part of the Russian soul. In Plyoss, a small museum has been created from a house on the Volga embankment where Levitan spent a few years with his mistress — a refuge from his family and a place to do his best work, painting after painting of Volga views, the river in autumn, or spring, the landscape under the lowering skies of October, or the lemony colors of May, the barges and bargemen, the gaily painted steamers, the fisherfolk; Levitan hunted and fished and walked in the woods, and left behind dozens of paintings of the fields and the streams and his beloved birches.

The introduction to a book of his paintings I'd bought years before in Moscow describes his sojourn in Plyoss this way:

> For Levitan, all the aspirations of previous years were real-
> ized when he lived on the Volga. The Volga is closely linked
> to his creative life. The broad vistas, the calm of the far-
> stretching land, the measured flow, the smooth curve of the
> banks, the epic scope and subtle lyricism — tranquil and
> mighty, he believed it captured the essence of the Russian
> spirit. Levitan's brush captured the pensive sweep of the
> Volga, the changing light patterns. His famous paintings of
> the period were: *Evening on the Volga* (1888), *Evening: The
> Golden Reach* (1889), *After the Rain: The Reach* (1889) and
> *Evening Bells* (1892).

There's a reproduction of *Evening on the Volga* in the Plyoss museum, and it's a lovely painting: a dark gray bank curving down to the water on the left; a few skiffs abandoned on the bank, a lowering cloud and the water, silver and purple, drifting away into the endless distance. *After the Rain: The Reach* I saw in Leningrad the previous year: a stormy gray sky, barges and fishing boats moored at the stony bank, in the background a square white house and the blue domes of a church.

There's another aspect to his life that the rather solemn book of paintings doesn't mention. Levitan was a man of uncommonly good looks, and was reputed to be a prodigious lover. The working routine he developed in Plyoss was the envy of the Russian intelligentsia: he'd ascend the steep bluff in the mornings, paint the golden landscapes until noon, descend for lunch, go to bed with his mistress for an hour or two, and get up in time to capture a Volga sunset. No wonder he did good work.

The museum is sweet. Upstairs is Levitan's apartment and studio (two rooms with a view of the Volga through a grove of birches) and downstairs the museum proper. I talked to the curator and her assistants, two giggling schoolgirls assigned to take the 5-kopeck entrance fee and to sell postcards. They're so proud of this little museum! A hand-lettered sign inside the front door told me it's "one of the newest museums in the USSR!" It was founded in 1972, and is clearly underfunded — the 5 kopecks from the occasional tourist don't add up to much of an acquisitions budget. There are two rooms on the first floor. In the outer room are old snapshots of Levitan and reproductions of his work, apparently cut from magazines and carefully framed. The inner room consists of paintings by Levitan and his pupils. Most, alas, are mediocre, pieces the metropolitan museums didn't want. There's just one powerful painting, a study of the Volga at dusk. I wanted to buy a postcard reproduction, but there weren't any. The postcards on sale were all banal things clearly churned out by some bureaucratic printing house at Center — cheaply printed photographs of the Moscow Kremlin, statues of Lenin, Red Square, anonymous modern buildings. I suggested to the curator that she make postcards from the snapshots in the outer rooms, informal shots of Levitan in hunting gear, or fishing, or sitting at an easel. She said there was no money for such things. "That has to be done in Moscow," and Moscow doesn't care about Plyoss.

While I waited for the *Novosti Express* to arrive from Kostroma I pulled out the pile of newspapers I'd been accumulating: *Moscow News*, *Ogonyok* (which translates roughly into Little Light), *Sovershenno Sekretno* (Top Secret), the establishment papers *Pravda*, *Izvestia* (Chronicle), *Sotsialistichiskaya Industria* (Socialist Industry), *Krasnaya Svesda* (Red Star, the army newspaper) and

Literaturnaya Gazeta (Literary Gazette, a weekly arts paper), the fly-by-night sheets with their "exposés" of the expenditures of Raisa Gorbachev, the local rags, the provincial versions of *Pravda* from Tver to Yaroslavl, the mimeographed one-pagers with their primitive political polemics, the new tabloids with their headlines about UFOs . . .

The liberation and proliferation of dissenting voices was one of the exhilarating, if fragile, consequences of glasnost. If silence is indispensable to oppression, conversely the new anarchy among Soviet journalists was a strong signal of liberation.

For decades, Soviet newspapers carried no news. They were propaganda organs. This wasn't just a Western canard — they were *proud* of being propaganda organs whose function was to educate, not inform, to publish polemics, not information. Everyone knew what they printed was lies. It was just the way it worked: Stalin would tell Khrushchev and Khrushchev would tell *Pravda* and *Pravda* would print it, and whatever it was became the official line, the only permissible "truth." Until very recently the top leaders, whoever they were, had a monopoly not just on information but on truth itself; reporters, therefore, wrote what should be instead of what is, in the Socialist Realist fashion, and were deeply cynical about their work; they performed their jobs mechanically, without joy or any notion of pleasure. The judge in Yaroslavl had made the point forcefully.

Gorbachev threw the rules out the window and reporters began to report whatever they pleased. Center is backsliding now, but the results were nevertheless joyous. Some wonderful investigative work got done, some imaginative polemics written, a good many outright lies printed. There was much banality and a good deal of sensationalism, but also a freshness and a sense of excitement and commitment: more than once a journalist compared himself not to just any current Western model but to the original muckraker of them all, Tom Paine. (To a cynic, this should give pause; Paine was hardly a reporter. He was a good, a great, polemicist. Soviet journalists who revere him are still in the service of a political idea, even if it is an oppositionist one.)

While I was in Russia the newspapers were seizing on every returning exile for his views; they gleefully published every word

Solzhenitsyn agreed to write; they sent reporters to snoop around the houses of the high and the mighty, and even sent them on missions into the secretive world of the KGB itself. *Moscow News* did a terrific piece, sensationally sentimental, comparing the estates of the Politburo with the housing of the women who cleaned them; in several cases journalists embarrassed powerful men into relinquishing privileges.

Custine wrote last century that "if freedom of the press were accorded to Russia for twenty-four hours, what you'd see would make you recoil with horror." Freedom of the press arrived, but people did not recoil: the horrors were confronted every day as more dirty stories emerged; as the newspaper *Top Secret* ("The journal of politics and detection") put it, "there are not enough rugs in the whole country to sweep the secrets under," and readers and writers both were having a wonderful time picking at the sores.

On the Raketas, in the squares and in the buses, on benches along the river, standing in line at the food shops, people were reading newspapers, a sight that would have been unthinkable a few short years before, when piles of useless and unread newspapers were commonly stolen and used for insulation.

I was working my way through a four-page sheet from the town of Kosmodemyansk, further down the Volga, when the *Novosti Express* chugged into town. The paper contained a thorough dissection of a local gas scandal, and an editorial calling for the Mari Autonomous Socialist Soviet Republic to throw its modest weight behind the reforms of Boris Yeltsin. The politics of change are everywhere.

That evening things turned somewhat sour on the *Novosti Express*. George, who was slightly drunk, had found a girl from one of the cruise ships and brought her back to the boat. He'd taken her shirt off a short while before, and then her bra, and was fondling her while drinking. She was cooperating, and returning the favor with some vigor. They disappeared behind the hatch, and I could hear scufflings and gruntings. The rest were drinking too. For some reason Plyoss depressed them — I think it was the very provincialism of it, its isolation from the events at Center. They felt cut off, restless. Or maybe they were just homesick, seeing the families on the embankment. They wanted to take it out on someone.

"What the hell are you doing in this country anyway? Really doing?" Vasilii demanded, looking at me, no teasing in his voice.

I guessed that the someone was to be me.

"I like this place," I said defensively, trying to head him off. "I just want to understand what's going on . . ."

"So spend a few weeks on a boat and understand everything? What arrogance!"

He launched into a rambling attack on the Western press, how it thought it was free, thought it was so bloody superior, but it was as conformist as anything, in the service of America's political elite . . . This was a tough one. I thought of debating the difference between the Western press's notorious "pack journalism" and political instruction, but my heart wasn't in it. I didn't want to defend Western journalism, which I figured could look after itself, but I found myself defending it anyway. Eventually, I shrugged it off. "Just ask George Bush if he thinks he's master of the American press . . ."

The girl George was with sat up, her naked white skin pale in the moonlight, and demanded a drink. Someone took her a bottle of brandy, and she subsided. She was already very drunk.

Vasilii persisted, prodding me in the shoulder. I shook him off angrily. I was growing tired of his tone.

"What the hell *are* you doing here anyway?" he repeated. "Going to write condescending things about us? You were . . . Valentin told me you were thrown out of the Soviet Union once for malicious reporting."

"Not true," I said.

"Well, what happened?"

"It was twenty years ago, for God's sake. The Brezhnev years. *Pravda* wrote a piece, said my activities were 'inimical to Soviet-Canadian friendship,' or some such, a typical *Pravda* sort of phrase. I was given a nasty lecture by the Foreign Ministry. That's all. It was bullshit of course. You know how it was . . ."

"There must have been something to it. What were you doing?"

"Just writing about stagnation . . ."

Of course, he did know how it was, he knew there wasn't "something to it," he knew perfectly well how the Years of Stagnation worked, and subsided. He grunted, and flung a beer bottle overboard. It smashed on a rock, and there was an angry shout. George and the girl started. Vasilii shouted at them, "Why don't you go downstairs to fuck, you pigs?"

I lost patience with him and got up to go back on shore for a walk. George and the girl, having paid no attention to Vasilii's cursing, were thrashing about on the deck.

I strolled up the embankment, watching the Plyossites taking the air and the hydrofoils coming and going. I was accosted by a drunk, to whom I gave a package of Marlboros, but he became angry, and berated me, for he hadn't wanted handouts, only to converse, and he insisted on giving me back a package of Russian cigarettes, rank and limp things that I discarded after he left. At the end of the town, near a small house with cartoon cats and squirrels and owls carved into the wooden fence, a stout lady was carrying an enormous cat. The beast's claws were out, digging into her back. She took the cat down to the Volga and washed it vigorously, to its howling dismay.

Vasilii would apologize when he sobered up, I figured. I didn't believe his hostility was real. At least, I hadn't detected any in the days that had passed. There was some slight nervousness on all their parts about having a foreigner on board, this had become clear. They refused to be photographed, for instance, and wouldn't even let me photograph the boat; the only picture I have of it was a grab shot I took from the deck of the *Rus* when no one was aboard. In vain did I say the pictures wouldn't be for publication. I also had to promise not to use their real names; even in my notebooks they wanted me to use pseudonyms. But I saw nothing beyond this, no animosity.

I sat on a bench a few hundred yards upriver and listened to a group of teenagers gossiping, their voices low in the sultry night. Across the water from a small boat there was a hoarse shout, and a shrill giggle. This was the first real quarrel with any of the others, I reflected. For my part, I found traveling with them useful, and a lot less stressful than going solo, as I discovered later.

The boat had proved to be unexpectedly comfortable. Everything worked as it should. The only problem we'd found was potable water, since the boat's plumbing systems used river water. It was a problem with a simple solution: we solved it by not drinking any — beer and fruit juices sufficed. After we dealt with the mysteries of siphonage, we had no further difficulties with fuel, though if we'd gone all the way to Kazan we might have run out, with little prospect of replenishment — Volya's "arrangement" for further supplies having come to naught.

We took plenty of canned food with us, which was just as well: supplies were hard to come by en route. We did manage plenty of bread, and by shopping at local peasant markets we were able to get enough fresh fruit and vegetables, mostly apples and cucumbers. Fresh meat was always difficult to find: there was hardly any in the stores or the markets, much of it was rancid, and it had to be purchased with coupons, which of course we didn't have. So we ate endless kolbasa, heavily garlicked. Twice we got a chicken from local farmers, though one insisted we de-feather and dress it ourselves, which the others made a holy mess of before I intervened. It was a scrawny, sorry thing, too. I've seldom seen such a collection of domestic incompetents; they couldn't even manage a barbecue right, even after I lit the fire for them.

But no, there had been no hostility, until tonight.

There were idyllic moments, too, mostly in the soft evening light. After we'd anchored somewhere safely out of the traffic lanes, and supper was over, we'd sit on the deck and there'd be murmured conversations from dusk until the small hours; usually they'd continue long after I went to bed, conversations that ranged from the minutiae of Center politics to ethnic policy to economic solutions (always inconclusive) to the novels of John le Carré, whose *The Russia House* they admired. "Its truth is in the small details," said Vasilii. "The story is just a story but he's found us out in our small anxieties."

I don't remember exactly where this conversation took place; I just remember the moonlight, and the slow rocking of the boat, and the deep rumble of the passing barges, their lights glinting on the river and their navigational strobes flashing into the distance — it must have been somewhere around Kostroma. Vasilii quoted a paragraph from *The Russia House* that he believed was such a small truth; he wasn't sure how it went, exactly, "but it went something like this . . . 'In the Soviet Union nobody any longer believes in action, and so words have become a substitute, all the way to the top, a substitute for the truth that nobody wants to hear because they can't change it, because they'll lose their jobs if they try, or maybe because they don't know how to change it any more. They've had all the lies, had Stalin, the Khrushchev chink of light, the long dark of Brezhnev. And they've only got one last shot in them.' " (I looked this passage up later, and though it turned out to be two passages he'd strung together, he'd got it mostly right.)

I strongly disagreed with this "truth." Yes, everyone in the Soviet Union was endlessly jabbering, but this jabbering was liberating, a prelude to action, not a substitute for it; yes, people were afraid this was their last real chance at making a revolution work, but the momentum was unstoppable now . . . Vasilii shook his head. "No one knows what to do," he said. "No one knows how to reform this place, and so they'll try this and try that and we'll end up once more in silence. Why else does Gorbachev talk so much? It's because he doesn't know what to do."

This was a bum rap. Gorbachev's endless speeches were not a substitute for action, I said, but a substitute for force. I said if he could quote from le Carré I had a better quote, to do with the endless talking and endless arguing and the endless fevered discourse. I looked this passage up later too: "You go for a walk in the country-side and end up arguing with a bunch of drunk poets about freedom versus responsibility. You take a leak in some filthy public loo, somebody leans over from the next stall and asks you whether there's life after death." I gave Vasilii the version I could remember. Doesn't that sound familiar? I asked. He agreed that it did, but said he saw no conflict between the "cynical optimism" of the one quote and the despair of the other. "You'll see," he said, "that I'm right. No one knows what to do," and he lapsed into glum silence.

After an hour or so, I went back to the boat. Vasilii had gone to bed. George and the girl had vanished. Only Anton was to be seen, smoking quietly in the bow, staring at the village. I didn't disturb him, and went below.

In the morning, as I'd expected, Vasilii was contrite, and apologized. By the next day he seemed entirely to have forgotten the incident.

Still, we remained wary of each other after that.

There'd been no such wariness on the *Rus*, where the relationships and routines had been utterly different. Partly as a result of the previous night's quarrel, I spent a few hours after breakfast reviewing notes I had made about the people I'd gotten to know on that ten-day swing from Moscow to Kazan and back. I have no experience of cruise ships elsewhere, but I found the daily life on board agreeable and unexpectedly informative. The crew made desultory efforts to involve the passengers in activities such as early morning exercises and jolly games, but these weren't pushed too hard and were easily resisted. The routine was simple and useful. The ship's crew produced three hearty meals a day (I was to look back enviously to these), and there was a daily tour of some city or town, conducted by the rented Intourist staff, Irina the tour guide, Zina the manager and little Svetlana, who was on her first trip as translator and was very nervous, particularly when she translated for the ship's captain, a no-nonsense type who was never very comfortable schmoozing with the passengers. I liked Irina: she had only a modest interest in the factories and enterprises of Socialist Construction, but she was very good at evoking the small matters of daily Russian life, and when she didn't know something she said so. Being a tour guide can be a frustrating business. I heard Irina attempting an explanation of Levitan to an elderly American whose take on Plyoss was to speculate how a good developer could convert it into luxury rural condos, and I admired her patience and forbearance. (I ran into Irina again a few weeks later in the southern resort town of Sochi, where she was with another group of Americans, and was attempting to explain to them why their "luxury" hotel was without hot water.)

In the evenings we had our "political lecture." Misha Lyubimov was our "professor," whose function, traditional on Russian tours, was commentary on the politics and history of the places we were to see, giving context to our own observations. Most such professors are hacks hired to trot out the current line, whatever that may be, putting new labels on tired ideas, or, as Arthur Koestler once put it, "dealing in slogans as bootleggers deal in faked spirits." In earlier years these people were generally dogmatists of the worst sort, rewarded for their narrow-mindedness with a cruise on the Volga and a captive audience. When I first saw his name on the *Rus* bulletin board, I assumed Misha was one of this sort. I recalled a passage from the Italian Communist apostate Ignazio Silone, who'd been appalled on his first visit to Moscow soon after the Revolution: "What struck me most about the Russian Communists, even in such really exceptional personalities as Lenin and Trotsky, was their utter incapacity to be fair in discussing opinions that conflicted with their own. The adversary, simply for daring to contradict, at once became a traitor, an opportunist, a hireling. An adversary in good faith is inconceivable to the Russian Communists." This was as true during the Brezhnev era as it had been under Lenin and Stalin. But Lyubimov's lectures, which were really low-key monologues, were refreshing in their candor, humor and insight.

He wasn't really a "professor" at all, though that's what we called him. He had been, at one time, but was now making a living as consultant to foreign businessmen and as a journalist, one of the co-founders and contributors to the extraordinary newspaper called *Top Secret*, copies of which I had in my luggage. He was a reserve officer, a colonel, in the First Directorate of the KGB, and was the possessor of a Distinguished Service Medal for meritorious services, unspecified, to that notorious body. Or he had been: he'd changed, been radicalized, had come, as he put it, "out of the dream"; like the Soviet judge in Yaroslavl, he admitted to being baffled by his earlier self, "surprised and a little ashamed." Later that summer he became briefly famous when he returned his medal to his former bosses and published in *Moscow News* an open letter to the KGB that was strongly critical of their conduct in the affair of Boris Kulagin, the former KGB general who'd lately blown the whistle on some of its internal activities against dissidents. Lyubimov was perhaps better known in the country at large as the father of one of the leading democrats in the Supreme Soviet; perhaps his son had radicalized him.

It was a tough job lecturing to Americans who'd heard of Lenin and Stalin but who had no idea how the Soviet Union is governed, or even how it's constituted, to whom "Russian" and "Soviet" were generally synonyms, and to whom "Communist" was merely a label for a failed system, but Misha managed it with good humor. I never really discussed with him his former KGB work. I was skeptical of the whole Kulagin affair anyway — "reform" KGB struck me as about as sensible a notion as "reform" Nazism. Still, one sometimes forgets that, just as there are real criminals in the Soviet Union and not just political prisoners, so there were real threats to their national security, most of them coming from us in the West.

If I never talked with Misha about his work, I discussed it endlessly with the crew of the *Novosti Express*. The KGB, the security apparatus, the secret police, the gulag, the psychiatric institutes . . . These things depressed them profoundly. I got the clear feeling that all over the country there were scores waiting to be settled; all over the country, there were angry men and women collecting the information that would help settle these scores, that would bring "justice," or, more likely, retribution and revenge. There are three generations of grudges to settle.

The Leninist system was based on snitching and on snitches, and the files of the KGB contain many millions of names, not only those who were informed on, but those who were the informers. This is the legacy of Lenin that depresses Russians most, the spiritual pollution that turned a whole country into a nation of spies — spies on their family, their friends, their workmates. The system forced Russians to become petty bureaucrats, mean-spirited, humorless, grasping, vengeful. As the journalists and the judges and the academics emerge from their self-imposed nightmare, as the sunlight chases the shadows, this pollution remains, sullying their lives. In Eastern Europe, or what used to be called Eastern Europe but is now more properly called Central Europe, the secret police files are being turned over to the prosecutors; in some places, one set of executioners is being substituted for another. The KGB is still a major power center in the Soviet Union, but the pressure to do something about the "internal violence," the systemic "abuse of the norms," is mounting.

The secret police were not a Bolshevik invention. Boris Godunov had invented the notion of the "internal spy"; in Tsarist Russia the police had informers everywhere, even in the schools; the arts were so tightly controlled that the police doled out permits and grants for theater companies. The Bolsheviks brought two extra ingredients to the Tsarist recipe: the technology of the twentieth century, and a self-righteous zealotry; they turned Siberia, the prison province, into the slave labor camps of the gulag. This is a legacy that doesn't dissipate overnight. It wasn't very long ago that dissidents were shot; even in the Brezhnev years they were exiled and imprisoned; and they are still, if in fewer numbers, being turned over to the witch doctors of the KGB's psychiatric institutes for "correction." Even the young people, even now, will not talk freely in crowds. They all assume the KGB is watching, and that their files are growing. "You think perestroika has dealt with this?" a young man in Volgograd asked me later. "You're wrong. They're waiting. They'll wait until the reforms fail, then they'll be back. Only this time *we'll* be waiting for *them*." He told me Rambo was one of his models, and I found this peculiarly depressing. But his is one of the many angers Gorbachev and his successors must deal with.

The KGB is such a creature of legend that it isn't easy to tell what real authority it has; as Khrushchev put it after taking power, "We have re-established proper control of Party and government over the organs of state security" — but had they? Best estimates place the strength of the KGB at more than a million, without counting its stooges and informers, and this figure includes a number of tank and artillery divisions and the border guards. The multiplicity of other Soviet police forces — the internal troops, convoy troops, guard troops, fire guards and forced-labor-colony guards — are run by the Ministry for the Preservation of Public Order, known locally as MOOP. MOOP also runs subsidiary networks, such as "rural executives," unpaid conscripts who serve three months, People's Squads, who serve as militia auxiliaries, and the housing administrators, who help control population movement. As the Kulagin affair shows, the KGB still runs informer networks in most major enterprises. They also perform duties foreign to Western police forces: the control of printing and copying machines, the control of address and information bureaus, the registration of foreigners and "the detection and exposure of persons leading an anti-social, parasitic way of life." These notions are still on the books, even if their enforcement is, at best, spotty. They could easily be reimposed.

Some things have changed, though. The control mechanisms are failing. People are moving freely about the country in a way that was unthinkable just a few years ago. That I could travel without documents and without apparent surveillance was a sign either that surveillance itself had diminished or that the organs of state security had considerably graver matters on their minds than a few errant foreigners.

Later, I caught up with news reports of a trial that had been going on in Yaroslavl, where a young man had been wrongly convicted after "confessing" to the militia. The judge wrote: "It's a great mistake to think that people will tell the truth when they're intimidated. People often lie when they're frightened." New norms for Soviet law, indeed.

From Plyoss the river flowed eastward; the south bank was still steep, the water clear, the farms and towns had a prosperous look: Kamenka, the resort town of Kineshma, Reshma, Yelnat, set picturesquely on the Yelnat River overlooking the Volga. Then, at Yurevets, we chugged round a headland into the Gorky reservoir and steered almost due south into a choppy body of water that seemed as big and as treacherous as an ocean. We crossed over to the left bank, 20 kilometers or more away, and moored for the night in a tranquil bay where the Mocha River flows into the Volga. We couldn't see the Mocha or the landscape around its mouth that night, for dusk had fallen. So we couldn't see that many of the trees were dying.

CHAPTER 9

Kilometer 1,281

Gorodets

From the Mocha River to Gorodets we traveled along the Gorky reservoir, and the Volga fattened into a comfortable 10-kilometer breadth. The banks on both sides were shallow, the landscape flat to the east as well as the west. The woods were scrawny, thin. For some distance there seemed to be no trees at all, or at least none alive. We didn't pay much attention. I suppose we assumed there had been flooding, drought, some natural disaster. We puttered along the left bank, passing the villages of Zabolotnoe and Taratshevo, seeing nothing that would persuade us to stop. The morning was cooler than it had been for some days, and there was an ominous cloud bank to the southwest. The topic of conversation over a breakfast of tinned sprats, black bread and cucumber was the Russian national character.

"Sprats are in the Russian genes," Volya said, as he scraped the can. "Not a Russian anywhere doesn't like sprats."

"We all love them," Anton said, grinning. "Like we all love poetry."

"And despotic leaders," said George.

"Sure. And what else? And vodka and the Russian landscape

and good writing and the winter, the broad hips of Russian women, *kapusta* [sauerkraut] and *kasha* [groats], Pushkin and Repin . . . We're all generous and communal and stubborn and slow to anger, we're all ruthless and we all love Peter the Great . . . We love plain food and strong men. We have our history and our land stamped in our genes too, do we not? We love — "

I didn't know the Russian equivalent for *Give me a break!* so I said it in English.

They soon tired of the game, the shopping list of national clichés. I found myself more interested in the consensus that eventually emerged than in the list itself: despite the sardonic tone, they all "knew" what Russians are, what the national character is. All of them rejected outright the notion, which had been popular in the West until well into Stalin's day, that the Russians were some awkward mix of West and East, of Western feudalism and Oriental despotism. This had seemed, at least to outsiders, a plausible explanation for the madness of Stalin, but the descriptions of Lenin and Stalin that describe the "Oriental cast" to their features now just seem dated and racist — the product of Western writers prone to equating Orientalism with primitivism.

And it wasn't just these Russians who rejected it. Most modern historians now dismiss the notion that Russian society was transformed in any fundamental way by the Tartars, or that Russians were somehow infected with a despotic virus by Asian invaders. Two centuries of occupation must have had some effect, but no one believes the convenient Western formulation that the Russians are somehow a bridge culture between the West and Asia. I never found a Russian who didn't think of himself as a European. Curiously, only one prejudice about Tartars seems to persist among young Russians (or young Russian men, at any rate): it's a common assumption that the most beautiful Russian women carry Tartar genes. Whether this represents Russian self-hatred, as Vasilii suggested, I couldn't say.

"This lack of self-respect wasn't produced by the Tartar yoke," said Vasilii. "A national character takes longer to form than that. It comes from, is made by, a long history, by a certain climate, by genetic traits, and also by social and political factors, isn't this so? For example, two centuries of tyranny under the Tartars and three under the Romanovs must have made some difference, don't you think? It would be unreal to think it had not."

"Two or three centuries isn't very long in the life of a people," said George. "But yes, the invasions were traumatic enough to impress themselves on the folk culture, to make the culture doubt its self-worth, its ability. So Russians learned to live day by day. So we're not a very strategic people. We've no talent for detail. We're not very good planners."

The others hooted at this; Gosplan, the State's central planning apparatus, and a Center-dominated planning system notwithstanding, a lack of strategic planning ability among Russians seemed to them entirely self-evident.

George ignored them: "And this is probably a response to centuries of oppression. We're also a very patient people, and this eternal patience is due less to the tyranny than to the climate and to the rural nature of the society — "

"Peasant society, you mean," said Anton.

"Peasants, yes. We've always been peasants."

I told them a story of peasant patience I'd experienced in Moscow in the early Seventies. A cholera epidemic in Iran had spilled over into the Soviet Union. To prevent its spreading, the authorities sealed off the south of the country from Moscow. It was simple to do in those days: they simply closed the roads and stopped the buses, trains and airplanes. Typically, however, they didn't tell anyone they were sealing it off, they just did it. I visited one of the Moscow railway stations a day or so later and saw long lineups of rural people, each with a bundle of goods to take home, patiently waiting for trains that never came.

"What puzzled me," I said, "was not so much that they were waiting, or that no one had told them anything — though there were no signs, no announcements, nothing. No, it was that none of them had thought to ask any questions. They just waited, for two, three days, content in the knowledge that eventually a train would come."

"Exactly!" said Volya. "But that's not peasant patience. Peasant patience is much more sly than that. That kind of ignorant waiting is only 'Russian' because curiosity has been beaten out of us since Peter the Great . . . Fear, after all, is in our bone marrow; you can't root it out with a few short years of openness."

I remembered what Misha Lyubimov had told the Americans on the *Rus*: "The main features of the Russian character are contradictory. Russians are prone to extremes. They're trustful and suspicious, gloomy and exuberant, desiring anarchy and demanding order." He'd also believed that because Russia is built on the notion of the community, of the small village, of the clan and the family, the communal feeling had survived intact among them. "This is at the moment a brake on development," he'd said. "We must now encourage a little selfishness among our people."

The people on the *Novosti Express* agreed. "This communalism was reinforced by the ideology of Communism," said George. "It was why Communism seemed so attractive to Russians, why they fell for its promises so easily."

There are three great Russian questions, he said, questions that all Russians have a fundamental need to answer, that they ask before and after all events, great and small. They are these: Who's to blame? What's to be done? And how to partition it (the "it" referring to almost anything anyone might possess, such as a sudden windfall, a harvest, a salary, a house, a country)?

"Like any people, we're more complicated than the clichés. There are warring tendencies in us as there are in you, and which tendency is uppermost is largely and historically accidental. At the present time, the old trends and the new trends, the trends towards order and the trends towards anarchy, are both working in Russia. This is what makes our politics so interesting. These tendencies have been warring in Gorbachev himself. And this is the best part of him: he resists as much as he can relying on strength, resorting to force.

"Also, Russians have a sense of humor. We're hospitable," George declared. "We've been generally defensive in our warmaking. We can organize ourselves well in difficult times, as was proved under the Nazi invasion. We're xenophobic, but this is inculcated in us, not a true trait. Gogol said Russians are by nature utopians, and I think this is true. We're a religious people — did you know that there are eighty million believers in our country?"

I said I believed there were probably more. I'd noticed that many young people were returning to the Church.

"Are these stereotypical 'national characteristics' at all true?" I asked.

"Of course, yes, in broad strokes. We Russians *are* like this. You Americans — "

"I'm not American."

" — you Americans *are* ignorant moralists. The Germans *are* self-righteous and arrogant. The Jews — "

"I don't want to hear any of this 'the Jews' stuff," I said.

"I was going to say, the Jews too are a product of their long and melancholy history, just as we are," George persisted.

Only one thing made them all mad, the accusation that Russians were in any way a cruel people. I'd asked the question obliquely. "It has been said," I said, ducking responsibility, "that Russians are both sentimental and cruel . . ."

"Sure, cruel like the Nazis, cruel like the Inquisition, cruel like Pol Pot, cruel like Idi Amin, cruel like . . ."

"Okay, okay," I said. "Just asking."

Vasilii changed the subject. "Moscow joke," he said. "Communism is the longest and most painful route from capitalism to capitalism. George?"

From George: "The Soviet definition of a job? Five people not doing the work of one."

From Anton: "How many Russians does it take to dig a hole? Ten. One to dig it, one to issue the permit and another to stamp it, one to examine it for political content, one to maintain its security, and five to line up behind the pile of earth, just in case there's anything in it worth having."

"Why are Russian jokes always so bitter?" I asked.

The others looked at me in surprise. "They're not bitter," said Vasilii. "They merely reflect our particular reality."

The dead trees continued. Along some stretches nothing larger than scrub seemed to live, and we began to understand that this was more than a localized natural phenomenon. The landscape itself was attractive — or would have been attractive, but it had a pinched, wan look. The guidebooks gave a clue, pointing proudly to the paper factories, glue-making manufactures, phosphorus and fertilizer factories and shoe factories that dotted the banks,

set down in their twentieth-century ugliness among the monuments to the fourteenth-century battles against the Tartars at
Mogiltzi, the ancient monastery at Navalok, and various estates,
monuments and villages.

On the right bank we stopped at the little town of Chkalovsk, an
exceedingly dreary place named after its only local celebrity, an
aviator named B.P. Chkalov, who in 1937 had made a non-stop
flight to America over the Pole and became a Hero of the Soviet
Union for his achievement, his picture appearing in *Pravda*, his
arm draped over his little aircraft while a beaming Uncle Joe Stalin
looked on. In a small hangar by the Volga is a "museum," in which
the little ANT-25, the plane in which he flew to a largely ignored
welcome in New York, is preserved, much to local satisfaction.
Further uptown is the house in which he was born, which has been
turned into a pathetic little museum of heroic memorabilia, shabby,
underfunded, creaking floors, a few dusty cases of banal personal possessions. There's also a monument to Chkalov, executed
in the classic Socialist Realist style, with the aviator staring into a
future redolent with the promises of Socialist Construction . . . We
bought supplies at the meager market there, and moved on downriver to the small city of Gorodets, where the great Russian hero
Alexandr Nevskii died in 1263, after a peace mission to the Tartar
capital of Bolgari.

Gorodets was first mentioned in the Russian Chronicles in 1152,
the year it was founded by Yuri Dolgoruski, but the modern city is
a disappointment. There's nothing left of its long history except an
earthen mound that's said to be the remains of the ramparts
burned down by the Tartars; it looked to me as if it had been made
by a bulldozer.

It was colder now, and beginning to rain, the sky low and threat-
ening. We ran into an unruly crowd outside a factory gate and went
over to see what was happening. This was the factory Gorodetskaya
Rospis, which made children's furniture and toys, and which stank
of glue and acrid chemicals. The unruly crowd proved to be the
factory's work force, who were on a wildcat strike, not on their own
behalf but on behalf of the miners at nearby Balakhna. This was
the first time I'd heard of a sympathy strike in the Soviet Union,
where until recently all strikes had been outlawed. The workers at

the gate were angry. They distributed posters that pointed out that the average Soviet mineworker will be dead at forty-eight (compared with sixty-four for other occupations). More than eight hundred miners die each year in accidents, mostly because of collapses — there's not enough wood to shore up tunnels. This, the Gorodets workers pointed out, in a country rich in forests.

"And what about us?" one demanded, pushing his face into mine. "What about us? We have wood, we work above ground, we work with wood. But can you smell the air? We have to breathe this every day of our lives, and it's killing us. The air we breathe, comrades, is killing us," he said, his voice rising to a shout.

It was true, the air was thick, with an acrid smell and a chemical taste. On the left bank, a huge chimney was pouring a thick plume of smoke into the atmosphere. By now the sight of the thousands of dead trees along the banks had become oppressive. The boat had traveled for several hours through an eerie stillness — no trees, no birds and no life. I asked the others what had caused it. Acid rain? Some other kind of pollution? Drought? Worm? None of them knew. I'd seen this before, I said, in northern Ontario, where acid rain from American industry and drought are killing the maple forests. For several years I'd faced the grim evidence as a hundred kilometers of old forest that I passed each weekend sickened and died; in the spring there'd be fewer and fewer buds, and hardly any leaves, until I grew to prefer the winters, when the dead trees couldn't be distinguished from the live. Along the Volga, the trees were mostly beech, oak and birch, but they were dying just as surely. None of the others on the *Novosti Express*, city folk all, had seen anything like it, and they were depressed; the image it conjured, of a Mother Russia poisoned at the hands of the Russians themselves, was a grim one.

All the towns along this stretch of the Volga were horrors; I noticed that Volya had unconsciously speeded up, opened the throttle, and we were leaving behind a bigger, angrier wake, in an effort to escape it and reach Gorky and beyond. We roared past the city of Pravdinsk without stopping. My old 1926 guidebook said the city had been famous for its lace. Now it seemed to consist largely of a pulp and paper plant, and a cellulose factory named, appropriately I thought, after the dreadful Felix Dzerzhinsky, who ran the Cheka, the forerunner of the KGB. The face Pravdinsk showed to the river was profoundly depressing. There was a railway line with a tottering trestle bridge leading to the factory; lumber had spilled off the trains over the years, and most of the neighborhood was littered with tree trunks that had been left to rot where they fell. Those that had been delivered to their destination lay in untidy piles, great jumbles of timber. The factory itself was falling down. Elevated pipes that were strung between buildings were sagging; they'd been patched with what looked like old tires, and some were rusting through.

The town of Balakhna, on the right bank about 30 kilometers from Gorky, was even worse. Balakhna is a mining and smelting center, one of the first large consumers of Volga hydroelectricity. Balakhna's factories were almost a parody of Victorian-era industrial exploitation, but worse — they were not only grimy infernos, they were falling to bits. There was grass growing from the masonry of the walls; storage tanks were crumbling; roofs were sagging; smoke poured from windows on all sides as well as from the chimneys. Downwind the air was yellow, a cloud of pollution that rolled over everything in its path, as relentless as a line of Nazi tanks, killing all vegetation in the way, shrubs and bushes and grasses and trees, all dying. Upwind, scrawny trees still lived. As we passed one factory I noticed a small gully leading to the river, a runoff into the Volga; it was actually steaming, and was a sulfurous yellow. A man was fishing just a few yards downstream.

We stopped. Volya cut the throttle without being asked, without discussion — this swirling, yellow, poisonous cloud was something we had to experience for ourselves; none of us could believe that anyone lived in its path, but there they were, little houses thick with the yellow dust, their yards bare of vegetation. I found it hard to imagine any of the children living in those houses growing to be adults, but they apparently do.

The workers at Balakhna were angry, as most workers in the Soviet Union seemed to be, angry mostly about shortages of food and consumer goods, and about the lack of firm direction from Center. They didn't seem to know of the sympathy strike upriver, and seemed to take the foul air they were breathing for granted, as if it were normal for air in the workplace to burn the lungs and make people dizzy. The town was buzzing with politics and rumors of politics. Had we heard that they were going to get rid of all the Bolshevik street names — Dzerzhinsky, Kalinin and the others? Had we heard that Moscow was going to name a street after Sakharov, who had been in exile only a few kilometers from here? Had we heard that the Tomb (there was no need to specify which tomb) was to be toppled? Had we heard that Moscow city council was going to insist on placing identifying plaques on all buildings in the city, including all those KGB psychiatric institutes, even including the dreaded Lubyanka Prison itself? Had we heard that Gorky was officially abandoning the Marxist doctrine of class warfare? Was it now all right to be bourgeois? Were the rich to return? What did we know?

They crowded around us, visitors from Center, for the latest rumor and gossip, the questions coming in a torrent, the assertions and arguments in a flood. They'd heard that the new buzzwords were to be "human issues," whatever those were, as opposed to class issues. What did all that mean? Had we noticed all the demobbed soldiers, here and everywhere? What was to be done with them? Half a million of them were in "East" Europe, soon to be coming home — would they be resettled with German Deutschmarks? This was an interesting question. There's no housing for these returning soldiers, no jobs in this "full-employment economy" where unemployment is the latest grim Western import.

We'd heard on *Vremya* that a few collective farms had been given "hard currency" (sometimes known here simply as "currency," in contrast to the ruble, which was just money and worthless) in exchange for grain, but that this had just disappeared into the bureaucracy instead of facilitating purchases of equipment from the West. Miraculously, the newscaster said sarcastically, new local taxes just appeared, and this marvelous Western money vanished. A week earlier, the Soviet prime minister had introduced a so-called "bread-price market solution," which had been disastrous, causing immediate shortages, rises in prices and civil unrest, and it was torpedoed immediately. In a country where the price of bread has remained stable for thirty years, how do you introduce market-value economics? Raising prices doesn't make a market.

But without a market they have nothing, and they have no other ideas except the market.

All this was buzzing about this small, polluted provincial town, a thousand kilometers from Center.

Balakhna is where Peter the Great had many of his wooden ships built. We learned this as we poked about with a couple of workers from the factory, looking at the few old buildings that were still standing — a couple of churches, and at least one house dating to the eighteenth century. I was interested to note that these industrial workers, "workers" who didn't seem to do much work (one of them with a plastic bag filled to bursting with beer slung over his shoulder), still held Peter the Great in high esteem. Peter, who with Ivan the Terrible and Stalin had been one of the three truly ruthless rulers in Russian history. I was curious about this admiration.

Peter the Great had invented in the seventeenth century the notion of an absolute ruler by merging the offices of church and state, but this hadn't had much effect on the Volga region — to the provinces, the organization of government was neither here nor there. Still, like all rulers with grandiose ambitions, Peter had needed more and more money for his ever wilder and ever grander schemes, and to get this money he taxed the peasants even more heavily, and the effect of this taxation on the Volga region was traumatic. Thousands escaped their burdens by hiding in the dense forests of northern Russia; others fled to the middle and lower Volga. Sometimes whole villages ran away, fleeing to the middle Volga just as they'd done a century earlier in the Time of Troubles. There was severe punishment for those caught, but the flight continued and this part of the Volga, around Balakhna, seethed with suspicion, turmoil, intrigue, treachery, cruelty and reprisal.

In the northwest, careless of the effect he was having on the middle kingdom, Peter constructed his new capital, St. Petersburg, "on the bones of his subjects." In order to get the work done, he needed a disciplined workforce, and to get that he essentially militarized the whole country, quartering a new and swollen army permanently on the provincial population. Which of course added another crushing burden of taxation and confiscation, which in turn increased the number of fugitives. Many turned to robbery, which led to further uprisings and the further need for repression and more money . . .

This monster was the man revered in Balakhna. They tried to tell me why: here was an absolute ruler who actually liked his people. As the man with the beer put it, "he liked the peasants, enjoyed being with them, liked working with his hands, would go down to the shipyards and pick up a hammer, a chisel, working as surely as the shipwrights." True, he did nothing about serfdom, but that wasn't really his fault. He would have done something about it if his attention hadn't been diverted by his grand projects, by foreign invasion, by the construction of an entirely new capital in the swamps in the middle of nowhere. The Russians love that sort of thing, the grand gesture, the noble folly; I'd often heard the same rhetoric years earlier when they were constructing another massive factory somewhere in the mud and chaos of a newly cleared forest, and they'd roll out the stats: so many turbines, so many tractors and trucks per hour, so many trillion kilowatt-hours, all the industrial statistics of entirely fictional growth that had become the music of the Soviet state in the Thirties and that was still reverberating here among the unhappy workers of Balakhna.

None of us wanted to argue with these workers, or remind them how Peter had codified the class system and locked his people into it. I did remind them that Peter had introduced police sponsorship of local arts and crafts, and that surely they wanted to move away from police sponsorship of anything, but I didn't push it. They loved Peter and looked back longingly to the days when a strong man knew what he wanted and mobilized a country to get it, and in this longing I heard echoes of the proto-fascist hero worship practiced by Pamyat, with its talk of the pure Romanov blood of the Line of Rurik (notwithstanding that Catherine, Peter's most formidable successor, had been a German). It seemed to me that Peter had become a kind of code word for Stalin, and Stalin himself, while increasingly the open target of revulsion and rage among the intellectuals at Center, was here becoming converted into a shorthand way of saying larger-than-life achievement, the "strong leader" that "Russians have always needed." This wasn't a Russia that any one of us wanted to believe in, and we were all subdued as we returned to the *Novosti Express* and let loose the lines, heading for Gorky.

CHAPTER 10

Kilometer 1,335

Gorky
(Nizhni Novgorod)

Allalong the Volga from Uglich I'd seen clues to a profound change in the river's character, but I hadn't paid sufficient attention. We'd been proceeding placidly downstream. We passed Kimri and then Kalyazin, with its old, cold Monastery of the Holy Trinity, its reputation austere and fanatic; parts of Kalyazin had been flooded by the Uglich dam, and we'd seen, as we chugged on by, the bell tower of St. Nicholas's Church, built in the 1800s, forlornly peeping from the river. (Ironically, the few feet still above water were surrounded by scaffolding — the top of the drowned spire, which has become something of a navigation landmark, was being restored.) This is where I should first have noticed the change that had been wrought on the river, but we merely continued, passing dozens of hydroelectric barrages, sailing through locks into huge reservoirs, and still I didn't notice. It wasn't until we were nearing Gorky, the Nizhni Novgorod of old, and I was reading my notes on the travels of Olearius that it finally sank in: the Volga wasn't really a river any more; the great Mother River had been tamed and turned into a series of gigantic ponds.

Olearius had gone overland from Moscow south to the Oka, and thence downriver to where the Oka joined the Volga, at Nizhni Novgorod. His party remained at Nizhni "until the end of July, at which time we became aware that the water level was rapidly shrinking." Ships on their way to Astrakhan, he reported, normally waited until the river was in flood or rising, which occurred in May or June. After that, the water fell very quickly, and Olearius's party passed many vessels grounded unexpectedly. The Volga, in Olearius's description, sounded like a small stream, a freshet in the spring, a collection of mud banks and sinkholes in late summer. It didn't sound much like the Volga I could see from the deck of the *Novosti Express*.

A few weeks earlier I had asked the captain of the *Rus* whether low water was a problem, and he shrugged. There is low water, high water, but it makes no difference, he said. This should have been a clue that plenty had changed since Olearius's day. After all, the levels used to fluctuate wildly. My 1926 guidebook, published before the river was tamed by dams, says that the fluctuations ranged from 23 to 36 feet on the upper Volga, from 39 to 46 feet on the middle Volga and from 10 to 49 feet on the lower Volga.

Many of the towns Olearius passed were set between four and ten kilometers back from the river. Why were they so far? Because they would otherwise have been flooded in the spring runoff. The modern Volga towns are on the riverbanks. Ergo: big changes.

It took a large ego and a large imagination to conceive of taming the Volga, and Stalin had both. He managed it in the same way he did his people: he pulled the river into a noose and put it to work. And a mighty worker it is: the four great hydroelectric projects of the "Volga Cascade" supply much of the electric power for Russian industry, and the so-called "water treasuries" or reservoirs that the dams have created furnish the irrigation water for agricultural regions that were for centuries subjected to droughts.

The uppermost dam, built in 1937, is northwest of Moscow, at Ivankovo. It's one of the smallest and earliest, and its reservoir is 200 square kilometers (a square kilometer is about 0.38 square miles). The Uglich reservoir, built a few years later, is a modest 150 square kilometers. Then come the giants: at Rybinsk, the dam created a lake that at 2,800 square kilometers was the largest in

Europe at the time; at Gorky, 970 square kilometers; at Kuibyshev, built in 1957, the reservoir is 3,900 square kilometers, an inland sea even bigger than Rybinsk; at Saratov the dam flooded 1,200 square kilometers; and at Volgograd, the last part of the Cascade to be built, in 1960, the reservoir covers 2,150 square kilometers. At present, the Volga dams altogether generate about 23 trillion kilowatt-hours per year. And it's not yet finished. There'll eventually be eight Volga reservoirs and four on the Kama, for a total of 40 trillion kilowatt-hours.

That will run a lot of toasters, everyone agrees. Still, no one I talked to ever mentioned the dams or the hydroelectric production, or spoke of the Volga Cascade in anywhere near the breathless tones of official propaganda. Most people merely took it for granted that there were dams on the river. No one cared that the Volga had been "tamed"; perhaps I'd unconsciously picked up the macho attitudes of the Socialist Realist proselytizers. The Volga was the Volga, and that it could be in places 30, 40, 50 kilometers wide seemed only natural. You could still travel from Moscow to the Caspian Sea, as they did in the old days, and that was all that mattered.

The first time I went to Gorky was on the cruise ship *Rus*. We reached it late one afternoon after steaming steadily down an ever widening reservoir. Gorky, which most people were once again calling Nizhni Novgorod, was still a "closed" town to foreigners, closed for no good reason any more, except that Stalin had closed it and no one had gotten around to opening it. This wasn't uncommon. When I lived in Moscow twenty years previously, much of the country was closed to outsiders, on the simple premise that unless there was a good reason for foreigners to go there, you should keep them out. This attitude had deep historical roots. Custine made the same observation traveling through the Russian countryside in the early 1800s; the principle of sealing off the provinces from prying eyes is firmly rooted in pre-Revolutionary practice. Cities and regions were closed for diverse reasons — because of national xenophobia, on grounds of military security, because they were places of internal exile where the state banished its dissidents (Siberia, which for so long has been a gigantic penal colony, was closed until very recently), because they were close to frontiers, because they were polluted or simply because no one bothered to open them.

There'd been some reason to close Gorky at the height of the Cold War. It was a major industrial center, not only for cars but for the aerospace industry. Now most of the military installations have official American observers stationed in them, and it seems pointless to be paranoid about a few foreign tourists taking snaps of the local kremlin. Sakharov had been exiled there, but that was because it was a closed city, not because it was some kind of urban gulag — it was chosen to keep Sakharov away from the foreign press.

The other reason Gorky was closed was more prosaic: there wasn't yet an infrastructure for tourists — no decent hotels, no restaurants, no tour buses with foreign-language guides. However, I was told the day the *Rus* arrived that by the following week the city would be open to foreign tourists. This meant it would be open by the time I returned on the *Novosti Express* (which at that point was still in some doubt; while I was parked off Gorky on the *Rus* the journalists were still back in Uglich trying to acquire their fuel).

From the deck of the *Rus*, all I was able to do was lean on the railing and peer at the city from afar. This was the port of registry for our ship, and we stopped here to reprovision, which activity was done by supply boat to the middle of the river. It was raining as the crew worked. The ship's storekeeper suspiciously inspected every case that came on board, especially the champagne. The barge-workers, most of them women, were given Pepsis as an incentive to get the job done quickly.

Nizhni (Lower) Novgorod was founded in 1221; and for a century or so afterward many people exiled from the other Novgorod, called by its own residents Novgorod the Great, were settled here by Ivan III. The modern city is handsome. It's a good size, about one and a half million people, set on the junction of the Oka and Volga Rivers. There is an impressive ensemble of nineteenth-century buildings along the waterfront, a massive fifteenth- and sixteenth-century kremlin spilling down from the hillside, a pretty ornamental staircase built by German prisoners of war and an attractive mix of old and new buildings. On the outskirts, as usual, massive highrise developments have been built, rank after rank of apartment buildings.

This harmonious look, too, was misleading.

A week or so later, as we approached from the north on the *Novosti Express*, the crew began to parody the rotund provincial accent that reaches its apogee in the Gorky region. This peculiar accent even has its own name, *okane*, said with an O as round as the mouth of an astonished fish. The Russian word for thank you, *sposibo*, which is pronounced "spasiba" in Moscow, is "spohsiboh" in Gorky, and even to a foreign ear it sounds slightly bovine. Alexei Maksimovich Peshkov, who wrote under the name Gorky, was born in the hills of Nizhni Novgorod and spoke with the *okane* all his life. So did the sinister Zhdanov, who later became one of Stalin's henchmen, but no one dared make fun of his accent.

Gorky straddles the Oka on the right bank of the Volga. The old part of town, the city proper, is on the south bank of the Oka. North, there is a line of marine cranes along the river, and behind them industrial terminals, freight warehouses, huge dumps of potash and minerals for loading into barges and, in the distance behind the cranes, an old church, covered in scaffolding. We tied the *Novosti Express* to a stanchion in the industrial quarter by the row of cranes. There was no sign of what Custine called "the most beautiful site I've seen in Russia." Nor was there any sign of what made Nizhni Novgorod the true border between Europe and Asia for so long, attracting to its shops and bazaars all manner of exotic peoples, Vikings and Danes, Frieslanders and Scots, Mandarins, Kalmyks, Tartars, Chuvash, Turks, Syrians . . .

Poor peddlers and rich merchants, beggars, adventurers, con artists, itinerant monks, thieves and Cossacks were all seduced by the "fabulous Yarmarka," the annual fair that from the Middle Ages until the nineteenth century made Nizhni the most cosmopolitan city in Russia. Up the Volga from Iran and China, down the Oka (which itself served as the frontier between Tartar and Russian) came the traders and the merchants; the Oka, which for 1,500 kilometers waters the most fertile plains of Great Russia, brought to the fair the produce of the artisans of Orel, Kaluga, Tula, Ryazan, Tambov, Vladimir, Moscow, their metalwork, woodcarvings, religious artifacts, leather, furs, lace . . . The famous fair was separated from Nizhni proper by the Oka, and covered a wide plain, turning itself into a self-contained town, with paved walkways and canals. At its height early in this century the fair attracted nearly half a million people each year; in 1911, the merchandise on offer was valued at about 260 million rubles.

All that remains is the Alexandr Nevski Church, which we could see in the distance with its scaffolding. Gone are the stalls for the furs, cotton, leather, spices and wine, gone the racecourse, the circus, the mosque. Gone are the taverns, gone the brothels with their exotic Levantine whores, gone the decadent traders who shipped blond Slavs to the slave markets of the Middle East. A contemporary map showed the market as measuring close to a mile across. All gone now, all vanished into an exotic history.

It was in Nizhni Novgorod that I discovered how much things had changed since my earlier visits, or at least how much the control measures had slipped. We on the *Novosti Express* had simply assumed that the city had been "opened" to foreigners, as I'd been promised earlier on the *Rus*, and paid little attention to the matter. I was still somewhat nervous about wandering about openly, since I had no explicit permission to be there, but if I'd known that the city was still closed, I would have been considerably more discreet. Yet it *was* still closed. I strolled about the city wearing Western T-shirts, with a Nikon slung around my neck, rubbernecking at government buildings, passing patrolling militiamen, taking pictures of the kremlin, asking questions in my awkward foreigner's Russian, and no one paid any attention. In retrospect, my very lack of deviousness was its own safeguard — no one that obvious could possibly be clandestine, and I suppose the cops took me for one of the American observers or academic lecturers. It was only as we were leaving Gorky late the following day that one of the others discovered the truth, and they started to laugh. I didn't think it was so funny; it was I who would have faced the chilly interrogations of the KGB, who'd presumably have expressed considerable skepticism at any protestations of innocent ignorance.

I spent the first day in Nizhni Novgorod on my own, poking about the city. The following day George, who'd spent the night ashore, came to the boat to see if I wanted to meet a friend of his, "very interesting person, very complex, part of the new way." What new way? I was suspicious of "new ways"; the phrase had become an empty cliché of the Gorbachev era, as if saying it often enough would make something new actually happen. Most of the "new ways" turned out to be un-doable, or criminal, or both, and many of the New Men, the ruble millionaires, were beginning to hide their wealth, or at least become more discreet about spending it, as the angry rumbling from the populace about "exploiters" and their inflated prices rose to a roar. To be an entrepreneur was okay now, but no one yet knew where the boundaries of legitimate enterprise lay, and many of the New Men were testing these boundaries in ways that would have appalled their fathers. I supposed that the greed merchants of Wall Street similarly played fast and loose with the rules of ethical business conduct, but at least in the United States the culture of the entrepreneur was well established. Here, you had only the gray market, the hidden bargain, the subterranean deal.

George's friend lived in an apartment building a few blocks from the university. It was a substantial Stalin-era building of about twelve floors, heavy with ornament, overdone in Stalin's obsessive way with corbels and columns and useless embellishment, but solid and well made. There was a man at the door in a suit, standing with his hands in his pockets, apparently doing nothing, but he eyed us carefully and checked us off on a short list of expected guests. This was an interesting sign. The only other doormen I'd seen were at state institutions and Party offices, and this one had the unmistakable smell of state security. The presence of official-dom made me uneasy, and I wondered fleetingly again whether the city really was "open," as I'd believed. But the KGB man, if that's what he was, showed no interest in my legitimacy in the city, only in this building. We took the elevator, and this, at least, was reassuringly normal — its floor dropped a heart-stopping two inches when we got on, as elevators often do in the Soviet Union. Then it clanked slowly upward to the tenth floor.

"What does your friend do for a living?" I asked as we approached the apartment door.

"He is a . . . I think you call him a broker," George said.

"I thought brokers were illegal?"

"Not any more. Not this kind of broker, the kind who just helps things happen. So far, people like this are the only real free market we have."

The door opened and a young man with longish blond hair and cowboy boots invited us in. Behind him was another young man, dark, smiling a mirthless smile, and on the sofa behind him sat a willowy young woman, in a short skirt and inexpertly applied makeup. There was music playing on a Bang + Olufsen turntable, Western pop music. On a Finnish glass table by the window was a spread of cold cuts, smoked sturgeon and a large pot of caviar with silver spoons. We were supposed to be impressed. I was impressed.

The apartment had six rooms, and the young man seemed to live there alone. I was even more impressed. I'd talked to people in Moscow who'd been on a waiting list for an apartment for six years; in Yaroslavl and Kostroma the housing squeeze was a constant complaint. I'd met young people who were living with their parents years after their marriage. Every city was desperately short of housing. I knew of an influential man in Moscow who was now reduced to one room, after two divorces in which he and his wife of the moment were forced to divide the flat in which they lived, because neither could find another; he was living in a corner of his former spacious apartment with his third wife, feeling squeezed and betrayed by his fate.

The food George's friend had on display impressed me too. When we lived in Moscow, in an apartment in the foreign ghetto on Kutuzovsky Prospekt, we'd tried at first to do our shopping in the "Russian" stores, that is, the stores where the ordinary person shopped. In practice it took too long, and we soon gave in and used the supermarket set aside for "coupon rubles" and hard currency. Coupons were issued to those influential in the Soviet state, to the new elites, who in the Brezhnev era were astoundingly open about their corrupt practices. This supermarket was . . . unusual, to say the least.

We were unable to buy hamburger, only filet. If we wanted a hamburger at home, we ground filet mignon to get it. I remember one day longing for a simple roast chicken, and seeing in the poultry racks only pheasant and the tender yellow flesh of willow ptarmigan. We bought caviar by the half-pound.

This aspect of Soviet life has been well covered by Moscow foreign correspondents — the special section of GUM, the biggest
department store, where the ladies of the elite go to be fitted for
Western fashions; the special shops for French perfumes and
Scotch whiskeys and Sony televisions; the special garages for the
special curtained limos; the "open accounts" (for unlimited funds)
at the State Bank for certain individuals; the school for children of
the elite where chauffeured limos wait to take the little darlings
home. That there was a class of rich and influential people
shouldn't have been surprising, but it was the schism between
rhetoric and practice that annoyed all of us at the time. I'd become
familiar by then with the peculiarly Russian concept that goes by
the shorthand term *blat*.

Blat isn't criminal corruption — not necessarily. Nor is it the
simple doing of favors. That there's a fairly fine line between crimi-
nality and *blat* is well understood; to have *blat* is to be able to use
influence and connections to get goods or services scarce or unob-
tainable in other ways. *Blat* is the whole system of the repayment
or exchanging of favors. Almost everyone possesses it in some
small measure, or at least anyone that Westerners would call
middle-class. Those who use it develop it into a system; those who
don't are forever walking away disappointed as they discover the
Aeroflot flight is full, or the last eggs were just sold, or the broken
light fixture cannot be repaired this year. Stores and restaurants
remain stubbornly closed to those who have nothing to trade, no
blat, nothing banked with which to dispense favors. The apparently
empty stores are not always quite as empty as they appear. The
shoe salesman has put a few pairs aside, for those who can provide
theater tickets, or a kilo of meat, or some planks for the dacha, or a
gallon of paint.

The system is intricate: *blat* can take on an abstract quality, just
like money or honor: favors can be stored up against need. If you
work in a paint store you might set aside two gallons for yourself,
one to trade to the dentist so he'll use an anesthetic next time, the
other to give to a friend to use for some other purpose, thus owing
you a service at some unspecified future point. This isn't bribery or
corruption. It's an understanding that a system this sclerotic needs
a friendly jolt to get its lifeblood flowing, an understanding that

everyone can use a little assistance in getting through life — assistance that will someday, in need, be repaid.

Whether or not the purist will call *blat* corruption, the Russians insist it is not. They point to the basic honesty of most citizens. Until recently, theft of personal property was rare in Russia. Purloining state property, on the other hand, is taken as a natural right — lumber, paint, bricks, even trucks are fair game, and disappear constantly; in one notorious instance a whole apartment building under construction was trucked away, to be traded elsewhere for unspecified favors.

The temptation to exploit one's position in the consumer distribution chain is almost irresistible. The system runs all the way through from the simple and relatively innocent *blat* to hard-line racketeering. No one who's lived in the Soviet Union, or even spent a week there outside the protection of Intourist, can help but notice how practiced ordinary Russians have become in circumventing the official command economy, in making do amidst chronic shortages. Nearly a quarter of the Soviet economy is estimated to work in this "gray market" fashion. In some sectors the proportion is much higher. Almost a quarter of new apartments built never get to the allocation system, and of those that do, a third more disappear through *blat*. Virtually all repairs are done in the gray market. It's estimated that doctors see twice as many people as they report, the "fees" from the other 50 percent ranging from hockey tickets to trips abroad. More than twenty-five million people make most of their living in the gray economy, making Soviet economic statistics difficult to interpret: even when there are official shortages, and the stores appear empty, goods can often be obtained in the gray market.

Which is where "facilitators" like George's friend enter the picture. Many of them are making money, sometimes very great amounts of money, through networks of co-ops and "distribution collectives."

It's often said, in an attempt to explain the notorious Russian reluctance to do any work, that cynicism is the enemy of enterprise. And it's true that Russians have become deeply cynical about promises to be "fulfilled in the next plan," and no longer believe in the State or in much of anything else, and therefore don't even try to respond to the State's exhortations. This is only half the story. Cynicism also breeds the fast operator, the quasi-criminal who manipulates the system to his own advantage. The sorry part is that these facilitators, these fast-ruble artists operating on the fringes of respectability, are the corporate elite of the new Russian market economy.

George and I stayed for an hour. The willowy young woman and the man with the fixed smile said nothing in that time; they were there as backdrop, not as featured players; she was referred to only as the *pizdka* (little cunt), and she didn't seem to mind. George's friend, who said he was a graduate of Kishinev University and a former Master of Sports in football, whatever that means, apparently got his start working the Moscow-Gorky trains with a pack of cards, and his real education paying off the train crews and the militia with the money he fleeced from credulous peasants. He monopolized the conversation, speaking fluently and gracefully of Western politics, economic theory, his admiration for Margaret Thatcher, his thoughts on matters of taste and style, while George and I ate sturgeon and drank champagne and wondered where the hell the country was going.

On the way out, the KGB man at the door touched his fingers to his forehead in an ironic salute. I wondered what he and his bosses were getting out of all this. I recalled a quote from Lenin: "No profound and popular movement has ever occurred in history without dirty scum rising to the top, without adventurers and rogues, boasters and ranters attaching themselves to the inexperienced innovators." Lenin would have recognized George's friend; he would have been astonished to learn that a good many people have applied the same quotation to his own successors.

In the boulevard outside the Communist Party headquarters, a building that rudely dominates the red-brick kremlin and has a commanding view over the Volga, I ran into an old fellow berating the doorman for something or other. I went over to hear what was going on, just as he left, fuming. I followed and caught up with him. When he calmed down, he explained that he'd owned a small car on which he'd taken out collision insurance (rare enough in the Soviet Union, where private insurance brokers are unknown). He'd never opted for theft insurance because "I have good locks and a place to keep the car inside." This, it turned out, was naive. One of the gangs that had plagued Gorky for months raided his garage and brazenly took his car while he watched. "And do you think the militia would come?" That's what he was going on about back there.

"Why harangue the Communist Party and its petty functionaries," I asked, "especially a doorman? Why not harangue the militia instead?" He looked at me askance. He may have been mad, but he wasn't stupid — it never pays to berate a cop. It interested me that he felt free to harangue the Party, however.

I was curious about this business of insurance. In a nanny state, where the government is insurer, banker, enforcer and judge, what role did insurance play? If the government intervened in everything, why would private citizens need insurance? There was supposed to be, in the doctrine, "no-fault" insurance — that is, automatic compensation for loss, without apportioning blame. He explained over an apple juice from a kiosk that no-fault applied only to liabilities, not to property losses. The State pays all medical bills, so liability insurance against injury to others isn't necessary. "If my apartment burns, they are supposed to give me another," he said. "But they won't replace my furniture. I must insure against damage to that, and I do. If I kill someone with my car, I can be charged and jailed. If I injure him and it wasn't my fault, I pay nothing. If he damages my car, I get no compensation unless I'm insured. This is normal, no?" I supposed it was. "Now my car is gone and I get nothing," he said, beginning to fume again. "If the militia had come when I called them they could have caught the hooligans in the act. But I suppose they have better things to do than help an old man."

Later that day I met a couple of young Russians in an ice cream store a block or so from the kremlin. One was a tall, muscular youth with a mustache, blond and hard-looking. He'd applied for permission to leave the country, to go to Toronto, and would be leaving in about a month. ("A Jewish friend from Moscow helped with the papers, and with being in line — you have to be there on the right day, or you lose your chance. Jews have been getting lots of practice lining up for visas.") This friend had relatives in the Toronto suburb

of Willowdale, and my friend had spent a month with them the previous summer, working (illegally) in a car wash for five dollars an
hour. He was absurdly proud of this car wash — he sounded something like a TV pitchman for it — and thought five dollars, which
was well under the minimum wage, was a fortune.

Permission to travel abroad is now much easier to get, but
because of restrictions on exporting cash it's still difficult for Soviet
citizens without relatives abroad, or sponsors, to travel to the West.
An emigrant is allowed only 2,000 rubles in Western currency,
which through some bizarre economics translates as about $600
American. The blond young man was quite prepared to work
below the minimum wage for however long it took, washing cars
while he studied English. He was full of questions about social
security, having heard alarming (but erroneous, because American)
stories about the high cost of medical care in Canada.

He was very pessimistic about his country, and was full of scorn
when he spoke of the "boss" or "our boss," as he called Gorbachev
— a man of the old times, he called him, "born in the old times, of
the old times, will always be of the old times." He also disparaged
Gorbachev's Russian, which he said was full of errors and spoken
with a poor accent. This disparagement struck me as a bad sign,
particularly coming from someone in the provinces. Russians are
snobs about language, and criticizing a politician's use of language
is a strong signal of disillusion. It was used against Khrushchev in
his last days, and against Brezhnev, who possessed a hard Kharkov
accent. It was one of the reasons the Russian people could never
bring themselves to disparage Alexei Kosygin, who spoke beautiful,
sonorous Russian with the desired Leningrad accent, before
Brezhnev shuffled him off to obscurity.

The young man's pessimism was very deep. He asked if I'd had
any trouble in Gorky. He said he was surprised I was there,
because he thought the city was still closed to foreigners and that I
should be careful, because it was a dangerous city, and Kazan too.

"How so, dangerous?"

Had I seen large groups of young men in the streets?

I said I had.

Then I'd been lucky, he said, because many of these groups
were "Mafia," they attacked people for no reason, they ransacked

shops and stole their goods, they even carried guns and knives, and there were many murders among themselves.

I said the gang warfare sounded like L.A.

"New York!" he said eagerly. "Mafia!"

In any case, he said, if I were to see a group of young men I should get out of there *skoro*, fast. And it was worse, much worse, in Kazan. I should watch for them there too, and I should be very careful; the gangs killed each other, the Russians fought the Tartars.

"Who are these people, these gangs?" I asked.

"The sons of the poor," he said, "who have nothing and don't believe what the bosses say. They don't believe anyone. I think by this autumn we are going to have big trouble here . . ."

I noticed that my young informant was wearing a medallion around his neck, an enamelled painting of the Madonna and Child. He confirmed he was Orthodox, and said there was an active Russian Orthodox community in Toronto, which I hadn't known. He asked whether I wanted to visit a working church, but I declined. I have only a sociological interest in churchgoing, and I'd seen enough churches for the novelty to wear off and to get a feel for the richness of the ritual.

Instead, he offered me a cigarette made from *anasha*, a wild marijuana shipped in from Siberia. I declined that too, so we ate another ice cream and then we parted.

"Watch for it," he said as he strode away, "there'll be civil war here before the year is out."

Civil war? Chaos? The Russians have been there.

In 1916, during the war to end all wars, and under the crazed rule of the last of the Romanovs and the mad monk Rasputin, Russia was in ruins. Drunkenness was endemic, on the job, in the field, in the army, in the police, in the authorities sent to put down drunkenness, everywhere. Before the Bolsheviks took the country out of the war, soldiers did so on their own, streaming home to their villages in hundreds, and then thousands, trudging home in the rags that passed for their uniforms. The country was falling into chaos, which only grew in dimension under the provisional government. Like the Tsars, the Kerensky regime collapsed less because of the Bolsheviks than because it had no idea what to do.

The Bolsheviks came to power, to their own astonishment, and the wild experiments that they came to call "War Communism" completed the chaos. War Communism was an attempt to transform the country instantly into Utopia. Lenin and his followers abolished all ranks in the army, all ownership, all enterprises, all landowners, all bosses except themselves. The ideologues took control, and never has the necessity of cynical and pragmatic politics been better demonstrated: the Bolsheviks' utopian theories took no heed of how societies actually work, or how men actually behave, or of the practical state of the country. As the disorder mounted, so did organized revolt. The Cossacks and the White Guards rose in rebellion against the Bolsheviks. Foreigners intervened in the west, in the south, in the far north. Civil war followed. Fantastic inflation ensued, industry was more than five-sixths destroyed, transport ceased, private trade was abolished, foreign trade disappeared. The peasants, with great brutality, "cleared" the countryside for themselves, seizing the great houses, killing their inhabitants and overseers. State farms were set up and run by Communist zealots who knew nothing of farming; peasants were moved there at gunpoint, but sulked and sabotaged wherever they could.

A few years later, the country almost a country no longer, War Communism — and the idea of Communism as an immediate, practical political goal — was abandoned. In 1921 Lenin, on his own initiative, brought in his New Economic Policy, the NEP.

The NEP was a full-scale retreat from the mad notions of Communist theory. It restored the idea of ownership and profit. With astonishing rapidity (reassuring in these times) the NEPmen emerged. Fast-moving, amoral, profit-oriented, decadent, the NEPmen filled the empty shops with a speed that took everyone aback, including Lenin. This was the period when the arts flowered, of the building of a "new way" (in the cliché of the Nineties), of the emergence of the Russian entrepreneur. Only to disappear a few years later in the grim silence imposed by Stalin's Great Terror, when gangs of Chekhist thugs would emerge from the Lubyanka at night like predators and go on sweeps of the city, and the frightened citizens would scurry to work in the morning, too afraid to ask why the person next to them wasn't there.

Can the NEP be reinvented? The post-glasnost question of the moment is, Can perestroika — restructuring — do for the Soviet Union what the NEP did for Lenin? How far along the slope is the Soviet economy? Is the country still falling into a kind of pre-NEP chaos? What can be done to avert it? What can be done to avert the counter-perestroika reaction? How to ensure — how to finally be sure — that another Stalin isn't waiting in the wings, waiting to unleash some new terror? These questions were haunting everyone; Bolshevik history was haunting them, the ghosts of the Bolshevik giants treading on their heels, the cold breath of revolutionary ideology on their necks. George's friend in his six-room apartment wasn't worried about the future, but he should have been. He should have been worried about the anger coming from the bread lines in the shabby shops below. He was wrong to be cynical about Gorbachev and his people. He should have been praying that what Gorbachev started, he or his successors would be able to finish.

The Duke of Nizhni Novgorod asked Olearius if he was suitably afraid of the Cossacks, the legendary horsemen who were then engaged in brigandage along the Volga and were "not apt to leave us in peace." As the duke put it, "They're a cruel, inhuman lot, who love pillage more than their God, and fall upon people as if they [the Cossacks] were beasts." For the rest of the voyage down the Volga, the German party kept a wary eye out for bandits, and the sight of a lone horseman was enough to send them for their arms. Every time they met a fisherman or a hunter, or passed a village, they'd hear stories of Cossack raiders who'd just been by, or were expected, or were lying in wait downriver.

The Cossacks, who as an organized culture are now largely confined to museums and folk dances, had their home on the great plains around the Volga and the Don. Their name comes from the Turkic word *kazak*, meaning adventurer. From the earliest times they developed a fierce tradition of independence, and for centuries they received privileges from Moscow in return for military service. Originally, the word *kazak* applied to the semi-independent Tartar groups who formed in southern Ukraine, but later it also applied to peasants who fled from serfdom in Poland,

Lithuania and Moscow to the Dnieper and Don regions, where they formed free, self-governing militaristic communities. By the sixteenth century there were four main Cossack armies: the Don, the Yaik, the Terek and the Zaporozhie. As a result of an arrangement made with the Tsars, their influence was felt beyond the Volga into central Asia and even Siberia. By the nineteenth century there were twelve major Cossack groups, among them the Don, Kuban, Terek, Orenburg and Ussuri.

Whenever their privileges were threatened, they revolted. The most famous rebels were Stenka Razin, Kondrati Bulavin and Emilian Pugachev. Their way of life deteriorated in the nineteenth century when the communal landholding system broke down as their hetmans, or leaders, were made civil servants and allowed to own land themselves.

In the nineteenth and twentieth centuries the Cossacks were widely used by the Tsars to quell revolts. In the south, during the Civil War, Cossack regiments formed the bulk of the White Guards. Cossack administrative units were abolished under Soviet rule, though regiments were revived during World War II.

We met half a dozen Cossacks by the river just south of Nizhni Novgorod. None of them knew anything about their history, except that they had once been great and now were not. They all worked in a nearby cement factory, but had stayed away from work on this day to lie on the riverbank in idle contemplation of their fate. None of them had ever been on a horse, had ever ridden across the great plains of the south. They thought this an idiotic question when I asked it, and it probably was.

Some 20 kilometers downriver, the Olearius party met a large boat from Astrakhan with two hundred workers on board. Olearius, a student of all he saw, was interested in the Russian way of doing things, so different from the Teutonic methods he was accustomed to. He watched the *burlaki*, the Volga bargemen, at work: "When the wind isn't directly behind them, the Russians do not go under sail. Instead, they carry the anchors, one after another, a quarter of a league [a league is almost five kilometers] ahead in a small boat, then, using the bast ropes, a hundred or more men, standing one behind the other, pull the boat against the current. However, they

can't go more than two leagues this way [because of exhaustion]."
The boats, he reported, were loaded with salt, caviar and salted
fish. The Olearius party passed the villages of Rabotki,
Chechenino, Tatinets and Yurkino before anchoring for a hunting
excursion ashore.

We passed some of the same villages on the *Novosti Express*. I
hadn't expected this — we'd decided earlier that our voyage would
terminate at Gorky, and that the others would return to Moscow
from there, leaving me either to make my way further or to return
with them, as I pleased. This didn't trouble me, since I'd already
passed this way on the *Rus*, on which I'd gone somewhat further
downriver, to Kazan. But when the time came for us to abandon
the *Novosti Express*, the others couldn't quite bring themselves to
do it, and after considerable argument we arrived at a compromise:
we'd push on for another two days. We looked at a map the
Rechflot crew had given me. Anton wanted to go at least as far as
Vasilsursk, a resort town another 150 kilometers further on. And so
we decided. We untied the boat from its mooring and headed on
down Mother Volga, following in Olearius's trail.

CHAPTER 11

Kilometer 1,423

Makarevo

It was dark when we stopped for the night. Just after dusk, a passing freighter had given us a scare — we'd thought he'd pass on the right, but we failed to see his left strobe flashing, and he missed us by a few yards, his wake rocking us violently. He apparently hadn't noticed us, though our running lights were in good order. George, who was at the wheel, pulled over to the left bank, and we crept towards the shore until we ran lightly aground, then dropped the anchor. From the map, we were near the mouth of the Kerzhenets River, just upstream from the town of Makarevo, about which none of us knew anything.

For most of the early evening we'd passed small villages and isolated hamlets; at each place there was someone on the riverbank, and whenever we stopped they offered to buy eggs, or meat, or whatever we had. No one was begging, but they had an impoverished air and a resigned look, as if they were used to being told no. Some of the women looked like Gypsies; they were probably Bashkirs who lived at the edge of the forest and relied on the river for their provisions. There was no longer any kolbasa to be had, one of them told us, and she looked frightened. This news depressed our crew more than anything. If they cannot even provide kolbasa, what hope is there?

After supper — in which kolbasa played some small part — we sat on the afterdeck and smoked and the Russians drank beer, while I opened a bottle of white Georgian wine and chewed on the heel of the sausage. As usual, the talk was of politics. I'd been trying to understand what had attracted Western intellectuals of the Twenties and Thirties to the Soviet idea. Some of it, clearly, had been revulsion from, rather than attraction to, something. They'd all been disgusted with the excesses and cruelties of capitalism as then practiced, but what was it about the chaotic Soviet state that lured them? To some degree it was the coherence of the underlying idea — the idea of equity for the small man. The Soviet Union was founded on a vision, and however chaotic and uneven its application, it was nevertheless an idea that could be applied universally, to all people, a vision that wasn't restricted to the boundaries of the traditional nation-states — states that had in the teens of the century destroyed millions of men in appalling and futile battles for mere yards of territory.

As the American journalist Louis Fischer had written, in a passage in which he was rejecting his earlier Communist affiliation: "The unique appeal of the Bolshevik revolution was its universality. It did not propose merely to introduce a certain number of drastic changes in Russia. It envisaged the world-wide abolition of war, poverty and suffering. In all countries, therefore, the little men, laborer and intellectual, felt that something important had taken place in their lives when revolution took root in Russia." This was naive, of course. It was also impractical. And later, those visionary revolutionaries would make the fatal mistake of equating force with wisdom and their own incumbency with the inevitable march of history, and so cynicism would triumph over honesty, and the "brave experiment" would deteriorate into the Great Lie, the Great Silence and the Great Leader. Still, the Soviet idea had been a noble one, and this made its perversion into a grotesque form of Tsarist tyranny even harder to bear.

"And now that the Cold War is over, there's no longer an idea, only a market," George said sadly. "All we're left with are economic mechanisms. That's why no one cares about anything any more."

"It was the Party," said Vasilii. "The Communist Party of the Soviet Union — glory to the CPSU! — that Party is the Soviet state's only achievement. Pretty remarkable, it was — an underground conspiracy, a monastic order, a military caste, all in one. Then it turned into nothing more than an enforcement arm of the tyranny. Now, it's just a way of getting by."

We'd been talking about the Party that afternoon, after we heard on the radio that Boris Yeltsin had left a meeting in Moscow early to travel to Leningrad, there to appear at the dedication of a new church. "That's the new reality of our country," Vasilii said. "The idea of the Party no longer attracts anyone, and people are turning back to the one institution left that has rejected materialism." All through the years of atheist propaganda the priests lived their lives of poverty; believers wore their crosses even into the basement killing rooms of the Lubyanka, and the executioners always tore them off before firing the bullet into the back of the neck. "The Party tried to be the Church, tried to be God, but that God has failed," he said.

At this phrase George hissed us to silence. "Look!" he said. "Look over there!" The moon was up, and a hundred yards away we saw looming out of the night a massive wall, and the moon glinting softly off the six blue domes of a church. Beyond it was another church. In the foreground, seen through an opening in the wall, was the yellow light of a small fire. We could smell the smoke, now that we'd noticed it; someone had lit a fire inside whatever building this was.

"Jesus," I said, somewhat inappropriately, "what do you think that is? Where are we?" I was startled — talk of the Church, and there it is . . .

No one answered.

We splashed ashore and walked towards the wall. Its base was set in what appeared to be a new concrete embankment, but there was nothing new about the wall itself. We came first to a round tower that turned out to be a corner, and the forbidding wall stretched off in both directions as far as we could see. It was cold and damp, and smelled old, as old stones do, for these were clearly very old stones that had very likely seen the passing of the ships of Peter the Great, and had watched the waning of the Tartar power so many centuries ago. I leaned against the wall, its white paint silver in the moonlight, and felt its cold sweat on my flesh, and shivered, although it wasn't cold. Fifty yards further the featureless wall changed, and a square tower was set into it, cold slit glassless windows staring from on high. A little further was a wooden door, heavy with studs and bolts, and inside the court, on the stones before the church, a man was sitting cross-legged before his fire, singing a melancholy hymn.

We quite forgot our arguments and the Party and the drinking and stood silent, struck dumb by this scene from ancient Slavic history, the flickering flames and the silver and blue night fire of the moon on the domes . . . I thought of the last phrase before we were interrupted by the moon, "the God that failed," and here we were in the house of the elder God, in the intimate sorcery of a church that had wrestled with its fate all though the long, tormented Russian history, a church that had survived purge and persecution for so many centuries, that had survived Stalin by going underground, which is where Russians always hide as their country descends again into a long, long night . . . I was shaken, for even as the cynical observer in me was saying, *This is a wonderful moment!* I saw a church behind a church, and behind that another could dimly be made out, and suddenly the world seemed overflowing with the stones of Byzantium, and I remembered all the stories of the monks who'd spread Christianity through Trotsky's "howling wilderness."

These reveries were interrupted by the abrupt cessation of the singing, as the singer sensed we were there, and he swung round, shining a large flashlight in our direction, and shouted, "Who's that? Who's there?"

"It's all right," Anton said, stepping into the light. "We saw the fire from our boat, and we came to see what it was. We're not robbers."

The watchman, or security man, or whatever he was, was angry at first, embarrassed to have been caught singing a hymn, but he soon accepted a cigarette and offered to show us around. "I can't get you inside," he said, "but I'll show you what I can." He seemed to be glad of the company.

The Makarevski Sheltovodskii monastery, he told us, was

founded on this headland sometime in the fourteenth century by holy men whose idea had been to send proselytizers into the lands east of the Volga. But the monks became sidetracked by affluence and developed instead a lucrative trade with the south. Spiritually, they were diverted by power. They owned in their heyday, the watchman told us, many thousands of serfs, "and the gold in those churches would've sunk a Volga barge."

He pointed to a smaller church whose outline could just be made out. "That one — the whole iconostasis was made of gold," he said. "They're restoring the church now, but of the gold there's nothing left."

By the mid-1500s, at the time of Ivan the Terrible, the monastery owned most of the left bank from Nizhni Novgorod to Kosmodemyansk, a distance of well over 200 kilometers. This was not uncommon; as it did for the Catholic church in the West, affluence became its own spiritual reward.

The early Orthodox monasteries were founded near towns and owed their existence to the "generosity of the boyars," though occasionally a group of wealthier peasants would endow a small monastery. As time went on, monasteries appeared even in remote areas. They would be founded by itinerant monks, some of whom developed holy reputations and attracted followers. St. Sergius at the town of Zagorsk, one of the greatest of the medieval institutions, was established when the saint took refuge in the forest after a Tartar raid and found himself surrounded by pious peasants. In other places, holy men would sometimes spend half a lifetime wandering in the wilderness before founding a monastery; Saint Paul Obnorsky, a mystic whose life was austere even by Russian standards, lived for three years in the trunk of a lime tree. Within a few centuries there were monasteries stretching east to the Urals and north to the White Sea.

In time, the caretaker told us, echoing an old saying, "a blight of wealth fell on the Church." The historian Bernard Pares, who made a study of early Russian Orthodoxy, recounts the tale of a prior who lived in a small cell but who extended his lands for eight kilometers on each side, after which angry peasants burned down his church. Another monastery owned twenty villages and ran its own judicial system. By the seventeenth century the Church owned two-thirds of Russian territory, and through the monasteries and priesthood dominated the lives of the people. In 1762 Russia's 921 monasteries owned eight hundred thousand serfs; St. Sergius owned a hundred thousand alone.

Even in the Byzantine heart of Russia the excesses of wealth led to protest. Monks split from their communities and disappeared again into the great Russian forests, there to found new ones. Fanatics and heretics appeared everywhere; out of the wilderness came the Skoptsi (Eunuchs), a sect of castrated fanatics. They lived in communes, dressed in white. They spent their days gardening and their nights in prayer, snatching sleep when they could. There's a marvelous painting in Moscow's Tretyakov Museum by the nineteenth-century artist Vasilii Surikov that shows white-garbed men, haggard but proud, being dragged off to the gibbet in Red Square in Moscow. In the foreground, women and children (presumably not their own, unless pre-castration) weep in front of the carts to which the men are lashed; off to the right, standing with the commanding officer of the militia, is the Orthodox Metropolitan, calmly supervising the executions. The chaotic opulence of the domes of St. Basil's in the background is echoed by the seething mobs of peasants who surround the martyrs.

In the cities, a rationalist heresy arose among a group called the Strigolniki (Shavers — signifying the importance attached to the beard in Orthodox thinking of the time). Through the centuries faint flashes of light pierced the gloom of obscurantism. In the West, these became Protestantism; in Russia, they deteriorated into arcane squabbles.

The greatest schism of Russian church life still has its echoes today. I once visited a Old Believers' church in Moscow and was instructed in the essential differences dividing them from the ecclesiastical authorities. To the outsider, these differences seem trivial beyond belief, but in reality the schism was political opposition in disguised form — the Church hierarchy, in the persons of the Muscovite clergy, were the champions of authority and regimentation; the Old Believers were more concerned with matters of morality and religious experience; they were the upholders of tradition and were closer to the feelings of the masses.

The split was begun by Patriarch Nikon, a harsh and arrogant

man born near Nizhni Novgorod. He set about "correcting" the
ancient liturgical books, which had remained unchanged since the
earliest of days of Saint Cyril, the monk who'd brought Christianity
to the north. By a clerical error, the early books spelled the name
of Jesus "Isus" instead of "Iuisus," and Nikon's effort to correct this
error set off a wave of revulsion among believers. Another dispute
concerned the number of fingers to use when crossing oneself: two
fingers represent the dual nature, divine and human, that hung on
the Cross; three fingers represent the Trinity, of which only one
person was on the Cross.

Open conflict broke out in 1653. It took root and spread in the
middle Volga regions and also in the lower Volga of the southeast,
where Old Believers were given refuge by the Cossacks. Archpriest
Avvakum, one of the leaders, was exiled to Siberia in 1655, and
counselled retreat for religious reasons:

> Fly, my dear ones
> Into the black woods
> Take refuge, my dear ones
> In the mountain and the caves
> Hide, my dear ones
> In the depths of the earth.
> Ah, if someone would but build me
> A cell in the heart of the woods
> Where no man went
> And no bird flew
> Where only thou, O Christ, wouldst dwell
> For the good of our souls
> And where I would no longer see
> All the scandal of the world.

"How come," I asked the watchman, "you know so much about
the Church? About religious life?"

He shrugged. "The monastery has been a ruin since before I
was born," he said. "It was a ruin before my mother was born. I
think it's been pretty much of a ruin since Peter the Great. But a
man has to believe in something. I don't trust a man who believes
only in himself. They tell us that's what you in the West believe."

I said nothing. I thought of what the judge in Yaroslavl had said, how "dogmatic" is a positive word in Russian, how no one trusts anyone without a set of guiding rules. Then I thought of how rank superstition was once again prevalent in Russia, with UFO landings reported on the Tass newswire, with monthly sightings of the yeti, with psychic healers and "extrasensory doctors" appearing in every town. The churches had never been fuller. Why, they were even turning Solzhenitsyn into a cult figure, the pan-Slavic zealots taking on a mystical coloration. How many times had I read Westerners speculating on this persistence of superstition among Russians, how it was allied to the old Russian tendency to take things to extremes, how in Russia emotions are open and almost tangible, an emotionalism verging on the manic?

Before we left, the watchman pulled out from his shirt his enameled cross with a small pastel figurine of Jesus glued to it. He offered it to me, but I refused. His need for a talisman seemed greater than mine.

In the morning we spent a few minutes ashore on the opposite bank, in the little town of Liskovo. Liskovo is also full of architectural monuments of the old times. Most of them bore scaffolding, but there was no sign of the workers, as usual. I asked a young man what was being done to the cathedral, but all I got in return was a tirade, apparently directed equally against the Church, or its resurgence, and the authorities, who apparently paid more attention to it than they should. Liskovo has at least three churches, the massive cathedral of the eighteenth century, which is under renovation, and two others, which seemed to be in moderately good shape. There was also a small regional museum, consisting mostly of folk art and battered agricultural implements of the older days.

The rest of the afternoon we traveled south, passing the villages of Prosek, Selskaya Maza, Barmino and Velikovskoe. I remembered Olearius mentioning Barmino: "August 5. Barmino, 90 versts from Nizhni Novgorod. Here we bought provisions from the peasants in boats. There were many more shoals and shallows." I saw no shoals or shallows thereabouts, but Barmino was a pleasant place, set on a long, sloping, steep meadow with many attractive blue houses and neatly fenced gardens. I saw an old man sitting in front of a small *izba*, a hut, with a tiny barn out back. There was new wood planking on the west side of his house, carefully laid in a herringbone pattern. I looked at the old man again. He was sitting on a chainsaw, its blade stuck into the ground as a chair leg. He looked very comfortable. I passed my binoculars to Volya, who looked, shook his head and steered the boat on south.

CHAPTER 12

Kilometer 1,505

Vasilsursk

J ust outside Vasilsursk we stopped at a small village whose
name I never did learn. It wasn't much of a place — a few
houses spilling down the bank to a meadow at the river's edge,
where a herd of Kostroma cows grazed placidly. I wanted to try
again to get a sense of the rural economy. I wasn't looking for
peasants who wanted — or didn't want — to be *kulaks*. I just
wanted to know how ordinary people got by, on a daily basis, in
their everyday affairs.

Officially, forty-three million Russians live below the poverty
line of 75 rubles a month. Much of this region of the middle Volga
had resorted to rationing. And yet, the peculiarity of this barely
functional economy is that there's far too much money parked in
savings accounts, and the government faces a major struggle to
prevent it leaking into the black market, sending up prices even
further. How did the villagers get supplies? Where did they shop?
I'd heard, we all had, the extraordinary stories about milk shortages in dairy producing areas, of wood shortages in the forests, of
meat shortages in beef country. Some of that we'd seen for ourselves in Kostroma and other places. I wanted to see how the

country people shopped, how they got things like tools, furniture, TVs, repairs, amusements of all sorts.

For many evenings we'd talked about the economy, but of course no one had any solutions beyond invoking "the market." All we had were buts. But . . . without free prices perestroika will fail. But . . . with a budget deficit of up to 10 percent of GNP and enormous pent-up demand from 300 billion rubles in savings accounts, free prices would bring huge inflation. All these buts, all these doubts, all this uncertainty, all this fear, all this disillusion. No one any longer believed what the Soviet government — including, apparently, Gorbachev — was saying; the words of Marx, Lenin, Stalin and his successors have papered over so many grotesque lies that the failure this time to literally deliver the goods has stretched credibility to the breaking point. Did any small reservoir of the "entrepreneurial spirit" persist among the rural people, in a society where the measure of success has been to beat the system, not to make a new system work?

The riverside villages were clearly better off than those deep in the forests. Residents could, and did, use the Raketa fleet of hydrofoil boats as commuter buses. They were regular, efficient, reliable and relatively fast, and went places one wanted to go, at least in summer. For virtually all non-food items, the villagers were forced to travel to the larger towns, to Kstrovo, south of Gorky, or to Gorky itself, a hundred or so kilometers away. They borrowed the local truck, hitchhiked, took the boat or waited patiently for the rare buses. Curiously, none of the local people had learned, even informally, to fix things themselves, with the exception of motors — they were good amateur mechanics. To get a TV repaired, you schlepped it a hundred kilometers. To acquire a chair, you went a hundred kilometers. To buy a sweater — a hundred kilometers. There are dressmakers on some of the farms, but sew-it-yourself clothing seems to be unknown. Some women have sewing machines, but they use them only for simple repairs. This is partly a matter of the shortage economy — fabric is hard to come by, and so are patterns — and *Vogue* isn't available at the corner newsstand, had there been a corner newsstand. On the other hand, travel really is cheap, and going to the cities has its pleasures. Sometimes they stay overnight, usually with friends. One woman said she'd gone the 200 kilometers to Kazan for an evening at the opera. The others were so proud of her that I was ashamed of my initial skepticism.

Tools, any tools, were very hard to come by. The typical "hardware store" seldom stocked tools, except the most basic — a hammer, perhaps, and a saw, but little else. It soon becomes obvious in any village that the villagers lack practice with tools, especially levels, squares and measuring instruments. I watched a young man building a wooden fence around his house. The house itself was an old one, a small log cottage with decorative carvings around the windows and an intricately arched doorway. Most of the carved moldings looked shabby, the weather having taken its toll in the absence of paint. Much of the rest of the house needed paint too, the sills were rotting and the whole thing had an alarming list. The fence he was making was rudimentary, horizontal beams with one-by-four vertical nailers. Rather, they were supposed to be vertical, but hardly any were. Nor was the spacing between the vertical planks at all regular. The whole effect was of instant disrepair, even before the wood had weathered. He owned neither a level nor a tape measure. He told me he'd have to go to Gorky for those, though he doubted even Gorky would have them. In any case, he pointed out, the fence would keep out dogs, which was its purpose.

From the boat, it was easy to be deceived about these riverside villages. The landscape around Vasilsursk was beautiful, steep banks covered with white and silver birches, broken by green meadows interspersed with little hamlets that from the water seemed tranquil and cozy. It was only when you got close enough to examine the dilapidated state of the buildings that the poverty became evident, and the deep unhappiness of the people with their lot. From each shabby roof protruded a television antenna, and I wondered again how the powers at Center were dealing with this simple fact: there are no truly isolated peasants any more. This point had occurred to me before, at the *kolkhoz* outside Uglich, and it was reinforced here: the baritone voice of Boris Yeltsin could be heard hectoring and haranguing in even the tiniest of hamlets, reaching directly into isolated homes. This makes the post-perestroika crisis different from any that went before. In earlier days, the peasants could be manipulated by landowners or their overseers or, later, by the local Party bosses. All discussions of the "Russian peasantry" and its historic isolation and legendary conservatism have now to take into account that the new politicians can address them directly, not just bypassing the local *apparat* that has run things in the countryside since Soviet history began, but also sliding into the peasant brain an insidious message far more powerful than propaganda, the notion that they themselves can make, remake and unmake the state.

In all the romantic writing about Russia, much has been said of how the immense open spaces instilled in the Russians their larger-than-life emotions, their communalism as well as their historic xenophobia. If there's any truth to these assertions, it lies not so much in the spaces as in the interstices — in the isolation the great space has historically engendered. This isolation is now only physical; the web of television has brought the peasant into the picture in a new way. It will be impossible to revert to the old-fashioned top-down management style the Party long ago picked out for itself from the thinly stocked shelves of Russian history.

How poor is poor, how deprived is deprived? Garri, one of the people on the *Rus* (his job had been ill defined but seemed mostly to be problem-solving — he was a fixer by temperament as well as employment), had suggested that the countryside was much worse off than it looked, that the villages had major problems just getting by, and that my experiences were incomplete unless I came to understand this. But then Garri's notion of what constituted a problem was unusual in the Soviet Union. He worried, for instance, that satellite dish receivers had become available but cost 15,000 rubles — "and who has that kind of money?" A monthly salary, after all, was around 200 rubles. The doctor from Chernobyl had told me she earned around 500 rubles a month, and considered herself well off.

My own view on the villages around Vasilsursk was that they were poor but not deprived, if the distinction is valid. They certainly felt themselves to be poor, and were clearly restless and unhappy, but they did have adequate clothing, and although food was scarce no one was hungry. I asked the chairman of the local soviet what he thought. Did Russian villages have major problems getting by? Were things getting better? Worse? What would the next winter be like? In response, he resorted to poetry, as Russians so often still do when words fail them or emotions threaten to overwhelm them. I didn't understand very much of it — the sonorousness of his delivery made it hard to hear — but I caught enough to get his meaning. It seemed to be a poem about how trials were meant to strengthen the spirit. I wondered whether the other people in the village felt the same way.

Food remained the critical problem. The chairman confirmed it: there were indeed places in this agricultural heartland where there was virtually no meat. Some places seemed to have plenty, some had none at all. He told us about one village, further up the river, where there was no milk, although the state farm 20 kilometers away raised cows. Why? No one really knew. They blamed it on the chairman, or on the quota, or on "them," whoever "they" were — no one really knew that either. All the milk from the farm was shipped out, because their quota was set at a level they were supposed to have been able to reach with the number of cows they were supposed to have, but since they never reached this quota, not having the requisite number of cows, they were always in deficit. In order to maintain the fiction that everything worked and everyone fulfilled their quotas, the figures would simply be falsified by functionaries higher up the distribution chain. This process would repeat itself as each stage noticed the shortfall, and it was only at the retail level that any attempt was made to match figures with actual product. By that time, it was much too late, and so mysterious "shortages" would be "discovered." The authorities punished the farmers for these shortages by not letting them keep a supply of their own. Local people would therefore have to travel up to 50 kilometers just to buy milk. Of course, the farmers have become wise to this trick, and so they indulge in falsifications of their own, hiding some milk from the inspectors. Unsurprisingly, that particular farm has developed a reputation as a troublemaker. The village chairman said blandly: "So life works."

This was one of the few places where the locals apparently regarded Boris Yeltsin as a wimp; their own politics were far more radical.

"You want to know why?" the chairman asked. "It costs the farmers about 4 rubles to produce a kilo of pork. The state sells the meat in town for 2 rubles, and helps to bankrupt everyone. The co-ops in towns will pay us 6 rubles for a kilo, and sell it for 8, thereby pricing it out of everyone's reach. So we sell for 6, and say the hell with it."

If enough co-ops existed, the competition would drive down prices. The price revolt among consumers makes this impossible. No wonder the farmers were saying the hell with it.

I still found it puzzling that even in the rural areas, there was no attempt at self-sufficiency. Hardly anyone seemed to raise chickens, for example, or pigs, even for their own use. Is this custom, practice or simple apathy? No one I asked had a response.

Many of the small villages along the Volga, which are all electrified, have at least one, possibly two, small factories and enterprises. Hereabouts they often make wooden things, ranging from implements (ax handles, brooms, spoons, bowls) to furniture. The distribution problems they face are immense. Few of these places are close to a railway line. Apart from the river, which is closed for half the year, trucking is the only way out, but the roads are dreadful and there are never enough operating vehicles. There's a lively debate in the local press about these small enterprises. Would a market economy kill them off? Or would they learn to supply local markets, instead of importing and exporting goods to and from the cities?

There are decent roads in the small towns, considering the ravages of winter and the high cost of repairs. In the more enterprising towns, stores have traveling sections — merchandise loaded onto trucks for sale in the hamlets.

The village we stopped at was nicely situated in a cove, a well-preserved Orthodox church on a high bank on one side, the central square behind it, the former manor house and substantial burghers' houses around the cove on the other side. We were offered lunch at the chairman's house, a robust meal of sliced pork belly, raw garlic, lemon and vodka. In this case, few of the locals seemed curious about a foreigner in their midst, except as a good excuse not to do any work. Not that there was much evidence of work having been done — most of the men had been planning to go fishing in the Volga after lunch, despite the obvious pollution.

The idea that the Volga, their beloved river, was becoming polluted angered them more than anything else. Our host pointed

After a quarter century of violent, ceaseless propaganda on the sinfulness and wickedness of private business, Russia is so alienated from the institution that young people under thirty, in conversation with foreigners, find it hard to imagine the system of private enterprise as it exists in the outside world.

Envy, yes, envy and terror both played a role, as the Bolshevik machine turned on itself and began to devour its children. The envy is still there, but the terror has gone now, and the Russians are developing their own instructors in the nuances of private enterprise. There's nothing to suppose they won't learn it fast. They've done so before.

CHAPTER 13

Kilometer 1,550

Kosmodemyansk

Vasilsursk, at Kilometer 1,505, was as far down the Volga as the *Novosti Express* reached; from there, we'd turn back, west to Gorky, where we'd do . . . something . . . with the boat, and the others would return to Moscow. I'd already gone past Vasilsursk on the *Rus*, past the towns of Kosmodemyansk and Cheboksari to Kazan, some 200 kilometers further, so I had no need to repeat that stretch. I needed somehow to cover the further 220 kilometers from Kazan to Ulyanovsk. I was "official" in Ulyanovsk — that is, my visa allowed me to be there — but how I'd subsequently get from Ulyanovsk (which was at Kilometer 1,968) to Astrakhan (at Kilometer 3,500) I wasn't yet sure. And how to get from Gorky to Ulyanovsk? The most probable route would be to return with the others to Moscow and fly from there to Ulyanovsk, picking up a boat once I reached it. A boat, or . . . something.

We were all impatient to be moving. I was impatient because I was only a third of the way down the Volga, and I'd already seen Gorky twice. I didn't particularly want to return to it — it was going the wrong way, upriver, and I wanted badly to go down. I wanted to see the Zhiguli Hills, where the Cossack bandits once lived, I wanted to see the Samara Bend, the Volga's last hesitation before its plunge to the Asian seas; I wanted to visit Saratov, where the Volga Germans had settled. Was Russia so limitless, so deep, so cold, that entire ethnic groups, entire nationalities — the Don Cossacks, the Volga Germans, the Crimean Tartars — could simply vanish from history, and their cries of outrage and pain go unheard beyond the endless frontier? I wanted to see where they'd been, and to find some trace of them still, if I could.

And Anton, George, Vasilii, Volya and Vladimir? They were impatient because they wanted to go home. They wanted to go back to Center, where momentous events were happening. They were impatient with the provinces, with the constant angry grumbling of the provincials. They knew it was this very grumbling that had precipitated and underpinned the changes they all endorsed and the other changes they now feared, but they didn't much like it. Provincial grumbling struck them as whining, a sly whining that had unpleasant echoes in Russian history and literature; it reminded them too much of Russia's peasant heritage. They understood that Lenin, and Stalin, and Khrushchev, and Brezhnev, and Gorbachev himself all came from the provinces, that their views were formed by the provinces and by the attitudes they'd learned there, but in their Muscovite snobbishness, they tended to dismiss all ideas emanating from "elsewhere" as somehow inferior. Above all they wanted to go back to the smell of their newsrooms, where they knew what was *going on* — they all believed their nostrils were as sensitive to the nuances of perestroika and post-perestroika policy as a canary is to coal gas, and they wanted to be part of the action again.

They'd all wanted to go on to Vasilsursk from Gorky, but they paid very little attention to it when they were there. As soon as the boat turned back, Volya opened the throttle as wide as it would go, and headed for Gorky, and home.

On the way west, we went through the provisions. There were still a few cans of Lowenbrau, and a dozen or so Zhiguli beers. The wine and the vodka had disappeared. There was a string bag of potatoes, a jar of cucumber pickles, a few tins of fish and the inevitable kolbasa. Anton hacked the kolbasa into chunks, and we each stowed a piece in our luggage for future use. The rest we'd simply abandon.

And the boat? Would we simply abandon that? This had puzzled me for some time. What to do about the boat? Who'd take it back upriver? Surely we couldn't simply leave it in Gorky, tied to a quay for any fast operator to make off with? Or didn't they care? Who *did* it belong to, anyway?

Anton had always been vague about it. I asked him again: Whose boat is this?

He became impatient. "Don't worry about it."

"I'm not. But you can't just leave it at the dock? What about the papers? Where do you leave them? On the hatch?"

He was evasive. "It's not a problem."

"What happens when the militia finds it? Someone will surely alert them?"

He grinned. "I'm sure the boat will have a good home," he said, and shut up. So did I. He had the papers, and if he wasn't worried I wasn't going to be either.

We moored the boat in the same place as before, across the Oka from downtown Gorky, just upriver from a series of commercial jetties where barges were filled with what looked like beach sand. We all heaved our bags onto the deck and took stock. Volya shut down the motors, we checked to see that the boat was fast, then we clambered ashore up a small ladder set into the concrete wall, passing our bags up ahead of us. Mine had gotten heavier. I was down a couple of cartons of Marlboros and one bottle of vodka (and the pantyhose I'd brought from Toronto, to the smirks of the Russian Customs officers, had long since been dispensed to the crew of the *Rus*), but I was up a guidebook to Tver (which I later discarded) and a huge pile of local maps and newspapers, which I thinned out, keeping only a representative sample. As we walked through the dockyard I was very conscious of these bags. The large one said in bold letters "Sportsac," and the smaller proclaimed itself the property of Pierre Cardin. These did not seem prudent items to carry about a dockyard in a city still closed — as far as I knew — to foreigners, and which, in any case, I hadn't been given explicit permission to visit. The few people we saw paid us no mind, but at the gates to the yard two militiamen were standing at a sort of sloppy attention.

"What to do?" I asked.

"Ignore them," Anton said. "Everybody does. It'll only be suspicious if you say hello. Just walk on."

Neither of the militiamen paid us any attention, though Anton was talking loudly as we approached.

As we passed, he suddenly slapped me on the shoulder and yelled, "*Yeb vas!*"

I didn't know what this meant, so I just laughed.

The cops ignored us.

As we rounded the corner, I asked, *Yeb vas*, what does it mean?

Volya laughed. "Don't use it in polite company," he said.

"What does it mean?"

"Fuck you," he said.

About half a kilometer down the road we stopped at a phone booth and Anton called a cab, haggling loudly over the price. "I told him we'd pay him in dollars, because he didn't want to come over this way," he said.

This meant I'd pay, since I was the only one with dollars. "Maybe he takes Visa," I said, snidely. The cabbie only needed five dollars to take us the many kilometers to the train station, and he deposited us there with a toothy grin of satisfaction, waving his dollar bills through the window in farewell. This wasn't prudent, but I'd given up trying to be invisible. No one else seemed to care, so why should I?

Two cops were examining documents at the ticket window, and for the first time the others shied away. "Better stay here," George said, "sit with the bags. We'll be right back." We piled the baggage in a heap, the Sportsac at the bottom, and I sank onto it. I was wearing a T-shirt that said, in Russian, "What Have You Done for Perestroika Lately?" on the front, which I'd exchanged on the street in Moscow for a *Toronto Life* shirt, but my Nikes were pretty obviously foreign. I shoved my feet under the baggage and read an old copy of *Kazanskaya Pravda* I'd wrapped around my camera.

It took them only a few minutes. George used his own documents twice to buy tickets at two different windows. The papers were scrutinized by two different cops, and given two different okays. The train left an hour later, and we had to stand for most of the eight-hour journey to Moscow. Apart from one more puzzle about the rural economy — half the people in the train seemed to be taking food parcels to the city, and the other half were planning to bring food back — the trip was uneventful.

There were no cops visible at the Moscow end.

We said our farewells at the train station. We exchanged phone numbers and addresses and promised to keep in touch, though we all knew we wouldn't. In truth, we were weary of one another's company. They were glad to be home. I was glad to be about to strike off on my own. Our differences were real, but they had nothing — or very little — to do with a Soviet-Western gap in ideas or perceptions. They had mostly to do with questions of intention and matters of personality. Traveling with them took me into villages I'd never otherwise have reached; and I likely wouldn't have risked Gorky without the support of their company and knowledge. So when I said thank you, I meant it, but I turned my back without regret.

I'd prudently booked a room at the Hotel Rossia earlier (I was used to austere accommodations, but returning to the Izmailovo, where I also had a room booked, was beyond my capacity for punishment). I checked in to find the room on the first floor overlooking the Moscow River and the main city power station, the room's television set "absented" (in the words of the floor duty lady), the plumbing working at half-gasp and roaches in the corners. I didn't care. I was to set off again in two days, for Ulyanovsk and points south.

I'd already traveled in a quick pass on the *Rus* from Vasilsursk to Kazan, a distance of some 240 kilometers, passing the towns of Kosmodemyansk, Cheboksari, Volzhsk and Zelenodolsk.

Below Vasilsursk, both banks of the Volga are thickly forested. About 25 kilometers from the city, on the left bank, is Yurino, which is just a village. Beyond it used to lie the magnificent estate of the Moscow Sheremetyev family, whose mansion and attendant buildings were put to the torch in the Revolution; its park is now completely overgrown. The Sheremetyev family was said to have owned a great number of ancient artifacts and the best library in

Russia. Part of the library and its collection were saved, through the intervention of local Bolshevik officials, who insisted on having them carted away before the building was destroyed; they're preserved in the Nizhni Novgorod and Sheremetyevsk museums.

The *Rus* stopped in Kosmodemyansk, on the right bank at the east end of the large peninsula whose western end is Vasilsursk. My notebooks contain only hurried snapshots: Kosmodemyansk was founded by Ivan the Terrible in 1583. It's the main Volga port of the Mari Autonomous Soviet Socialist Republic (or ASSR, a second tier of governance that is neither truly autonomous nor a republic, and falls somewhere between a region and one of the sixteen constituent republics of the USSR). The Mari people speak a language of the Finno-Ugric family, akin to Hungarian and Finnish. They have wonderful almond eyes and are generally blond. The head of the local soviet is called Gorbachev, for which he takes a fair amount of ribbing. The street leading uphill from the harbor is called Pugachev's Mountain Street. There's a museum and art gallery with mostly mediocre works in it, and a few good portraits. Another museum, this one of local artifacts, is set up like a peasant village.

There's no running water in the houses: I saw a man with two buckets on a yoke at a communal tap. Every house has a woodpile. In the newer part of town, up the hill, there is natural gas. A woman with two baskets on a yoke, going shopping. Men building a log house (or not actually building it, sitting on a log drinking tea. Two hours later they were still on the log, still drinking tea).

Most of the older section is made of wooden houses, some of them more than two hundred years old. I saw a number of horses and buggies carrying freight. There was a "propaganda and agitation center" in a pretty bright blue house. Up at the ethnographic museum a sinister-looking man tried to sell me a cross and, when I refused, hissed at me: "Dirty Jew!" Party slogans still adorn buildings. There are shortages of every commodity. A small brown man in a shabby suit, who looked like a thin and anxious Lenin, saved me from being hustled by an old woman who wanted gum for her kids, and we fell into conversation. He was an engineer and had been in Kosmodemyansk for twenty-two years. He was emerging from the local bookstore when he bumped into me, and he told me the Kosmodemyansk store has more books than most such places in Moscow.

A group of us from the *Rus* visited a department store, where a long line of sullen women were forced to wait while we checked it out for bargains, which were non-existent; this privileged access embarrassed all of us. A couple of the Americans bought ice cream for the kids playing out in the yard. *Rambo* was showing at the local moviehouse. The houses in Kosmodemyansk all have TV aerials and electricity. There's a platform near the boat dock where the townsfolk do their laundry in the Volga. I took a photo of a couple rinsing baskets of clothing.

Most of the Mari ASSR is northeast of its capital, across the Volga in the forests, which here stretch unbroken for hundreds of kilometers. The houses in Kosmodemyansk are truly beautiful, showing a love for detail and ornamentation and intricacy and color that's playful and lighthearted. Here's a small apartment building, a pale eggshell blue with dark blue trim and a red drip cap; there are circles and swirls under the eaves and four rows of geometric patterns under that. The windows are capped with ornamented pediments and surrounded by medallions and complicated moldings. Below the windows are more severe patterns, then the metal drip cap, beaten into a fold. Here's another building, this one housing a store that sells secondhand goods. The background color is chocolate brown, the trim cream and white and the shutters green. The upper floor is logs, mortised at the corners, and the windows are hardly visible for the carved pillars and pediments and fretwork that surround them.

On a narrow street with wooden sidewalks three or four blocks in from the river, the smallest cottages had intricate ornamented windows. An elderly man sitting on a bench smoking asked me to photograph his house, which was across the street, and give him a print. I explained that I'd be leaving in an hour or so, but he insisted, though he wouldn't give me his name or address. I took a photograph from high up on the hill, looking back towards the Volga. It was misty — there was rain about — and the greens and browns looked soft and inviting; the air of shabbiness that hung over the town, as it does over most Russian towns, can't be seen in the picture. In the foreground are long grasses and wild roses in pink and red. Beyond them is a fence made of woven reeds, and down the slope, in a tangle of brambles and raspberry canes, is a random collection of small barns. The red roofs of the residential quarter appear through the trees, with the massive red-and-cream church (which is now the art gallery) in the background, its domes breaking the line that separates the river from the land. Then the river, a hazy white, three or four kilometers across, a deep smudge marking the far bank. Trees and flowers were everywhere; and even if the roads were a mess and the shops decrepit and three quarters empty, it was easy to see that life here would not be as hard as in the proletarian rigors of Center.

On the hill, at the collection of traditional farm and village buildings that is the ethnographic museum, there were a band of Mari girls rehearsing for a concert, wearing machine-made versions of the traditional national costume: white scarves, white boots, white skirts with blue and green and pink embroidery, and yellow and red epaulets on their blouses. The linen has been replaced by nylon, but the pride is still there. Each carried a stringed instrument that looked something like a triangular washboard. I wanted to ask them about the Maris and their culture, but they were guarded by a fierce choirmistress who chased me off. Later at the art gallery I ran into two urchins, pretty children in brightly colored dresses and red knee socks, who requested and got bubble gum (which I had begged from a fellow tourist). In return, I got them to speak a few words of Mari for me. It sounded like nothing I'd ever heard, though I knew it was related, if distantly, to Finnish. As soon as they saw my bafflement they chattered away some more, breaking into childish giggles at my incomprehension.

I reflected that I'd known nothing about the Mari people before I reached Kosmodemyansk. I asked people up at the museum to tell me about them: Who are they? What are the relations between the Mari and the other Volga ethnic groups and Center?

For many years Slavic Russians have fretted about the "nations" of the Soviet Union and the "ethnic non-Russians," whose birthrates are generally higher than those in Russia proper. Ever since Stalin's time there have been fears that the Russians will be swamped in their own country. When I lived in Moscow non-Russians were scarce, but this time I'd noticed a clear difference. The city was becoming more ethnically diverse as more Soviet minorities find their way to Center. Russian Muscovites are no more tolerant of "ethnics" in their midst than, say, the residents of London or Los Angeles, and they've taken to expressing their indignation — their prejudice — openly. By some estimates, almost 20 percent of the capital is no longer Russian-speaking. Which means two things: the city is more cosmopolitan and sophisticated, and at the same time, in a certain narrow Slavic view, it is filling with profiteers, men on the make, gangsters and thugs.

It also seemed to me, at times, that ethnic anarchy was pervasive in the Union at large. While I was there, Moldavia was crippled by riots. Georgians were demanding an end to the Soviet empire and feuding with their ancient enemies, the Armenians. The Armenians were almost at war with the Azerbaijanians and having it out with the Turks. The Lithuanians and Latvians were on their way to prickly independence; a crackdown by Center was feared imminent. Ukraine was already testing the limits of centralism. In Kazan, there were stirrings of the old Tartar animosities as that formerly proud people held pep and protest rallies against Russian domination. There was racism and ethnic anger everywhere. Not just in recent folk memory (the State-encouraged genocide against the Kalmyks, the Crimean Tartars, the Checheno-Inguts) but in recent months: Pamyat's attacks on "cosmopolites," on Jews, the visceral hatred everywhere expressed against Gypsies. Even in Kosmodemyansk there was a "nativist" movement, pushing for more schooling, more independence for the Mari language. There was a mood of pessimism everywhere. From media reports and casual conversation, it appeared the Soviet Union was coming apart at the seams, the last of the multinational empires on the point of collapse, with no one — not even the Russians — willing to resist its demise.

The museum's staff was endlessly willing to explain who was who. One of the curators, a portly woman named Valya, sat me down on a wooden bench in one of the exhibits, a replica of a traditional Russian *izba*, and laid out the broad picture: the Slavs, she said, are found throughout the Volga lands. The other main group, called the Altaic, is derived from the Turkic-speaking parts of Siberian Asia. The mix includes, on the middle Volga, the Chuvash and the Tartars (with a small group of Astrakhans stirred in); the Mari, the Udmurks, the Bashkirs, the Mordvinians and, lower down the river, remnants of the Kalmyks. The USSR's largest oil fields are in the Bashkir and Tartar ASSRs, near Kuibyshev.

She gave me a yellowing pamphlet on Kosmodemyansk, put out by the local tourist authority and containing photographs of the Volga that were barely recognizable, so bad was the printing. It sketched in a picture of the Mari:

> The Mari, sometimes called Mariis, and also called Cheremis, are a Finnic people on the left bank of the Volga across from the Chuvashes, around Kosmodemyansk and Cheboksari. Mari is their own name for themselves; they were called Cheremis by Westerners in pre-Soviet times. There are currently more than half a million of them. They've been ethnically and socially very close to the Chuvash people since 700 A.D. There's a strong "nativistic" movement among the Mari.

The Chuvash are a Turkic-speaking people generally south of the Volga between Gorky and Kazan. They claim descent from the Bulgars, who came here in the early Middle Ages from what is now Bulgaria. They're isolated from other Turkic peoples since they long ago converted to Russian Orthodoxy, and their language is only distantly related to the other Turkic ones (they're probably the product of a merger with a Finno-Ugric tribe). There's some local speculation that Chuvash might in fact be an old Altaic language, similar to the one spoken by the fourth-century invaders, the Huns. The Chuvash today mix freely with the Russians but are not at all assimilated, maintaining their own language and customs.

A bit "inland" from the Volga, beyond the Chuvash and west of the city of Ulyanovsk, are the Mordvinians, another Finnic people. There are almost two million Mordvinians, but only about a third live in the republic, where they're considerably outnumbered by ethnic Russians. The majority have lost their language, but an extensive literature of folk tales exists, many recounting stories of the famous King Tushtyan, a contemporary of Ivan the Terrible. The Mordvinian faith, which has mostly vanished, was a thin Christian veneer over worship of the sun, a water divinity, the moon, thunder, frost and a home god. According to Valya, the traditional faith survives in the remote villages and farms, and elsewhere there are somewhat self-conscious efforts on the part of ethnic leaders to revive some version of animism as a part of their ethnic heritage, but it's hard to say how successful this is.

The Tartars, a name out of legend that lives on in the Russian cliché "under the Tartar yoke," are a Turkic people, a mix of the tribes that boiled up out of the East as the Golden Horde, and the native Khazars, whose capital was Itil on the lower Volga. But the name Tartar has often been given to many other nomads with no relationship to the people around Kazan, and in common Russian speech it's still sometimes applied to all Mongols and Turks, all migrant tribes of Central Asia, and pretty well everyone east of the Volga. The Tartar ASSR, with its capital at Kazan, covers some 41,000 square kilometers on both sides of the Volga.

There are other, smaller groups, related in some ways to the major tribes: the Udmurts are a Finnic people on the Kama northwest of the Tartars; the Bashkirs a Turkic people further east, to the Urals. The Bashkirs have had a written language since the Russian Revolution and since 1939 have used the Cyrillic alphabet. Religions are Islam and Eastern Orthodox. The Kalmyks are a Mongolian people northwest of the Volga-Caspian junction with a tragic history.

Over and over, as we surveyed the small and largely forgotten histories of these ethnic groups, I learned that their language and customs had only been written down in this century, during the Soviet period. Many of the written languages were developed by Soviet ethnologists. When Lenin and the Bolsheviks drew up the political map of the Soviet Union they made room for the ASSRs, which were supposed to recognize and salute ancient national boundaries. I thought of my own country, Canada, and the United States, and how they treated their thinly scattered aboriginals, and wondered whether they'd have done as well as the Bolsheviks.

Our view of Russian and Soviet history has been stereotypical and clichéd, colored by the rhetoric of McCarthyism and Nixonian chauvinism, by closed-minded broadsides at the "evil empire" (in the Reagan era) and by our glee at our "victory" in the Cold War (in the Bush era) — or at least more colored by these than by reality. It's true that the Russian empire was built by conquest and colonization; but then the Apache have the same view of the Americans, and the Basques of the Spanish and French. It's true that the Baltic states were incorporated into the empire cynically and against their will and are being kept there the same way. It's true that the infamous "Question 5" on the application form for Soviet internal passports, the question that requested the applicant's "nationality," was just a code for a racial identification the authorities were too ashamed to ask for openly. It's true that the Russians carved out a "homeland" for Soviet Jews in northeastern Siberia as hypocritically as the South African government gave "homelands" to its black citizens after apartheid was invented. It's true that Stalin, a Georgian who was an avatar of Slavic centralism, exiled the Crimean Tartars, mostly for the crime of having invaded six centuries earlier; exiled the Volga Germans for speaking the wrong language; exiled the Cossacks in revenge for the Civil War.

Still, the Soviet record is not all bleak. The "nationalities question," as the racial and ethnic problems are called, vexed Lenin and the founders of the Soviet state. In 1923, when the Party concerned itself with the problem, Lenin was already incurably ill, but he had dictated his views to his secretary a few months earlier, and Bukharin defended them at the Congress against the onslaughts of the centralists led by Stalin. Lenin asked that each republic in the union be granted extensive rights; the Union should be maintained, he believed, only in military and foreign policy. He wanted non-Russian languages to be placed on an equal footing with Russian, and local "People's commissariats" to be restored and invigorated. The Ukrainian Party head, Rakovsky, warned that "the nationalities question will unleash civil war if we do not display the necessary sensitivity and the necessary understanding"; and the Georgian delegation protested strongly against "out-and-out colonizers and Russifiers" in their republic. The Congress therefore condemned the "deviation towards Great Russian chauvinism" pushed by the Stalinist forces. As we know, Stalin eventually won, and considerable Russification followed. But that the ethnic groups never gained any political power wasn't a fault of the Soviet theoretical model or of Leninist views towards other races; it happened that way because the whole Soviet state was perverted. The fatal identification of the Party with the State was the critical error that fed the Revolution — and its nationalities policy with it — into the jaws of terror. Despite that, there are nationalities and languages now in existence because ethnic Russians protected them. That should be remembered too.

The Russian empire is disintegrating. But then the Russians aren't the only ones to suffer from ethnic and nationalist ferment. The problem — the explosive obsession with self-determination — is worldwide. I was forcibly reminded of these things when, in the middle of the Mari republic of the Soviet Union, I turned on the television one night and saw there the premier of the Canadian province of Newfoundland, who was in the process of attempting to frustrate one small nationalism by asserting the existence of another, even smaller one; Canada, after all, is an improbable country, existing only as an odd construct based on the largely mythical virtues of tolerance and acceptance. The tribal demand for power is expressed not only by the *indépendantistes* in Quebec dreaming their foolish dreams of self-sufficiency (as if such a thing were possible, or even interesting, as if the trappings of nationhood — the flag, the embassies, the state visits, the anthems, the banks and national utilities — meant anything any longer). It's also seen in the atavistic dreams of the aboriginal people (the "natives") with their illusions of Arcadia Lost, and in the little pockets of pathetic ethnicity in the west, the north, the east.

Those who support the inclinations of nationalism are trafficking in illusion, and dangerous illusion: tribalism is always regressive. The ideology of the Communist International was in this regard superior to Western models: cooperation is a morally better ideological goal than Darwinian competition. The "Communist" part of the Communist International turned out to be a crock, but the "International" wasn't half bad.

Are we to throw all this out — all this searching for international amity — and to put all the weight of our longings behind the sour dreams of self-sufficiency? Is the dream of the Baltic states, for example, to *skep u eie toekoms*, to build your own future, as South Africa's Prime Minister Hendrik Verwoerd put it in the 1960s when he defended the nationalistic dream that he called separate development and that we called apartheid? Is this dream of endless mini-states to supplant the longing for a better understanding between peoples? If so, I'm not sure we've moved very much forward.

In Kosmodemyansk, walking through the old quarter, I peered into a courtyard, past a woodpile and laundry on a line, and saw two babushkas sitting on a step, their round peasant faces beaming, their heads covered with the traditional scarf. Between them were two fat and lazy cats, their faces as round and contented as the babas. I nodded and said hello, and asked them about their house, which was one of the older wooden buildings in town, with intricate patterning and ornament. It's two hundred years old, they said.

"You're Russian," I said, pointing out the obvious. "Do you speak Mari too?"

"No," one of them said. "But she does" — an elbow in the other's ribs. "But it doesn't matter, does it? Mari, Russian, what does it matter as long as we get along."

That wasn't such a bad way of putting it, I thought.

CHAPTER 14

Kilometer 1,609

Cheboksari

I left my bags in a locker at the Kazan river terminal and made a quick journey a hundred kilometers or so back up the river to the town of Cheboksari, which the *Rus* had passed by at night. I used a series of Raketas, which proved to be a quick and comfortable way of traveling, with a rotating series of captive passengers to practice conversation on — very few were going more than 30 or 40 kilometers, and at every stop people embarked and disembarked.

Cheboksari is the capital of the Chuvash ASSR, though I saw no sign of any Chuvash people. It's a typical rundown Soviet provincial town — the usual river terminal, the usual factories (a combine harvester factory, a textile factory, an electrical machinery factory and others), the usual philharmonia, the usual theaters and monuments and architectural relics of the seventeenth to nineteenth centuries . . . I remember a particularly banal statue of Yuri Gagarin, mostly because a group of small boys with plastic buckets over their heads were playing cosmonaut around it. And as usual, the open spaces were well provided with benches. There were parents with strollers among the trees.

I bought a map at a kiosk down by the Volga terminal. Like most Russian maps, it listed only the main roads, was misleading as to scale and was not really oriented by north and south. But it was adequate for getting around, and I was trying to find a specific address. I'd seen a notice on a bulletin board nearby about a meeting that morning of UFO enthusiasts, and since the newspapers were full of UFO stories and I'd met an astounding number of people who believed in them, I thought I'd see what was up among the buffs. One of the common stories going the rounds was an old chestnut that had been circulating in the U.S. for decades: in the Fifties (or Forties, or Sixties) the U.S. Air Force had captured a UFO and was still either interrogating its crew (Russian version) or studying its scientific revelations (German passenger on cruise ship). The Cheboksari UFO group meeting was to be held at Number 2 Korpus 2 at an address that proved to be in a courtyard through a crumbling arch behind one of the town's food stores.

The group was surprised and delighted to have a foreigner in its midst, even if he wasn't an American and therefore not particularly good on leaks from the Pentagon's secret investigations. The leader of the group was a severe man with a fierce beard, who himself wasn't sure of the validity of these stories of capture. Clearly, this was an old argument, and a source of some friction among the group. The bearded man couldn't believe that if Western science was good enough to capture one UFO, we couldn't capture more. (No one was surprised that Soviet science hadn't yet managed the trick, though it was accepted by the group that the Soviet Union was favored by the aliens for visits — there were too many reports from the provinces of recent sightings for them to doubt this.) "Maybe the captured one had broken down?" a young woman suggested. "In that case the others would've rescued it," the severe man said severely, bringing that discussion to a quick end.

The meeting was run to good parliamentary order, by what passed for Robert's Rules. All got a say by strict precedence, and there were many objections and points of order, each punctiliously adhered to. The tone was one of intense earnestness. The substance was that the old-time UFO watchers, the saucer people, had been naifs who hadn't understood anything about science. What about the sightings of saucers? What about the landing rings, which were of course absolutely authentic? Here the consensus was clear: what the old-style people hadn't understood is that no advanced science, that is, no ethical science, would risk people in that way. These craft were merely drones, set up to test our defenses and perceptions. So were the "appearances" of small men (none of whom seemed to be green in Russian sightings). All of this was illusory. They, whoever they were, were testing us. These sightings were psychological tests of Earth's people. The alien dossiers must be growing, must by now be immense. At first, naturally, the aliens had concentrated on the United States, because obviously science there was much ahead. Some time ago, they finished with America. Now they've been appearing in the USSR: perhaps it has something to do with glasnost — perhaps they only appear where people are free to speak their minds? Soon there'll be no more sightings. They'll all disappear. They'll never bother with Japan or China. The test will be over and a new test will begin.

It was the main belief of this group, why they met, that Phase Two of the alien plan would be to initiate contact. It was the purpose of the group to imagine this contact, so as to learn ways of dealing with it. "We're not naive enough to believe we'll be involved personally," the leader said earnestly. "This is in the nature of a philosophical exercise, you see."

"There are people in the U.S.," I ventured, "who say they were captured and returned to Earth by UFOs. What do you think of this?"

This was obviously a contentious point. The leader disbelieved. "These people are just trying to make themselves important. We had a woman who said she was pregnant by aliens, but no baby ever appeared. And wasn't there a whole village in Azerbaijan or somewhere in which all the women were impregnated by aliens? And it turned out to be an overactive farm boy? You can't believe everything you hear."

There were dissenting voices, and the discussion closed inconclusively. After a while the women busied themselves with a cheap electric samovar. "They say," the leader said, seeing my look, "that Cheboksari women are the most beautiful in the Soviet Union." He laughed, somewhat humorlessly. "Maybe it has something to do with the thick air here. Do you agree with this observation?"

This was a hard one, so I mumbled something about how I was sure he was an expert and I wasn't, and shut up. One of the women at the samovar, who was indeed very beautiful, with translucent skin showing a delicate tracery of veins, the enormous almond eyes of the Tartars, and a dancer's taut walk, shot him a dirty look, but said nothing. One of the others, a homely woman with startling blue eyes, giggled nervously. The men and the women were occupying stereotypical gender roles, but clearly this didn't make for harmony — there seemed to be less agreement on these matters than on Earth-alien relationships. Indeed, they seemed much surer of the aliens than of each other. This gender fractiousness is not uncommon in the society at large. Soviet sexual politics are as archaic as the formal politics.

Many of the women I'd talked to in the Soviet Union were in one way or another angry, generally angrier than the men. The women still had to do most of the housework, and most of the lining up. There was less gender-typing in jobs, but most jobs in which females predominated, like medicine, were assigned low status. There was a strong feminist movement in Moscow, Leningrad, Kiev, the great cities of the Soviet Union, and even a few provincial cities had groups of women who had come together to protest this, yet another level of Soviet injustice. But, nevertheless, along the Volga the rhetoric of Soviet women was often quite different from the feminist rhetoric of America: what they most wanted was free time, a little leisure, a rest from the endless grind of daily life — rest above all, a respite from daily harassments and frustrations of every waking hour — frustrations caused, exaggerated and exacerbated by the system, but also by men. They also, to an astonishing degree, wanted a chance to be pretty, and admired. Work wasn't something in which they invested much emotion, and I found that in the smaller cities particularly the whole notion of a "career woman" was met with nothing but bafflement: the idea that you are what you do met only with incredulity. Work was just something you did in order to get by, in order to feed yourself and your family. The iron Bolshevik dictum "He who does not work, does not eat" forced out of their houses even those women who hated work, and they are still reacting against it. Perhaps once the grosser injustices and inequalities in the Soviet Union are on their way to settlement, perhaps once there are enough goods in the system to make a consumer society even plausible, matters will change, and questions of gender identity will get more complicated. In any case, the women served tea and sweet biscuits and conversation continued.

I left soon afterward. I could detect no real difference between these UFO buffs and similar ones in the U.S., with their silly mix of pseudo-science and quasi-religious mysticism. In the U.S. there was the added ingredient of a pseudo-Indian cosmology, and in the USSR the messianic message was much stronger ("They'll save us from ourselves"), but in essence they were the same. The beautiful woman with the almond eyes came over and kissed me, thoroughly and for some time, to my unease and to a dead silence from the rest of the group. I left right away.

I came to call him the "the man on the log," because I never learned his name, only that he'd been a professor of philosophy in Ulyanovsk and now lived in this small city and did nothing very much other than read. I found him in a splendid park near the river terminal, on this day widely used by mothers with small children, by strollers, by young couples, by people gathering wild chervil and dandelion greens. Deep in the woods a great tree had fallen. It had been dragged off the pathway and made a perfect bench; on it a man sat, reading. Typical Russian dress: brown suit, blue shirt buttoned at the collar, gray shoes and socks. He was florid of face, with wild nose hairs and a thick graying thatch. I sat down next to him. He was reading the weekly newspaper *Ogonyok*, and beside him on the log was a book. I couldn't quite make out the title. We sat for a while in companionable silence, listening to the white-throated sparrows in the woods and watching the red-winged blackbirds speed about a clearing.

"What are you reading?" I asked.

"*Ogonyok*," he said, slapping the paper. "Perestroika, what else. *Ogonyok* shows us how they're restructuring the cadaver . . ."

"Interesting newspaper," I said, lamely.

He sat quietly for a while. I told him what I was doing in his country, and he wished me luck trying to understand what was going on. He thought I'd need it, since no Russian knew what was going on.

"The leadership," he said, "is filled with the rhetoric of the
market. This is what you people have put in our heads. The magic
solution of the moment. I've seen leaders come and go, you know,
and it's important to remember that although we're waking from a
seventy-year nightmare, and there's no going back, it all began, the
Revolution began, with a dream. That's why, despite it all, Lenin
won't fall into disfavor with people like me. He had a dream of
equality, and that's all gone. The rhetoric that talks of market solutions, of demand instead of command economies, is just another
materialistic theory."

I told him of a passage by Dorothy Thompson, written before
the Stalinist Terror began. "This brave experiment," she wrote,
"isolated spiritually, mentally, and commercially from the rest of
the world, a country which occupies one seventh of the land mass
of the world and includes 193 nationalities with as many languages,
is trying to lift itself by its bootstraps in one generation from an
economically and culturally backward and half oriental nation into
a modern industrial state, fancying itself at the same time a mis-
sionary to the world."

"I'm not sure about this Oriental stuff," I said apologetically. "It
was a cliché of the time."

"But she puts it exactly!" he said. "Look around you."

I looked.

People were reading. A father and daughter were playing bad-
minton in an empty parking lot. A family was picnicking. Two
teenagers were skateboarding on a pathway. Everything looked . . .
normal.

"They don't have very much," he said, "but they're fed, they
have toys for their children and though they see the corruption
they don't see huge disparities in wealth. Equality: is this such a
bad dream? People have to make do, it's true, with not very much.
But must we set off on the path that you in the West have taken,
with its homelessness, envy, greed, speculation, billionaires whose
only social talent is dealmaking?

"Don't get me wrong," he said, though I wasn't about to, "I'm
not saying our system is right. I said it has been a nightmare, and
thankfully we've woken up; we're still sweating from the terrors,
but we can feel the morning sun on our skin and we know we

won't fall back into that horror. Still, if we are waking up, if we're going to change everything, we must remember why we slid into this nightmare in the first place; yes, we must remember what we set out to do.

"And maybe we still have some teaching to do for the West, as well as a great deal of learning."

He fell silent for a moment, thinking.

"Much stupid propaganda has been made of the so-called instinctive cooperative nature of the Russian. Stupid, stupid stuff. Now they're saying the reverse. They're saying, These miserable peasants! We give them every chance to be *kulaks* again, and they're not taking it, the cows. But the Russian peasants *are* conservative, and maybe they're right not to want *kulaks* again. Perhaps you in the West can't understand this. You Americans were never serfs — you owned slaves, so you remember only the guilt, never the pain. Here, family memories preserved the trauma of serfdom. My family, for instance. My grandfather was in his late thirties during the Revolution, but his grandfather was a serf, the property of his landlord, and he was sold to pay off a debt. My grandfather remembers his grandfather talking about how much he respected the nobleman, and the nobleman's man in the big house in the village. He even respected the Church, the agent of his masters. My grandfather hated this servility, this craven servility, even while he understood it; it was that servility that drove him and his father before him to take the path of revolution against the Eternal Autocracy. It all went wrong, of course — the Party became the State and the State the Autocracy again — but we remember the impulses that drove us to revolt.

"Now, do we want people in Mercedeses driving past our little park, here in Cheboksari? In the West, they say, anyone can have a Mercedes if he wishes, is this true? Yet you're beginning to see the cost, no?"

I said nothing.

"Yes, I know, I know, we're going to get a free exchange of ideas between ourselves and the West, no? This is what your propagandists have been demanding, secure in the knowledge that self-interest is the most powerful of ideas. So smug they are! So superior! So superficial! They don't really mean exchange. They mean for *us* to learn from *you*. Well, before we're swamped with the benefits of non-dialectical materialism, let me make a small protest. I don't believe, even as we all stampede to earn more money to buy more VCRs, that our Russian people will understand that they're also abandoning a noble dream. It'll be the triumph of the small of spirit; of those who say human nature is at best selfish and cannot be harnessed except through selfishness . . . That's what Americanism means."

At this point he smiled sheepishly. "I don't mean to preach," he said.

Of course, he did. I told him I'd read something similar in an American magazine.

"Similar to what?"

"To what you've just been saying. I remember the quote well, because it seemed quite relevant. It went something like this: 'Like Communism, capitalism is a materialist and utopian faith; also like Communism, it has shown itself empty of moral imperative or spiritual meaning. To the questions likely to be asked by the next century, the sayings of Malcolm Forbes will seem as useless as the maxims of Lenin.'" I explained who Forbes was.

"What newspaper is that?"

"*Harper's*. A kind of American *Ogonyok*."

"Well," he said, "very good. But no one in this country seems any longer to be saying any of these things. It's as if we've all come to believe the propaganda of your Western pundits that you've somehow 'won' some kind of a victory. This is a singularly narrow-minded view of human activities, don't you think?"

I thought of a piece I'd read in some Western magazine about how it was "clear" that the Russians had lost not only the Cold War but the fruits of victory of World War II. And I thought, No, this is wrong, the Russians have lost nothing, they're finding something, they're merely at the beginning of their journey . . .

We fell into a ruminative silence. I thought of the twenty-five thousand homeless people in my own city, and the story I'd heard of the young man, scion of a very rich family, who'd bought a huge house, torn it down, bought the huge house next door, torn that one down too, and built an even bigger house, with a huge swimming pool. And it troubled me that the celebrities in our country were the real-estate developers, although it seemed to me we were veering away from our adulation of mindless profit-making, that the endless coverage of the democracy movement in the former Evil Empire was bringing a healthy tinge of skepticism and even disgust to our own attitudes. I thought of food banks for the hungry in the West, where the supermarkets were crammed with the produce of the world, of the long lineups in Russian food shops, with the counters barren, of Boris Yeltsin and his constitution-making, of angry demonstrators, of the sour, pinched faces in Soviet stores. I thought of LBOs and the arbitrageurs. I thought of Gorbachev's revolution and of the many ways he could retreat from it, of the way local politicians in the West so often give away the common heritage of clean air and open spaces in the holy name of "growth," bowing to the icon of the tax base. I thought about how this growth was destroying our planet, and how we should be learning to make a society that didn't depend so much on growth: Adam Smith was as wrongheaded as Marx.

Economists have long ago recognized that there's no independent "market" in the West. The market is all interventionism on a massive scale, protectionism, monopolies, subsidies, hype, popularity contests. It's all managed; there's not a businessman anywhere who really wants free competition. It was becoming less and less clear which of the two systems had the claim to moral superiority. In the Soviet Union the whole question of morality is being ignored, submerged in the follies of economics. In throwing out Marx, the zealots of perestroika are forgetting that not all of his lessons are irrelevant. Marx believed, as many Westerners do, that morality flows directly from the economic order. The spiritual poverty of the West is in some relationship to its runaway economic "success" (recessions notwithstanding), and only now, as the man on the log said, are we beginning to count the costs. The endless pressure for growth must in the end be counted as a serious threat to the continued existence of mankind.

After ruminating for some time, my man on his log began again:

"We are in deep crisis here," he admitted. "You can't have one foot in the market and still centralize power. I'm with Yeltsin there, while admitting that Gorbachev is a great man, a revolutionary.

Revolution? We're a revolution-prone people. But civil war? I hear the young talk of civil war. Where do they get these notions, except from their sense of high drama? These are mostly just threats from the *apparat*, not real — it's clear who'd fight *against* the party, but who'd fight *for* it? If we had free elections tomorrow, the democrats would win. This is clear. Are we near collapse? It's true that if a Soviet bureaucrat went to the Sahara there'd soon be a deficit of sand — you've heard this old joke? We have shortages, rationing. This is necessary in a transitional economy, perhaps. A stock market would help — people put all their savings into banks now — let them put the money to use."

He stretched. "Poor Russia. Can it survive more well-meaning reformers? Can it survive not reforming? Can it, on the other hand, join the Western economies without losing its soul? You know that Trotsky described Lenin as 'an adroit statistician and slovenly attorney'? Maybe that's our trouble . . ."

I told him of the foreigners I'd met here. A German-American who was obsessed with bargains. All the Americans who only wanted to know (and to tell) what things cost. And the Canadians, who always want to tell, not to ask. He just laughed.

"Don't be hard on your own," he said. "We're not so very different."

I wandered away, sat on a bench. There was a young woman on the other end, feeding the birds, dressed in a khaki suit in Western pseudo-military style, attractive and self-possessed. As usually happened, she spotted me for a foreigner immediately and stayed to practice her English. She was a "qualified" aerobics instructor, whatever that meant, and a former competitive gymnast. She gave up her sport at age fifteen. She wanted to go to the West. She'd been on a trip to Italy and a couple to the socialist countries, and she wanted to go to England to work. "We're just waiting for the emigration law, the law that will allow anyone abroad who wishes," she said quietly. "We think it's coming. They *promised*. Maybe next year: the U.S. has asked for it in return for lifting economic restrictions, so maybe it'll come. Free to go! We're all just waiting, and when the law comes, we'll go."

I repeated something I'd heard twenty years before, when I was living in Moscow, knowing then the pent-up demand but also the Russians' notorious incapacity to like any other place. "Probably," I said, "if they opened the borders tomorrow, 80 percent would leave immediately, and almost all would be back in a year."

She laughed, a trifle bitterly. "All the brains would go, that's what they're afraid of," she said.

"Maybe," I said. "But if there was freer access, there'd be less need to go."

I remembered Britain and the "brain drain," how they'd been afraid in the Fifties that the entire intelligentsia would depart for America, leaving the lumpenproletariat behind to manage the sickest economy in Europe. Still, she remained glum as I made to leave. "No, please don't go," she said. "Until a few years ago we weren't allowed to talk to foreigners. Now we're allowed. Not encouraged. They don't like it much . . . but there aren't so many foreigners in Cheboksari that we don't take every chance we can . . ."

I sat with her for a while, making inconsequential small talk, then she walked me back to the dock and waited until my boat arrived. I saw her waving as the captain opened the throttle and the boat lifted itself from the water and roared off in the direction of Kazan. This whole country has a sadness to it, I thought, a melancholy, a wistfulness. I found myself looking around with fierce affection, hoping they'd be able to find a way, any way, from the ocean of troubles that awaited them.

CHAPTER 15

Kilometer 1,750

Kazan

I woke up one morning on the *Rus* and we were in Kazan. The previous night, as the boat plowed steadily eastward past Marinskii Posad, past Volzhsk and Zelenodolsk, I lay in my bunk reading about Ivan the Terrible and his capture of Kazan in the sixteenth century, a story of heroism, cunning and great barbarity. Ivan had caused the best carpenters of Uglich, a thousand kilometers away, to construct a fort, which they floated down the Volga and erected across from the Tartar headquarters, where the Kazanka and Volga Rivers joined. Ivan brought with him as a lucky talisman the cross of Dmitri Donskoy, the thirteenth-century Moscow prince who had become the archetypical Russian hero by actually defeating the Golden Horde in battle, and at the end of September he began his assault.

His imported fortress was thrown up overnight, held together by wooden pegs; the army, which had come separately by land from Moscow with Ivan himself at its head, was immense, more than a hundred thousand men under arms; it stormed the Tartar stronghold, took the citadel, massacred all the males (he didn't have time for his favorite sport, impaling, so he contented himself with evisceration followed by a messy beheading). He enslaved the women, first turning them over to his soldiers, then passing them to the slave factors from the East. Most of the small children were butchered — too much trouble to do anything else with them. The mosques were pulled down, the fortress razed and the Tartar remnants scattered. Well, it wasn't as if the Horde didn't have it coming. The Horde had indulged in its own atrocities; by the time the great Tartar leader Tamerlane died in 1405, towns from Hormuz in India to Chistopol on the Volga lay in ruins for defying him, ruins marked by towers made from the skulls of his victims.

To celebrate his famous victory, Ivan built the Cathedral of St. Basil in Moscow's Red Square, now the backdrop for tourist snaps, its candy-cane domes and towers twinkling in the thin Moscow sunlight. The legend has it that Ivan put out the eyes of his master builder so he'd never be able to duplicate the cathedral's magnificence. No one knows if this is true, but it would have been perfectly in character. Whenever Ivan was drunk thereafter, which was often, he'd sing a song about the conquest of Kazan and Astrakhan.

I pushed aside the curtains in my cabin and stared outside at an altogether more prosaic sight. Two of the American tourists padded by in their slippers on their morning jog; on the embankment below, old women were slowly sweeping several acres of tarmac with birch brooms. We were moored in front of the Kazan river terminal building, an edifice in white stone and glass, with Tartar motifs picked out in the stone and the name Kazan in red on the top, in Russian and Tartar. There was no other sign of activity. The inevitable row of small kiosks, for beer, candies and newspapers, had been set up behind the terminal building, surrounding its parking lot. Only the newsstand was open, and I went down to buy my usual guides to a new town: the local newspapers and a street map. I sat on a bench to read *Kazanskaya Pravda* while I waited for breakfast to be served on board. There was a strong editorial opinion on page one in support of Lithuania's demands for independence; and there was a photograph of a demonstration that had taken place the previous day in favor of "Tartar self-sufficiency." So, I thought, the long fight still isn't over.

Olearius reported that Kazan "lies most picturesquely 7 versts inland from the Volga, on several hills. The surrounding plain is inundated in the spring by the Volga and the river Kazan." He visited the city to see what he could buy, but found nothing at the market except some fruits, especially melons as large as pumpkins, and old, putrid fish "that gave off a stench so foul we were unable to go by it without holding our noses." The city is now perched on the banks of the river itself, the spring flooding controlled by the dams of the Volga Cascade. I visited the same market Olearius did, and though I found no melons, pumpkin-sized or smaller, I found the same putrid fish and held my nose just as Olearius did. The locals were amused. The "putridness" was deliberate; this fish was a local delicacy, akin to the infamous Bombay Duck of India.

In the countryside, in these post-Ivan centuries, there are now only ghosts of Tartar greatness, ruined places and secret shrines where Tartars gather in summer, hidden by the trees from prying Russian eyes, a pathetic remnant of a proud people making pilgrimages to the burial places of their heroes. Such places existed in Olearius's time, and they still do. One was the ruin of an old Tartar town, now in the middle of a copse on a *kolkhoz*, and Kazan Tartars visit it at midsummer. A group of students took me there one morning for lunch; to them, unlike the country folk, the mood of the place is no longer nostalgic or sad; it's just a place for picnics. I saw nothing much, only grass tufts where cold stone had been, and a glade where traders had bargained, trading kumquat preserves for intricate carvings from Kosmodemyansk.

Tartar history has become mere legend, and the "wild saints of Batu," the mythical heroes the Horde carried into battle, are dressed up in picturesque detail to populate the stories of children; there are sporadic though feeble efforts to recapture the heroic moods of old; most of the Tartars have grievances against the Russians, but more of them share grievances with the Russians against Center, against the system, the *apparat*, against those who'd keep them down, against the bureaucrats who are blamed for the impoverishment of a proud people and the denuding of a fertile land. I sat with an old man on the Volga embankment later, and he told me stories of the old days, how they'd pulled sturgeon from the Volga, three, four, five meters long — "one fish would be enough for a boatload of people for a whole journey," he said. "There are no fish like that any more. There's nothing like that any more."

"Well," I said, "I don't think this has much to do with Center. This has to do with the modern world. It's the same in our country."

He didn't want to hear this. Center was the villain. Gorbachev and his people. Communists.

I didn't know what the Russian was for "bum rap" so I let it go.

I'd spent a few hours earlier in the day at Kazan University. I knew it was the oldest in the Soviet Union (founded in 1804), that it had a strong English faculty and a powerful Green movement. But mostly I wanted to get a fix on Kazan and Tartar history.

Kazan historians, both Russian and Tartar, are scornful of the skulls-and-pillage popular image of the Mongol invaders. The stories of Tartar atrocities are mostly unreliable folk memories, they believe, fed by centuries of xenophobia and paranoia. Yet they themselves seem to recount the more lurid tales with some delight, so perhaps the revisionism needs revision too. In any case, when the first outriders of the Mongol empire under Batu appeared abruptly in European Russia in 1223, they swept all before them. The Russian principalities of the time were in a state of political anarchy. Kiev was in chaos. Petty dynastic quarrels between princes and dukes were frequent. The towns of the region were constantly at war, and they relied on a poorly equipped and ill-trained peasant militia that was no match for the skillful bowmen of Asia; it's not surprising that after Kiev and Vladimir and Suzdal fell without a struggle to the invaders, the Golden Horde was regarded by its opponents with superstitious awe: the hail of arrows that opened Russia to Mongol conquest must have seemed like a miraculous and deadly rain, and the wielders of the bows appeared as devils incarnate. Batu ranged along the Volga, upstream to the old Bulgar country of the Kama and the trading town of Bolgari. His camp near the mouth of the Volga later came to be Sarai the Great, the capital of all the Horde.

The revisionist view of Russian-Mongol relations is somewhat different. It's accepted that Batu sacked Kiev in 1240 and left only two hundred houses standing of a city that had at the time made

Paris seem like a primitive village. But, in the Kazan view, Muscovite apologists and monastic sources grotesquely over-estimated the destructiveness of the first raids, and at the same time over-sold the bravery of the resistance. The invaders were mostly interested in trade, not conquest, in facilitating and reviving trade routes that had been lost, and it was control of these routes they were after. A more cold-blooded look at the history traces the network of alliances the invaders made, not only among the Moslem merchants working the upper Volga but among the Russian princelings themselves. Most of the occupied cities prospered under the Horde; and new centers, such as Moscow and Tver, flourished. In the Kazan view, the Tartars never tried to impose alien rule or foreign princes on the Russian people.

Some Tartar revisionists go further. They delight in describing in great detail the centuries of petty treacheries that were the daily lot of Russian towns. Twice in one afternoon I was asked if I understood how the Muscovite princes had allied themselves with the Tartars to impose their hegemony on Russia. Had I heard this? Did I know the details? No? Then they repeated the story I'd already heard in Tver of how Alexandr, the ruler of that city, was murdered by Ivan Moneybags of Moscow, who had enlisted the Horde as allies. This, I was told with an air of great satisfaction, was an absolutely typical story. It was how many Russian cities got where they were. It was how Moscow got where it is today . . .

The Khanate of Kazan, the rump that Ivan the Terrible conquered, was formed as a result of the disintegration of the Golden Horde. In 1437 Ula Mehmet was ousted from the Sarai Horde and started his own Khanate, building at Kazan the greatest fortress between Moscow and the Urals, with thirty thousand men in its garrison. Ivan the Terrible sacked it in 1552. And since then the Tartars, once feared as "Gog and Magog, devils incarnate, agents of Satan, as cruel as the wind," have been quiescent.

That morning I'd taken a three-hour tour of the city by bus. Our guide, Boris, was hired by Intourist as a freelancer. He wasn't really a tour guide but a cartoonist, photographer, English instructor and musician, and planned to set himself up in business teaching English and conducting tourists around town. He gave me a book called *Places Associated With Lenin on the Volga*, which he himself called "a good example of Red propaganda." And indeed, that's what it was, a panegyric to the Great Leader, couched in those familiar prefabricated phrases that make thinking unnecessary. Boris was a Tartar, though he only wore his black-and-white Tartar cap after he got to know us, and looked otherwise completely Russian.

We started at the kremlin, which is a copy of kremlins else-where; it could easily have been in Kostroma, or Yaroslavl, and had nothing in it of the Mongol. Its most interesting building is the Zuyumbeka Tower, which is a red-brick confection 70 meters high. There's a legend attached to it, of course: it's said that the Princess Zuyumbeka, in despair at the sacking of her native city, sprang from its height to her death on the stones below. Like many such legends, it contains a grain of truth: the princess had gone to Moscow to the court of the Tsars (Ivan the Terrible having invented the title) to plead for her patrimony; she'd been seduced by the decadent court life there, and never returned.

Boris was a fount of useful and trivial information. There's a fac-tory outside town that makes jet planes. The oil pipeline to Berlin crosses the Volga here; it's called the Friendship Pipeline (although maybe the Fraternal Socialist Countries, as they used to be called, don't see it that way any more, since part of Gorbachev's economic reforms were to make them pay for Soviet oil in hard currency, which meant a billion-ruble windfall for the Soviet economy and hardship for the Europeans). The region near Kazan is semi-desert, with primitive, scattered villages and few cities. There are not many real Tartars left. Boris told me that the Russians lied when they maintained that the Tartars of the Crimea had offered to collaborate with Hitler and kill all the Russians. "They were sup-posed to have sent a letter to Hitler. This is another of Stalin's fabrications." The Tartar language, which is Turkic in origin, has been transliterated into a peculiar mix of Cyrillic and Mongolian. Steak Tartare is not a dish you find on any Kazan menu. Kazan is now on the banks of the Kuibyshev Sea, which backs up almost to the walls of the kremlin. There are picturesque hills on the right bank. The word Kazan means "border of state" in Tartar. Pugachev the Rebel tried to capture it and failed. And so on and so on and so on . . . Boris, words finally failing him, resorted to poetry to show his affection for his city.

Kazan saddened me. It has its university and its symphony orchestra, its theaters and its houses of culture, and the people I met are so desperately proud of them. The citizens of Kazan are trying their best to preserve what they have, with pitifully few resources. There's an ordinance forbidding highrises on the main street that runs from the kremlin to the university, and the civic authorities have designated a "cottage belt" around the central core in which the old wooden houses will be protected, as a souvenir of the ancient days. There's scaffolding on many of the monuments, but there's no work being done: there's not enough money. This place is so poor! Walking past these little log and wood houses, with their peeling paint, their doors and sills sagging, their roofs bowed, I found it hard to imagine that there was enough money in the world to fix it up, to put it back together.

There were flowers in small pots in the windows, and little collections of *objets*. One of these weary houses must have contained the brothel where Tolstoy lost his virginity, to his own great shame and disgust. Many revolutionaries and writers lived in lodgings nearby. Maybe they still did. I felt excluded and, for the first time, lonely. Who knows what secret life these houses contained?

I walked down from the kremlin walls to the main shopping street, called Bauman after one of the early Bolsheviks. As usual, the stores were four-fifths empty and the shortages were severe. Meat, at 3.60 rubles a kilo, was scarce. There was some fruit juice and a few sausages, but not much else. There was no fish anywhere, not even the stinking delicacy found in the market. Kazan calls itself the center of the Soviet fur industry, and there were plenty of fur hats for sale, at prices ranging from 20 rubles for rabbit to 500 rubles for something I didn't recognize, a pale gray fur, silky smooth. Muskrat was selling for 200 rubles, about $20. There was a long line of women in front of a clothing store. Bras, I was told. Just as in Tutaev, women were lining up a hundred deep to buy bras, anxiously pushing forward, fearful that the precious supply would be gone before they reached the head of the queue.

That afternoon I went with the tour group from the *Rus* to a concert at the Kazan conservatory, the orchestra performing variations on Russian and Tartar national songs. The soloists, some of whom were very good, were from the conservatory and the Kazan opera; they appeared in tails and formal wear; the orchestra was in "national" costume, which appeared mostly to be Russian. Maybe it was my mood, but I wondered, not for the first time, why all the Russian folksongs were so sad. And why do the few happy ones make the Russians weep?

The next day I left the tourists to Boris and slipped back to the university in the center of town. I'd heard it described as somber and neoclassical, "like a midwestern American college," but I didn't find it somber. The library building was a baroque confection with intricate wrought-iron balconies; only the main lecture hall is at all sober; it's where Lenin studied, and the school governors preserve it as it was when he was there, "as a monument to the Great Brain of Simbirsk" (a phrase from one of the Kazan students). The students pay little attention to this monument.

Leo Tolstoy was a student here in the 1840s, long before Lenin's father pulled himself up by his own bootstraps from the slums of Astrakhan; Tolstoy studied in Kazan for five years before he decided the professors were ignoramuses and he returned to his estates. Lenin never actually graduated from Kazan; he was expelled for taking part in a student demo (and for refusing to recant). Gorky had come here from Nizhni Novgorod, but the university refused to admit him, so he lived in cheap rooming houses with the Volga roustabouts and whores as his teachers; his lodgings were filled with revolutionary students who were in ferment over the need to throw all aside in a great frenzy . . . Gorky loved them all.

"We have a reputation to uphold," one of the students told me as we sat on the edge of a monument in a park across from the main university building. His English was excellent, flawless, his accent British "from the films," as he put it. "A reputation for radicalism, for revolution; though our professors of course believe we have only to study the revolutions of the past, not to make one of our own . . ."

He and his friends had gone to the demo the previous day for Tartar self-sufficiency, but he hadn't been impressed. "It's all romanticism," he said. "No rigor on their part. Only anger."

I asked him what he and his fellows believed.

"We're not revolutionaries in the way Ulyanov was," he said, deliberately avoiding the name Lenin. "We're part of a much larger movement that cannot be called a revolution. Revolutions are made by conspirators, bomb throwers, cadres; revolutions lead to Stalin. We want none of this. We're part of a mass movement away from violence, force, insistence . . . We're not stoppable. We'll never have to fight. We're the future —"

"Yes, yes," I said, interrupting the flow, "but what changes are you looking for?"

"Devolution," he said. "You know the term? It's English, I think. Not separatism. A Commonwealth of Soviet Nations. We want the British idea with the West European reality. Little Belgiums, everywhere, with their own languages and their own customs and no one to bully them, in cooperation with others . . ."

"Belgium has severe racial and language problems," I said.

He waved me aside impatiently. "They're overcoming them," he said. "But all right, take Holland as our model. Why cannot the Tartars be like Holland?"

That was a tough one to answer, images of Tamerlane and jolly Queen Juliana jostling in my mind . . . So I said nothing. Why not West Europe indeed? Sovereignty-association, to use a cliché closer to my own home, from Quebec, is not an ignoble idea, taking for granted as it does that tolerance would be exercised on both sides. "Do you think the ethnic Romanians of Moldavia will accept a peaceful accommodation?" I asked. "Or angry minorities elsewhere in your country?"

"That's what we believe. When we've won they will."

Three or four more students joined us. They were all part of the English faculty, and I gave up attempting to speak Russian — they were much more fluent in English than I'd ever be in their language.

I asked them what relationships between the Tartars and Russians were like. "How many of you are Tartars?"

There was only one. He looked Russian to me. I asked him about that.

"Centuries of mixing have taken place," he said. "That should tell you something about how we get on."

They wanted me to come that night to a meeting at one of their professors' flats to draw up an agenda for "Green action"; they were trying to set up links with Western ecology activists, so far without much success. "We have no money and no access to technology. But we'd like to take part in the international movement." I declined. I knew I'd have to return to the ship, which would depart later that night, and I wanted to explore the city a little more.

I walked back to the kremlin, and with some difficulty clambered onto one of the ramparts overlooking the Volga below. I peered across the river, trying to imagine the armies of Ivan the Terrible massed on the other side. It was hopeless. This was no longer the Volga but the Kuibyshev Sea; Kazan had been kilometers from the water in those days. Still, Ivan fascinated me, as he did all the Russians — the first Tsar to rule all the Russias, the unifier and the madman, the first of so many holy heroes and mad fools . . .

It was Boris, something of an Ivan fan, who told me that "Terrible" was in fact not a very good translation of Ivan Grozni, his name in Russian: *grozni* can just as easily mean awesome, or awe-inspiring, formidable. "But I suppose he was terrible enough, so no one will change it now." Ivan was born in 1530, and ruled until he died in 1584. He came to power in a century that was cruel to Russia, beset as it was with wars and invasions on all sides. "It was from this," Boris said, "from these hammer blows, from these hatreds and invasions and cruelties, that Russia was formed. Is it any wonder Russia came to believe in a national dictatorship?"

Enormous resources were poured into these wars. The hundred thousand men Ivan took to Kazan were not his largest army. There were up to three hundred thousand men under arms in some of his western campaigns. Every year the provinces were expected to provide sixty-five thousand new recruits, numbers that are not so very different from those of modern armies. They were paid for by landowners, who in turn taxed their peasants and serfs. Bankruptcies mounted until at times the whole country seemed on the point of economic collapse.

Ivan's first marriage was long and apparently happy. His wife was Anastasia Zakharina-Kobila, from whose family the Romanovs would later come. She died, and Ivan never quite recovered. He married five more times before the end, each union short-lived and filled with turmoil and brutality.

In his last years madness began to overtake him. He was no longer satisfied just to be Tsar of all the Russias, governing a huge empire through his bureaucrats. He wanted to sweep away all opposition, and in the presence of the gentry, the boyars and the nobles, he sensed an opposing power. Out of this paranoia came his decision to set up what was in effect a parallel government, separating the country into a portion for the state and a portion as his own personal fief. This division came to be called the *oprichnina*, "the apart," a word that derives from the concept of a widow's portion of an estate.

This lunatic scheme was imposed with great ruthlessness on the country. His *oprichnik* enforcers rode black horses and wore black clothing; they carried a dog's head at the saddle and a broom as their emblem, and their business was terror and murder; it's no accident that Stalin's infamous police under Beria were sometimes called the *oprichniki*. Ivan even set up a tame Tartar on the throne of the "rest" of Russia; everyone who disagreed with him, however mildly, was taken to the dungeons, tortured and thrown to the dogs. At one point he suspected that the city of Novgorod had done a deal behind his back with the Poles (a suspicion completely unfounded). He took his *oprichnik* army there and threw whole families into the river, stationing officers in rowboats to push them under until they drowned. Later he sent a letter to the survivors: "Men of Novgorod who are left alive, pray God for our religious sovereign power, for victory over all visible and invisible foes."

Soon afterward he killed his cousin, then he beat his wife insensible and killed his son and heir with a blow from his staff . . . After this he slept no more and spent his nights howling through the palace, until he died in despair in 1584, to the great relief of the country and especially of the people who surrounded him.

Their relief was short-lived. The Time of Troubles followed, for Ivan had killed his legitimate heir and left only the feeble Fedor in Moscow to succeed him, and little Dmitri in Uglich . . .

The invasions of the Tartars were forgotten in all this chaos, and they subsided back into the long ethnic slumber from which they have not yet arisen.

People in Kazan, Tartars and non-Tartars, had insisted that Kazan was a seat of inter-ethnic harmony. Despite these assurances,

Kazan was the other place I was warned about in Gorky. The previous day's demonstration in the town square by militant Tartars pushing for an independent Tartar republic had drawn an approving mention in *Kazanskaya Pravda*, together with a front-page photograph, but it had attracted only a few hundred people, many of them jeering Russians. A number of the students had confirmed that there was gang warfare in Kazan, warfare more violent than Gorky's. Only some of it, they said, was traceable to Russian-Tartar tension. Much of it seemed to be Tartar gangs fighting each other, and was generated by nihilistic attitudes among the young who have no faith in the system. For the several days I spent in Kazan I was watchful and wary, but I have no firsthand evidence of clashes.

Only once did I become really nervous, when I spotted an unruly group of young men, yelling and shoving one another and heading my way. I ducked into the nearest doorway; it turned out to be the baking operation of a bread shop and was filled with burly women in white smocks and headdresses kneading massive lumps of dough. There was a wonderful smell. To their indignant inquiries at my intrusion I used the word *khoolighani* (hooligans), which is archaic but the only word I could dredge up to cover the case. That they responded at once, one of them slamming the heavy door and ramming home a massive bolt, made me think there was something to these stories. The women were solicitous. They made sure the coast was clear before they let me out, and insisted I take a loaf of bread hot from the oven. Solicitous, but also amused by my folly.

CHAPTER 16

Kilometer 1,861

Kuibyshev

K uibyshev sits on a great horn of land that juts into the
Kuibyshev Sea at its narrowest point, where the sea is only
about 10 kilometers across. This is the Kuibyshev that until
1935 used to be called Spassk-Tatarskii, not the much larger
Kuibyshev further down the river, which was renamed Samara
after I left; the old Bolshevik V.V. Kuibyshev had been Party boss
in Samara at the time of the Revolution, and there are busts of his
severe and overstuffed form all over this district. It seemed somewhat excessive to name two towns after him, but I wasn't going to
argue the point. I wasn't much interested in Spassk-Tatarskii itself
(even the Rechflot guidebook had little to say about it, except that
it was "a city in the Tartar ASSR, founded in 1781").

But on the outskirts of the town, on the north flank of the horn
facing towards Kazan, was the site of the ancient city of Bolgari,
which had been the capital of the Bolgar state from the tenth century until the coming of Ivan the Terrible. At its height, it had been
a city of internationally minded merchants, who'd taken on themselves the responsibility of keeping open the trading routes of
European Russia.

I found an old man who agreed to take me to Bolgari in his little outboard. I stowed my bags with his family and we packed a picnic lunch, setting off around noon. I was the fourth tourist he'd shown around, he told me. "Rush hour in Bolgari," I said, but traffic jams hadn't made their way into the consciousness of the citizens of Kuibyshev, and the phrase didn't mean anything to him. The other three were all writers, he said. One was French, the other two English.

There was nothing very much to be seen at Bolgari except a few ramshackle buildings and the detritus of a major archaeological dig. Clearly its workers were on leave, for there was no one around. "Usually there are many experts here," the old man said, disappointed. "They find all kinds of rubbish that they take to their museums." We sat on the shore and stared northward over the sea that had once been a river, and I tried to picture the dumpy Turkish trading vessels at anchor, and the sleek ships of the Vikings, which had made their way to Bolgari as early as the tenth century. A merchant from the Levant, Ibn Fad'len, took home a description of the Viking primitives "as tall as date palms, red in hue"; the Vikings frightened everybody with their wild ways, filled with violence, sacrifices and urgent sexuality, and the city was relieved when they headed back north, to whatever savage place they'd come from.

We were joined on the bank by a couple of fishermen from a *kolkhoz* on the other side of the Volga, each with a homemade rod of willow and a jar of worms. They sprawled on the grass near us, each accepting a cigarette as his due, and stared out of the corner of their eyes, looking away whenever I glanced at them. They both wore padded jackets of some rough blue material, denim trousers and heavy farm boots. Their faces were round and florid, sly and calculating.

So much has been written about the Russian peasant! This slow-moving, cautious, suspicious personage has dominated the thinking of the Russian intelligentsia for centuries, and his freedom has been the main burden of revolutionary politics since the Decembrists in the Napoleonic period. In an odd way the peasant, the "rural population," still dominates Russian thinking. The journalists on the *Novosti Express* had been fascinated by peasants, if somewhat repelled; peasant traits had been a frequent topic of conversation.

I looked at the two *kolkhozniks* again. They were supposed to be working on the farm but were "ill" this day. Their faces were closed, neither hostile nor friendly. They said little, keeping their own counsel. Serfdom, I reflected, is only four generations removed. One of the prime purposes of the Bolshevik Revolution was the liberation of the rural workers. They were to be the backbone of the State. And here they were, taking their ease. I wondered how the peasantry's legendary evasiveness squared with the fact that the New Politics appealed directly to their self-interest through the insidious medium of television . . . The peasants have taken what they want before; they're a powerful weapon for any politician who dares to unleash them.

On an impulse, I asked, "Didn't Stenka Razin operate around here somewhere?"

Razin was a renegade Cossack and peasant rabblerouser, and his revolt represented an early battle in the long war between bosses and peasants, the war that was supposed to end with the Bolshevik Revolution.

"Yes," the old man said, "he sailed past this place to burn Kazan."

He lit another cigarette. The two *kolkhozniks* lay back on the grass and snoozed, their rods weighted down with rocks, their hooks, unbaited, left in the water just in case.

From the 1650s Russia's peasants were always on the verge of ruin, and a bad harvest would bankrupt them. Since they had no legal recourse, flight was their only escape. Some would hide in the woods, others would gather in large bands, still others made their way to the Cossacks. Peasant risings became a kind of background noise, a violent static. In 1664 the Tsar ordered the first national hunt for runaways; these hunts were to be held on and off for another hundred years.

The legendary peasant patience was hardly anywhere in evidence in this period; frequently they murdered their owners, set fire to their houses, "expropriated" their fields. In 1648 there was a tax revolt in Moscow and Tsar Alexis escaped only by surrendering tax officials to the mob. Other tax revolts were reported in provincial cities. War and chaos at Center increased the burden. More and more peasants fled. Large estates became overgrown by forest, as increasing loans at increasing interest rates, impossibly heavy fines and hopelessly unpayable debts were added to the crushing burden of taxation.

With Stepan Timofeyevich ("Stenka") Razin, the notion of class war boiled up from the deep peasant resentments and shook the state. Razin terrorized the Caspian Sea, capturing Russian and Persian ships, murdering their crews and burning ports. Just outside Astrakhan he seized a flotilla owned by the Tsar. In 1670 he descended on Tsaritsyn with seven thousand followers. Next he sacked Astrakhan. After drunken orgies and many atrocities against nobles and military — reported in Moscow with horrified relish — he murdered the governor and proclaimed Cossack self-rule. He took and burned Samara and Saratov. He looted Kazan and burned it down. He incited the peasantry to revolt against the nobility and the bureaucracy (but not against the Tsar). His revolt spread to the Don and Donets and to the major towns of heartland Russia. He was widely regarded by the common folk as a hero. To some degree he still is: Soviet schoolbooks have promoted him as the precursor of the righteous anger of working peoples everywhere. But some aspects of his character don't sit too well with modern sensibilities and are prudently omitted from the Soviet school curriculum today.

I asked the old man if he knew the song of Stenka Razin. He said he knew a few verses. He poked the *kolkhozniks* awake. Did they know the song? They grumbled but said they did. Everyone did. Everyone knows that. "So sing!" the old man said. They sang. The old man sang.

> *From beyond a wooded island*
> *Into the river wide and free*
> *Proudly sailed the famous barks*
> *Of Razin's Cossack yeomanry*
>
> *In the first one Stenka Razin*
> *With a princess at his side*
> *Drunken, holds a joyful revel,*
> *With his beautiful young bride*

Stenka Razin hears the murmur
Of his discontented band,
And his lovely Persian princess
He has circled with his hand.

His dark brows are drawn together
As the waves of anger rise,
And the blood comes rushing swiftly
To his piercing jet black eyes.

Volga, Volga, Mother Volga!
Deep and wide above the land
I will give you all you wanted
Life and heart and head and hand!

And that I might rule as ever
All my free-born men and brave
Volga, Volga, Mother Volga
Volga, make this girl a grave!

Volga, mother of the nation!
Volga, Volga, Russian river!
Take with spirit this great gift
The Cossack, Razin, is the giver!

And in his mighty grip he took
The slender figure of his bride
Over the ship's side he hurled her
And into the heavens leapt his pride!

The legend says that after his "great gift," Razin climbed a cliff on the Volga that no one else could climb, and pledged that he'd never falter until Russia was freed and all the squires were dead. Many of the revolutionaries of a later century attempted to find this cliff and mark it for pilgrimage, but they were never able to agree on which it had been. This place, Bolgari, was a candidate, though there were no cliffs hereabouts, only banks. Wherever it was, this cliff-climbing helped Razin not at all. He was defeated in battle near Simbirsk in 1671, captured and taken to Moscow. There Tsar Alexis had him tortured, quartered alive and hung outside as a warning. Without him, the revolt collapsed.

"Well," said the old man, when our song had petered out, "so much for that. But the peasants are all gone now, aren't they?" He nudged the *kolkhozniks*. "Aren't they? We're all just workers on the land now, aren't we? Rural workers, that's what they call us. The peasant of Russia is gone. The past is gone. The villages are gone. We're all orphans . . . orphans of the past . . ." He was declaiming, a poem he knew, though he didn't know its name. He started to sniffle, and then to weep. I thought of a word Anton had used once, when he was describing the Russian confrontation with its appalling history. *Bezizkhodnost*, he called it, and when I asked him what it meant he struggled for a definition. A sense of hopelessness, he said at last, of ice-cold monotony without end, that the Russian frost will endure forever . . .

I told the old man this, and he stopped sniffling. "Our country has been flying apart as long as anyone can remember," he said, "and here it still is."

The *kolkhozniks* had fallen asleep again. The most they would ever do, I thought, was grumble. Never weep.

Razin's death didn't stop the revolts. In 1705 several new uprisings confronted Peter the Great. The Bashkirs rose on the middle Volga. The Cossacks on the Don murdered the tax collectors and fought back when Peter's army turned up to restore order. Other Cossacks ransacked Saratov, Tsaritsyn and Kamyshin. And in the north a holy ascetic, one Goli (the Naked One), called on all "the naked and the barefoot" to rise against the boyars, and some of them did.

When Anne succeeded Peter, more storms swept over Russia. There were famines, epidemics and great fires. Anne expelled hundreds of thousands to the prison province of Siberia — as many as twenty thousand at a time. Half of them died on the road, but no one cared.

In 1770, while Catherine the Great was waging war on the Turks, plague broke out in Moscow, adding to the war burdens, huge taxes and famine to create what the Bolshevik historians, with rare understatement, called "a climate of popular indignation."

Three years later, in 1773, Emilian Pugachev incited the greatest uprising in Russian history until the Revolution of 1917. It began in the Ural Mountains and spread rapidly through the impoverished Volga regions of the southeast, around Tsaritsyn and Saratov. By the following summer Pugachev had placed the whole country into an uproar and was marching on Moscow itself. Catherine hastily concluded her warmaking against Turkey and turned her troops on this new and more potent threat.

An illiterate Don Cossack, Pugachev had fought for Russia in the final battles of the Seven Years War (1756-63) in Poland. He returned home as an invalid. For three years after his recovery he wandered among the people of the Old Believers, absorbing their mystical and stubborn oppositionism. The Cossacks around the Yaik River on the lower Volga revolted against attempts to tie them to the land; Pugachev, following their lead, stirred up the Cossacks in Uralsk. He was arrested, imprisoned at Kazan and deported to Siberia. Through the complicity of his guards he escaped, and in 1773 he reappeared on the Volga. There, as "Tsar Peter III," he "decreed" the abolition of serfdom and soon gathered an immense following of Cossacks, peasants, mine and factory workers, Old Believer clergy and dissident Bashkirs, still seething from their failed revolt against Peter the Great. Pugachev was defeated by a force sent by Catherine, but he regrouped and burned Kazan, captured Saratov and besieged Tsaritsyn. Finally, General Suvorov captured him and sent him to Moscow for execution.

The net effect of these tremendous upheavals was, in the Russian manner, tragic irony. Catherine abandoned her tentative attempt at the reform of serfdom. The peasants became worse off than ever — in fact, history regards Catherine's reign as the very culmination of the last system of slavery found in Europe: the vindictive gentry, who no longer had to fear the peasants, turned to hating them instead. They were allowed unlimited authority over their serfs; they could remove them from their families, marry them off to whomever they pleased, whip them at will, banish them at their own pleasure, starve them and even, under certain conditions, kill them. On the surface of this ocean of misery lived the aristocracy, in immense palaces, unknowing and generally uncaring about their human cattle; the state enforcement apparatus, the agents of the aristocracy, was massive and cumbersome and ponderous, built on the soft and treacherous ground of national despair.

We know what happened in 1917. In the Revolution's frenzy the peasantry, that vast, illiterate mass boiling over with revolt and revenge, had little grasp of political parties and little need for them. They simply seized the land and smoked out the landlords; any political party that dared to stand in their way would be made to suffer. In the Civil War, the peasants discovered that the Red Army was the only organized force that could prevent the landlords "re-liberating" the newly liberated land, and they threw their support to the Reds. This support quickly evaporated when the war was over and Bolshevik squads appeared in the villages, rummaging for food.

But even the Russian peasantry was no match for the technology of modern repression, backed by the single-minded purpose of Stalin. A life of infinite humiliations, Pasternak said of the Russian way, and the Russian peasants' response to infinite humiliations was the retreat into the sullen silence Russians call *priterpyelost*, silence in the face of massive injustice.

We returned before sundown to Kuibyshev. I sat in the old man's two-room house and wondered about the past. I asked him if anyone remembered the gentry, but he wasn't interested. In the provinces the idea of the gentry has gone forever. Only the priests survive. And the *apparat*. The idea of the peasantry is confined to political texts. Stalin accomplished that too: there are only "people who live in the country," not peasants. Or so everyone says. But the country people do remember the old angers, the anger and the reasons for the anger. Maybe the *kolkhozniks* were still snoozing, up there on the bank by the old Bolgar capital. But I'd be afraid of them, if they begin one more time to come to the boil.

CHAPTER 17

Kilometer 1,968

Ulyanovsk

Kosmodemyansk

Kazan

Vasilsursk

Cheboksari

Kuibyshev

Ulyanovsk

Zhiguli

VOLGA

U lyanovsk was further down the river than either the *Rus* or the *Novosti Express* had taken me. I'd flown into Ulyanovsk from Moscow's Domodedovo Airport, after my farewells to the crew of the *Novosti Express*. It was a two-hour flight, and crowded, as all Aeroflot flights seem to be. I made friends with an off-duty Aeroflot pilot in the next seat; he was on his way home to Siberia. He persuaded me not to fasten my seatbelt (that was only for wimps) and offered me a drink of atrocious Armenian brandy. He said he loathed Moscow and all its doings, and also all other cities, including Ulyanovsk. He thought the Volga was okay, though he himself lived in Krasnodarsk in Siberia, there was no other place on Earth as wonderful . . . The flight passed amiably, and I was met at the airport by a helpful, if confused, Intourist staff person who spoke good French but very little English, and for the rest of the stay Zhina, a small blonde guide with hairy legs and a terrific smile, chattered away in Russian, French and a few words of English.

I'd read many descriptions of Ulyanovsk. Most of them referred to the city's 500-foot bluff, stunningly situated on the right bank, and it was the first thing I made for after I unpacked. The Volga is about six kilometers across at this point. Upstream, in the haze, it widens into an inland sea; downstream, where the pleasure boats go, through the bridge, it widens into another sea. Ulyanovsk is the stem of the hourglass, somewhat ironically, for the city appeared frozen in time.

I strolled along the crest of the bluff, trying to orient myself. My notebooks contain only scattered images: giggling schoolgirls doing their homework on a bench in the Volga park; a young woman trimming a hedge with clumsy shears, wearing heavy boots, coveralls and huge golden loop earrings almost a foot across; the agricultural college with a great view of the river (but it's downtown, a long way from the farms). The Ulyanovsk Philharmonia is an elegant white building perched on the edge of the bluff; there was a Tchaikovsky concert that night, followed by a string ensemble playing music by composers I didn't recognize. There were little cable cars from the crest down to the beach.

The reason my notebooks were scattered was that the town I'd read about . . . wasn't there. There was just a very pleasant park, a wonderful view, a few institutional buildings. The town, as a place where people lived and worked, has vanished. In its stead is a Lenin theme park. On the edge of the embankment, where it can be seen from the river, Lenin's name is proudly grown in hedge. Lenin was born Vladimir Ilyich Ulyanov, to a father who was a gruff superintendent of schools and a mother, Maria Alexandrovna Blank, who was a devout Lutheran of Volga German descent; the house in which they lived is now a museum. This museum-house has been moved to the edge of the bluff and is almost invisible, encased in a long, low structure in the anonymous international style of airport terminals — the house has been entombed by the administrative offices of the museum in the same way Lenin himself has been smothered in the embrace of the bureaucracy set up to study his life. I found this entombment a striking metaphor for the Soviet system, a system frozen into inaction.

The whole town — or at least the formal one — has a frozen feel to it, as if it were in Lucite. It's not a place that seems likely to encourage iconoclastic examinations, least of all of Lenin himself. His name is everywhere: in a town named after his family, one of the four administrative districts is also named after him. So is a school, a street, a park and at least one factory. There's even that hedge named Lenin.

Later, I discovered that real life does go on in Ulyanovsk, just not here along the bluff. Further inland, beyond a small river that enters the Volga, there's unruly life, where ordinary people live. This other town is tumbledown, thoroughly polluted, its factory chimneys belching black smoke, but at least it seems real.

Lenin was born in Ulyanovsk, though he never lived here as an adult, didn't die here and wasn't buried here. They are still piqued about this in Ulyanovsk; their pique is expressed as indignation that his wishes to be buried next to his sister in Petrograd were ignored: the mausoleum in Moscow's Red Square is looked upon with great distaste in the town of his birth. Still, there are interesting artifacts in many of the little Lenin museums around town. For instance, there's an ivory tusk, intricately carved, with Lenin's face on it, a gift of some foreign government. There's a lacquer box in the traditional Old Russian style, with Lenin's face worked into the motif. And, my favorite, a painting of Lenin that turns into Marx if you view it from the left and Engels if you view it from the right.

The school where Lenin spent a year or two still stands, no longer a school but a museum to the great man's brainy boyhood, in much better shape than other Soviet schools, though altogether without pupils; it's all roped off so we can see exactly where Lenin did his sums . . . and how tough his exams were! And how well little Volodya performed! (This is the only place where Lenin is remembered as "little Volodya," a diminutive for Vladimir, because when he grew up he went away and never came back. My Moscow friends were disbelieving when I told them about this. It's got to be an ironic usage, they insisted, though I don't believe it was.) The guides in the schoolrooms were schoolgirls themselves, already primed with the stock phrases of Communist cant — no sign of glasnost there. The director of the school in Lenin's time, and the man who signed his diploma, was Fedor Kerensky, the father of Alexandr Kerensky, whom Lenin later deposed as head of state.

Many of the people I spoke to in Ulyanovsk were grateful for the fact of Lenin; the accident of his birth had brought them relative prosperity. The celebration of the centenary of his birth in 1970, at the height of the pompous Brezhnev era, had taken veneration for Lenin and his works to ludicrous heights. I remember, for instance, that a light bulb factory had produced a new line in Lenin's honor and called it the Light of Ilyich series; a metropolitan bakery produced a special Lenin chocolate cake, with Lenin's head picked out in frosting. In the end, though, this veneration had been good for Ulyanovsk. During the centenary celebrations the long arm of Moscow poured largess into the town, building several institutes, a huge museum and a new hotel, among other things. To some degree the prosperity persists, has become self-sustaining.

I'd asked for a guide to the museums, since I was curious about the tone the official line would take. The most tragic event in Soviet history, the guide told me, was Lenin's premature death — before he had a chance to deal with the monster Stalin. She talked about Stalin in the way one talks about a scorpion, as if stamping him out would have avoided the poisons that followed.

"But it was the structure Lenin set up that allowed Stalin his grab for power," I said.

She'd have none of it. "Lenin loved people," she said. "He'd have solved the problem, as he did with the NEP. What was NEP, after all, but an early version of perestroika?"

This was clearly the new line among the Lenin establishment. I wasn't going to argue. Not that I agreed. After Lenin's death the State he'd created fell into the trap that faces every dictatorship, the inexorable narrowing of its political pyramid. The Bolsheviks, who'd suppressed all rivals and eliminated any possibility of political discussion in the soviets, themselves suffered the same fate — they fell victim to their own Party machine. Everything flowed from that crucial circumstance, even the physical extinction of minorities, the emergence of the Infallible Leader and the paranoia and madness that followed. The Revolution, which had extinguished its enemies, began to devour its favorite sons, as revolutions are prone to do. But in Ulyanovsk, why push the point? Perhaps, as the guide said, Lenin would have managed things differently . . .

In our tour of the museum we ran into a crew from CBS News, who were in town to do a documentary, to film the progress of a conservative delegate to the Party Congress, then only a week or so away. It was interesting that even the hard-liners had become mediawise, and had agreed to cooperate with the strategies of the bourgeois press. For the first time since I left the quarrelsome Moscow journalists I felt cut off; the CBS crew were primed with all kinds of juicy (and, I discovered later, erroneous) Moscow gossip and speculation. They also told me blandly they'd heard that Canada was falling apart, that massive demos were filling the streets . . . This sounded unlikely, and indeed it turned out to be so, but I had no way of knowing then.

That afternoon, I'd had enough Lenin for a while. I'd spent the morning tiptoeing through all the museums (the museum where He was born, the museum where He lived, the museum where He went to school) and later, it being a lovely sunny day, I had a pleasant picnic lunch on the bluff, watching the passenger steamers and the Raketas ply the river and the trains rumble across the bridge. Lunch over, I took myself off to the non-Lenin parts of Ulyanovsk, or at least to the parts where ordinary people lived and worked. More specifically, to the auto factory named after Lenin. Outside the factory gates a small Jeep-like vehicle was set up on a pedestal, its nose pointed skyward, a reminder of what the factory made. Unlike the workers at many of the other factories I visited, these people invited me cordially inside — I'd arrived during their mid-afternoon break. The working conditions seemed acceptable: the building was decrepit, as usual, but the actual machinery seemed in pretty good shape — the parts that moved, moved easily, they all gleamed, and the noise level seemed tolerable. I was offered a drink of uncertain provenance. They called it beer, though I could detect no beer flavor and there was no sign of alcohol, nor did the workers seem drunk, and they had great jugs of the stuff.

I can't say my visit was very enlightening, but I did learn a few things: they have great contempt for Moscow and all its works (the city, its people, its noise and size, its politicians, again with the exception of Yeltsin). And Lenin? None of them had anything against Lenin exactly. None of them wanted to abandon the name Ulyanovsk and reinstate Simbirsk — it just didn't seem worth the effort. There was plenty of animus against the other Soviet leaders, Brezhnev especially. There were even people critical of the

Revolution itself; and most of them found sardonic things to say about socialism. But Lenin? To them, blaming Lenin would have been as futile as blaming the weather. Had any of them been to any of the Lenin museums recently? None had. To them, Lenin might as well have been a collection of Paleolithic dinosaur bones, for all the relevance he had to their lives.

I took one more shot at it: "But Lenin created this system you've all just told me is holding you back," I said.

No one took this seriously. Lenin didn't cause anything. Lenin just *was*.

Most of them were pessimistic about the future of their country. Their consensus was that those in charge, at Center, didn't know what they were doing. "Those with ideas are weak, and the strong ones are idiots," one of the workers said.

Said another, "All Gorbachev's done is make the Georgians and the gangsters rich: allow them to exploit you and they'll do it, and before you know they're living in palaces on the Black Sea and telling everyone else what to do . . .

"If you ask me," he added, "I wouldn't wait for Georgia to ask to leave the Soviet Union. I'd kick them out right now and tax them every time one of them wanted to come in. Georgian gangsters are running every restaurant in Moscow right now, did you know that?"

No, I hadn't heard, I said, but I did know that a Belgian firm, Stella Artois, had a couple of new ones there, open only to foreigners, true, but . . .

"It's a fact," he insisted. "Gangsters everywhere. Georgian gangsters and foreigners too."

"What's to be done?" I asked, asking one of the Three Great Russian Questions. "What would *you* do?"

He never got a chance to answer: the hooter signaling the end of the break sounded and the foreman came over and asked me, cordially enough, to leave, which I did.

I was staying at the only Intourist hotel in town, the Venits, built in 1970 at the centenary of Lenin's birth. I ate my supper there that night.

How to describe the banquet at the Restaurant Venits? I venture to believe that nowhere else in the world are banquets like this possible, and here they're frequently probable, alas. I've been to many, and though in the end they all blur together in an incredible (I use the word truly) din, I do remember a particularly grotesque one at the Hotel Bug, in Brest, some years back, at the end of which a Soviet air force pilot and I swore, at the top of our lungs, eternal amity between our two countries before he collapsed in a stupefied heap on the floor and his fellow flyers dragged him away.

I've already described some of the less agreeable aspects of Soviet hospitality at the Izmailovo hotel complex in Moscow, and the Hotel Venits seemed to distill all the unpleasantnesses into one venomous dose. Ulyanovsk — to set the picture — has three or four hundred thousand inhabitants. It has two restaurants. Sure, there are some cafés, and a goodly number of *stolovayas*, cafeteria-style eating places of very low quality. But of real restaurants: two. So the first problem is getting in. Outside most Soviet restaurants an hour or so before opening a knot of people appears; by opening time this knot has grown to perhaps fifty or more, sometimes considerably more. The Restaurant Venits is part of the Hotel Venits, but, typically, you can't get from one to the other without going outside. Oh, you could — that is, there's a door — but it's always locked. The restaurant is on the second floor, and like all Soviet restaurants, is huge; there's room for four hundred diners. You reach the dining area by a street-level door and then up a winding staircase.

Since I was in Ulyanovsk legally, I had Zhina at the local Intourist office make a reservation, and she did so cheerfully. This is prudent, since it provides one with a piece of paper to wave.

I arrived at eight, as instructed. There was a seething mob outside the door, which was made of thick glass and firmly locked from the inside with a huge padlock at least six inches across. The door was guarded by a gorgon, one of the legion of petty functionaries whose jobs are apparently designed to make everyone miserable. I fought my way to the front, banged on the door and waved my paper. She peered at me suspiciously, then turned away. I banged again, pressed my paper against the door. After a few minutes of this, as the crowd muttered restlessly behind me (clearly hoping I'd get in, which would force the gorgon to open the door, which would allow them to . . .), she finally condescended to open the door. As I slipped through, the crowd heaved and the door opened wider. The gorgon bellowed and put her shoulder to it, forcing it closed, and snapping the padlock into place. I was in.

I went up the dark spiral staircase to the restaurant level. Loitering on a landing were half a dozen young men and women, the women in skirts about the size of a facecloth. The din began its assault about halfway up. At the entrance to the restaurant proper, I paused. The room was full. The individual tables had been rearranged into three room-long tables running parallel. The band was playing, and though I was at the other end of the room, I was shouting at the upstairs gorgon with my mouth an inch from her ear, and still she couldn't hear. Finally I produced my reservation paper, and she nodded. Over by the wall were three or four smaller tables, unoccupied. She ignored these and showed me to a seat near the end of one of the long tables. There were revelers to both sides of me, already thoroughly drunk, and they ignored me, as did the waiters.

The crowd was dressed for partying, or at least the women were. It seems a truism of Soviet parties that the women usually dress up, and the men usually dress down. There were women in shiny fabric like space blankets; there were women with flyaway hair, there were women with huge breasts and plunging necklines, there were slim young girls in tight pants, there were stout women with rough hands in fancy stout dresses, there were men in shirtsleeves, men in T-shirts, men in rough workpants and heavy boots. Many of the women were pretty, with refined features (here in Ulyanovsk with strongly Tartar overtones), but the men looked as if they'd been drinking a little too heavily for a lot too many years. Here and there couples were cuddling and kissing, and others were slopping toasts at each other. There were groups of hard-looking men with bulging muscles, groups of farm boys, cheerful groups of Asiatic-looking men in ill-fitting suits. The woman on my right had hennaed hair, an aggressive mien and a neckline to her navel; the man on the left could have benefited from liberal applications of Right Guard.

In front of every place, a riot of bottles and glasses, big jugs of juice and an endless supply of *limonad*, which tasted ghastly, with a burned licorice flavor. Bottles of sulfurous mineral water, cloudy to look at and vile to drink, stood in clusters. Officially the restaurant served no liquor, but there were endless bottles of Armenian cognac and Russian vodka on the tables. Drunks reeled up and down the room, yelling. An absolutely stunning young woman dressed in not very much was dancing with her girlfriends. Everyone was shouting, yelling, toasting, drinking; when the band played, which was often, the crowd simply cranked up the volume even more until my ears started to ache. It was thirty minutes before a waiter noticed me; my table companions ignored me, and in any case conversation was impossible.

I ordered a "filet," which turned out to be a gray slab of what I think was beef, with cold, undercooked french fries and a green tomato on the side. I had a decent salad of cucumber, followed by an ice cream topped with some appalling syrup. For lack of anything else, I had one of those awful licorice drinks, though while my neighbor was dancing I poured a generous dollop of her cognac into my glass to help it along.

Most of the three hundred or so people in the room knew one another: I was in the middle of a company banquet. The revelers were passing around copies of a group photo of the factory workers, to shrieks of laughter. I hoped the Red Star Machinery Works, for that's what it was, would be closed the next day, for if it wasn't, its allotment of tractors wouldn't hold together more than a few hours when finally loosed on some unsuspecting *kolkhoznik*. Many people were signing and scribbling notes on the photographs and on spare scraps of paper. Three people borrowed my pen and the last one forgot to return it. Three young women asked me to dance. My meal cost 5 rubles and 3 kopecks, or about 53 cents. Later, in my hotel room, my ears still ringing from the din, someone phoned me to ask whether I wanted a "girl" (herself). I declined, but she phoned back and asked me again, in English. I hung up and went to sleep.

Back at the Lenin auto factory, the workers had been complaining of the difficulty of finding vodka. Even beer had become scarce. The local brewery had converted to lemonade, in a zealous desire to cut down on drunkenness and absenteeism (I shuddered, thinking of the licorice *limonad* in the Venits), and the vodka shops had been shut down entirely for a year or so. The only results of this campaign had been the appearance of homemade liquors (and the virtual disappearance of sugar from the stores) and the instant evaporation of Gorbachev's remaining popularity — a blow from which he never quite recovered. I in my turn had complained to the auto workers of the lack of alcohol in the hotel dining room, and they'd promised to take me to a store the following day — the stores were once again open a few days a week.

Tobacco was the other great complaint. Everyone in the Soviet Union seems to smoke, and the tobacco shortage has led to major brawls outside shops. It was caused directly by the central planning system — it followed an arbitrary decision to "reduce consumption," which caused a run on the product that the factories couldn't keep up with; at the same time the manufacturers ran out of paper, and then ran out of filters. One major factory simply shut up shop when the promised credits for Western machinery didn't come through, and the factory's own machines, as per its manager's dire forecast, seized up (on the other hand, Center likely had more important things to allocate its precious Western currency to).

Alcohol? Well, they've been trying to cut back consumption by reducing production and by brewing large quantities of weak beer. To complicate things, there's a flourishing moonshine industry as part of the shadow economy. This stuff, called *samogon*, varies from awful to not bad; it's uniformly high in alcohol and doesn't actually seem to poison many people. The *samogon* seller was, in fact, parked around the corner from the wine shop I visited with my factory friends, and was being blandly ignored by the militiaman on duty. I suspect he knew he'd be very unpopular if he made a move to stop its sale. And it wasn't as if *samogon* was depriving the state store of business — the lineup was a hundred feet long, and the *samogon* prices were much higher.

The store, which stank of sweat and vomit, sold beer, vodka and Armenian brandy. There was no sign of wine, though it was called a wine shop. This was not shopping for the faint of heart. If you hesitated you were lost, and were shoved aside by burly, sweaty drunks. There wasn't a woman in the store except for the cashier, who looked as if she could take care of herself. Vodka was selling for about 6 rubles a bottle. After securing our bottles — I paid, since 6 rubles comes to less than a dollar — we retired to a park bench to sit and consume it.

As so often, the conversation turned to politics, defined here generally by the twin phenomena of the rise of profiteers (the new rich, the "co-ops," the speculators, the suppliers and middlemen) and their prices; and by the parallel feeling that things have gotten out of hand. The arcana of institutional and Party politics was left to the "big boys" and to Center, but I got a clear sense that a leader of spirit, a populist with a simple message, would capture their devotion, and I once again came to see Boris Yeltsin in a new light (this time as a man who was exercising some restraint, because he has the populist appeal to be that man). Anyone with that kind of populist appeal who also had a messianic message would be a potent force.

Later, I met a young couple over dinner — I'd been placed at their table in the Venits. He was a student in Moscow, at the Economics and Foreign Trade Institute of the Ministry of Foreign Affairs. She had a child of her own, and worked at the Pedagogical Institute in Ulyanovsk. He told me that none of his friends were interested in politics (he became finally disillusioned with Gorbachev when the law on free emigration failed to come through on schedule, even though it was still promised). He said he knew a number of "ruble millionaires"; one of his friends had become rich importing computers. He had a bottle of Siberian vodka, bought on the streets for 22 rubles, and he poured me a stiff drink.

When I returned to my hotel room that night, the phone immediately rang again. Again she asked — in English — whether I wanted her in my room. Again I declined. Sorry, she said, and hung up.

The following afternoon Zhina and I went for a drive up the north Volga shore, through the village of Isheevka, through Poldomasovo, Shumovka and up to Undori, which until the Revolution had belonged to the family of the poet N.M. Yazikov, a lesser literary light who'd been a friend of Pushkin's. The Yazikov family used to breed trotting horses for the gentry of St. Petersburg; now the villagers bake bread in an ancient bakery, and poets are forgotten. We hadn't gone very far when I saw by the side of the road a row of small buildings, about a dozen tiny cottages. We stopped to see what this was. It was a model dacha display — you chose your model and it was delivered to your site. When? "Within a year." These tiny cottages are quite cute, looking more like children's play-houses than the real thing. That they *are* the real thing it doesn't take a genius to figure out: on a long sloping hill down to the Sviyaga River to the left of the road, the hillside was covered with them, each with its little plot of ground, where good-sized tomato plants grew, and ripe strawberries, and sometimes cucumbers.

While Zhina waited in the car, I wandered down a steep mud road; as I descended, a man passed by on a motorcycle, with a full pail of strawberries strapped to the pillion. I walked on until I saw a babushka weeding her little plot, and stopped to chat. I kneaded the earth as if I knew what I was doing and (I think) passed for a son of the soil. In any case, she invited me in for tea. Her husband and son-in-law sat on a bench at the rear of the hut, drinking beer. Her daughter, in stretch sweatsuit and hairpins, made the tea; her fingernails were black, the sign of a gardener. The daughter grew the fruit, the mother the vegetables. And the men? Both women simply sniffed. Men? *Men don't actually do anything, they just sit.* After a pleasant half-hour I moved on.

I had a feeling I was traveling through the heart of the heartland here, the Russian aorta, the country's lifeblood. This is where all the tribes of Russia come together. On the far bank of the "sea" is the former Mordvinian village of Karatai, now alas drowned; not far away are the sulfurous caverns of Syukeyeskiye, where there are mysterious lakes of hydrogen sulfide, curative waters for the Chuvash ill. A few kilometers downriver is Tetyushi, a mix of Russian and Tartar; then comes the Chuvash village of Prolyei-Kasi, the Mordvinian village of Uryum and on the left bank Staraya Maina, which was once a garrison to protect the Russian colonists from the raids of Bashkirs and renegade Tartars who'd hidden themselves in the clefts and folds of the Zhiguli Hills.

On the hills called the Simbirskaya Gora there was supposed to have been a town destroyed by Tamerlane; no one remembers what it was called, only that a tall tower of human skulls marked the spot until scavengers took them away and plowed them into their fields, a grisly compost. In a picturesque gorge there's a great rock, which has attached to it a story that is peculiarly Russian. This enormous rock is about 30 feet in length and a little less in breadth. On one side are the words: "Lift me up and you'll have luck." The legend says that once, when a Russian barge was moored here, unable to advance against a headwind, its crew, thinking to find a great treasure, undermined the rock with prodigious effort and toppled it into a pit. There was nothing on the underside except the inscription, "What you are looking for is not here."

At Isheevka we turned right onto a smaller road and headed back in the general direction of the Volga. To the right, the flat terrain was clawed up by tracks and at the head of a field there was a small control tower. As we crested a hill I could see, in the fields to the right, a dozen sleek tanks going hell-bent for a distant copse. Not long ago this would have been an impossible sight, army maneuvers in open view of foreigners. Not that it's a secret they make tanks around here: we passed the factory, with a tank proudly mounted on a plinth.

We passed through the tank range and arrived at a major state farm, or *sovkhoz*. A state farm differs from a collective farm in that, at least in theory, the collective farmers jointly own the land in the name of the people, and it's managed by an elected chairman, though in reality the Party runs it and selects the only candidate for the election. In a state farm setup, the workers are simply employees of the state, civil servants, and the farm is managed by a director appointed by the local administration. In practice, there's not a great difference between them: the workers are salaried, and the scale of the farms is typically huge.

This one was an interesting mix of modern and archaic methods: there were horse-drawn carts, an old dray with a wooden barrel on it, geese and cattle wandering everywhere, old-fashioned bucket wells (perhaps foolishly, I risked a drink from one of these, and the water was so cold and clear that I drained a large tumbler of it, without later ill effect). Yet there was an extensive machine shop, huge combine harvesters, a general store, a small bookstore, a food store and several other services. The general store stocked everything from kitchen goods to rudimentary furniture; the stock was adequate, though the tool section had hammers but no nails, a drill but no bits, only one size of screwdriver, a hacksaw only and no power tools. In the food shop I saw piles of bread and honey and salt pork, and not much else. The workers' housing was a higgledy-piggledy array of small two- or three-room wooden cottages in varying states of repair. One had just burned down. There was also a row of gaily painted modern houses. These were built of brick, and appeared to have natural gas piped in for heating and cooking. The workers were all wearing long boots, to cope with the pervasive mud, but standing in a line at a bus stop waiting to go into town were stylishly dressed young people — there's a fabric store on the farm too, so presumably many of the women make their own clothes. There's a small lake. All the houses have a few fruit trees. All have TV antennas.

We returned to the Venits in the early evening. It was pouring with rain, and as we pulled into the parking lot Zhina put her hand on my arm.

"Our system is not right . . ." she said, completely out of the blue, for we'd been talking about housing and town planning. "Nothing works as it should. You know . . . you have to know someone before they'll do anything for you, before you can get anything done, before you can get what you deserve . . ."

"What do you mean?" I asked.

"There's no fairness here, no fairness in our country," she said.

"That's it?"

"No, I mean . . . I mean no matter how we try, we cannot . . . we must . . . it's not fair," she said, and started to cry. "Someday," she said, "someday someone will do something about it."

She was weeping quietly, with her head on the steering wheel. I didn't know what to do.

"I'm sorry," I said awkwardly, and passed her a paper napkin I found in my pocket. "I'm so sorry . . ." And I meant it, but she was still crying when I went out into the rain and across the Venits parking area to the door where the sour little commissionaire sat to keep out the unauthorized. From inside the lobby I looked back, but she was gone.

I ate my last supper at the Venits as I'd eaten the others while I'd been here. As usual, only about twenty of the sixty tables were occupied, but the waitress still insisted on seating another four people at my small table. When I'd eaten, I got up to leave, walking down the dark staircase to the street door. The door was padlocked. True, the padlock was on my side, but there was no key in sight. The door lady told me peremptorily to wait. Sheeplike, I did. What else could I do? There was a seething mob outside the door waiting to get in, though of course the restaurant was three-quarters empty.

She kept yelling at them, "There are no places! Absolutely no places!"

"Only people with reservations will be allowed in!" she yelled. This was a nice trick, since they'd refused to accept reservations that day — I know, I'd tried earlier.

Finally, she opened the door for me to escape, yelling at the heaving mob, "Let the foreigner out!" and gave me a hard shove to get me through. The mob plunged for the door, but the door lady succeeded in yanking it shut and locking it triumphantly.

I left Ulyanovsk that night.

CHAPTER 18

Kilometer 2,098

Zhiguli

As Hitler's armies rolled through Poland, Stalin's government lifted the Mummy of Red Square and built him a temporary mausoleum in Samara, not far from where I was skimming along in a hydrofoil; then they shipped whole factories, entire towns, floating them down the Volga, setting them up in the mud flats this side of the Urals, the productive industry of a nation shifted wholesale a thousand kilometers eastward into the Russian deeps . . .

I was reminded of these achievements by an old man on the hydrofoil as we approached the Zhiguli Hills. He said he'd been here as a boy, lying on a hilltop with his comrades watching the endless barges steaming past on their way to the railhead at Samara. I wasn't sure whether to believe him, but his descriptions of the view from the hillside, the black smoke from the tug funnels, the hoarse shouts of the roustabouts, the untidy piles of machinery exposed to the elements were all as vivid as if he'd seen them the day before, and they all rang true. "They seemed to go on all day," he said, "coming round the bend from Ulyanovsk, one after another, endless streams of them . . . It was exciting. I was just a boy, and didn't know that the great storm was coming, I just thought this was normal, that the Soviet people could move whole cities whenever they wanted to . . ."

"You sound nostalgic for those days," I said.

"We were poor then, we had nothing, we knew things were bad, my parents were always afraid, but we knew we were going somewhere, that our country could do anything it wanted, that we were always first in everything. We're still poor, though people are not afraid any more, and it doesn't seem to me we've made progress."

"Did you really think of 'the Soviet people,' and not 'the Russian people'?" I asked, curious.

"Oh yes," he said. "I know everyone now thinks this is horse manure. But we did. We believed it all."

The Raketa skimmed down from Ulyanovsk, passing the little village of Shilovka and the industrial city of Sengilei, described in the early books as "a place for a summer break in beautiful natural surroundings and fruit gardens" but which now seems to consist largely of a cement factory. This cement factory has its own place in Soviet legend: it was a product of the central planning system ("Hey, let's put a cement factory *here* . . ."), and the factory sat on the banks of the Volga for a decade before it actually made any cement; soon after startup its machinery needed replacement. This was a precedent often followed in this area, as the Soviet planners resolutely determined to bring the benefits of modern industrialization to farflung provinces, without waiting to see if (a) the people there wanted or needed these things and (b) there was anywhere to put them. The city of Togliatti, just downriver, is the most egregious (yet successful) example of this process.

Across from Sengilei on the left bank is the village of Belii Yar. It sits on an outcropping that faces south and west and was once a strong point of the Zakamskaya fortification line against the Tartars. A little further south is the village of Novodevichiye, named after a scion of the Moscow monastery that once stood on this spot. The monastery has entirely vanished, and the Rechflot book I consulted didn't mention it. "Large village in the Kuibyshev region," it merely said, "with a monument to the Red Army." I passed by this monument without stopping. In earlier times the village was known for its agriculture, especially eggs and bread, but in these days it suffered from the same grotesque shortages as other parts of the Union.

We whizzed by Klimovka and then Usolye, which is famous because Lenin's father opened a girls' school here; the village was founded in the sixteenth century by migrants from the Kama River district, attracted by the fabulous fishing, by the chalk cliffs, salt springs, sulfur springs and other natural wonders. Thereafter the Volga takes a sharp left turn and heads east in the first curve of the Samara Bend, which is probably the most picturesque section of its 3,500-kilometer length.

I got off the boat at a place called Yablonevii Ovgar and joined a group of day-trippers from Togliatti who were heading for an outcropping called Molodetskii Kurgan, near the site of an ancient burial mound. There were high white chalk cliffs on both sides of us, and across the bay I could see hills painted in the palette of pastels of a Russian evening. Here for a change the Volga had shrunk to the proportions of a river. Our group hiked along a sandy beach and a line of poplars, and I shut my ears to the litany of industrial splendors my hiking companion, clearly a Komsomol, thought I'd like to hear: so many tar pits here, so many chemical factories there, exploiting this and exploiting that, the Togliatti car factory extending for so many hectares. Finally I lost patience, and said I'd travel a good distance not to see another factory pouring another chemical mess into another river, and would he kindly shut up and enjoy nature? Wounded, he subsided, but later I heard him lecturing someone else in the group on the many sanatoriums in the area . . .

The Zhiguli Hills rose up behind us. Some of the more inaccessible summits are topped with "Stenka kurgans," cairns raised in memory of Razin, whose dispersed followers established themselves in this natural stronghold after he was taken and killed. Many of the hills rise to 1,000 feet, and a few to 3,000, their slopes covered in birch and pine. We passed Maiden's Mountain and Two Brothers Hill (where my Komsomol friend tried once more to interest me in an asphalt plant that he said was to be found on the other side). I loved these little hills, which weren't dramatic, just velvety smooth with spring growth and thick foliage, here and there a rare naked hillock, outlined in limestone. The impression was one of placidity and calm, very like the Volga itself.

My early guidebook to the Volga said of Togliatti (then still called Stavropol) that it was "a small and serene town, which, thanks to its location, is convenient for rest and treatment; there are 6,000 residents chiefly engaged in crop growing and trade; the town is surrounded by pine forests where well-known cottages and *kumiss* hospitals are located."

Well, that might have been so. But the old town, with its muddy streets and old wooden houses, is at the bottom of the Kuibyshev Sea, and in its place is this . . . horror called Togliatti.

The Soviet Detroit, the newspapers have called it, not yet having learned of Detroit's eclipse by Nippon. In 1965, there was only a swamp here. Now there's a city of half a million. The town was named after the Italian Communist leader Palmiro Togliatti, who after the war had tried to persuade Stalin to help him launch an armed insurrection in Italy, convinced as he was that the Italian people were ready for Communist discipline after the excesses of the strutting Fascists, but Stalin had sensibly declined. Later Togliatti fell out of favor with Moscow by making a speech to the Soviet Central Committee urging an end to the duplicity and moral double-dealing of world Communism's leaders. During his harangue, he repeated the words of the dying Goethe, "Light, more light!" The Central Committee, watching Stalin's impassive face watching Togliatti, quailed, and the next day they urged him to leave the country before something serious happened to him. That speech was Togliatti's one vain attempt at overcoming his conspiratorial roots, and he soon fell back gratefully into the lies and deceptions that were the staple of international Communism. This brought him back into favor with the Soviet leaders, and when the central planners in Moscow decided the country needed a huge car plant to anticipate the coming consumer boom, and they located it near a drowned provincial town on the Volga, the name Togliatti popped into their minds as a cynical if hopelessly inept way of rewarding Fiat for agreeing to a joint venture.

I was living in Moscow when the trainloads of machines and machine tools came through, bound for the Volga. The planners were determined to emulate the heroics of the wartime Soviets and build a gigantic factory from nothing, in no time at all, complete with garden suburbs and palaces of culture for the workers. They would "lay the rails of the future" and never mind that the rails sank into the mud and had to be relaid the following year — just so long as the photographers had captured the scene in time, the triumphant Young Communists Building the Future . . . The trains steamed eastward, followed by hordes of *Pravda* photographers, but there was nothing there when they arrived, and the Italian production line was dumped in the mud, where it waited for a year or two until there were buildings in which to put it. Another blip on the plans of Center. Still, the journey across Russia made good newspaper copy, and the fact that the factory wasn't working didn't stop reporters from writing glowing reports of its efficiency and modernity.

Eventually, of course, they got it going, and it still is, churning out Ladas and Nevas and Zhigulis in their many thousands. More than half the auto workers are women, mostly young. And the garden suburbs are there, the endless rows of drab apartment buildings, marching seemingly forever between scrawny trees and weedy gardens; there are bus tours of the factory and its environs, but I declined, and instead returned to the Volga to head round the Bend.

A few kilometers on we passed through the locks that formed the massive presence of the Kuibyshev Sea; below were the upper reaches of the Volgograd Sea, whose own locks were still more than a thousand kilometers away; this sea took decades to fill, partly because of its length and partly because the engineers tried not to disturb the biological balance of the Volga fisheries and of the Delta itself: for once reality had lived up to the propaganda.

On the left bank, just before the river makes its sharp bend south and then west through the narrows called the Zhiguli Gates, is a table mountain, Tzareviy Kurgan; from the left, near the village of Tzarev-Kurgan, the Soka River flows into the Volga. Higher up the Soka are natural sulfur springs, where tired Russian bodies go for mud baths and massages. On the right bank, at the blade end of the shovel-shaped peninsula, they've made a national park; the hills to the west, on the left bank, are called the Sokoli Hills. In the old days this was perhaps the most picturesque spot of all, and the rich and powerful of the Ural provinces built cottages on their slopes, most of which either are sanatoriums or have been overtaken by the sprawling industrial development of Samara itself. These are high, rocky hills clothed in thick forest: at their peak a broad white rock forms a landmark and a place small boys still go to dream grand dreams.

Samara, which had borne the name Kuibyshev from Stalin's time until the month I was there, is a strange study in contrasts — an industrial city that was, and to an extent still is, a fashionable beach resort, the Yalta of the Volga, though the local press complains of scrap metal on the Volga beaches, and the fact that bulldozers seem to choose Sundays to do all their work on the river's banks. I could see the beaches from the boat, kilometers of sand, small boats, lockers, thousands of bathers in the glowing summer sun, the usual minuscule bikinis. Many of the Volga beaches, which looked clean and fresh, lie below factories that would have gladdened the hearts of Victorian industrialists. There's belching smoke here, but a short distance away nature seems clean and untroubled, and on holidays half the town seems to go berrying and mushrooming in the forests.

So untroubled was Samara, so placid and conservative, that it annoyed the propagandists of industrialization, for whom grinding machinery was the music of the future, the overture to the new society. Maurice Hindus, who had visited Stalingrad, where they were carving immense factories out of the sandy Volga banks, called it backward and desolate, "with none of the energy, the enterprise, the vividness of Stalingrad, or of present-day Baku, or of Ivanovo or of other cities which the [Five-Year] Plans have recreated." Even Hindus, who seems to have loved factories more than trees, acknowledged its serene setting.

All round are woods, hills, flowers, fields; and as I went walking with Russians along the river front or talked to them of the Volga, their language spilled over with love for this mighty and beautiful Russian river and everything within its environs. Often they resented my comments that the city was wretched, with battered sidewalks, mud holes in the streets after rain. Invariably their answer was, but look at our landscape and our nature . . . Daisies in the meadows, corn-flowers in the rye fields or hedgerows, birches in the forests, the steppes, the rivers, the thatched huts in the villages, the smoke rolling from their black chimneys.

Hindus couldn't resist one more industrial image.

The guidebook had mentioned "*kumiss* hospitals," and they seemed to be thick on the ground in this area. These days, as in Chekhov's time, *kumiss* is usually made from mare's milk, but is still served in the immense sanatoriums of the region; there are places of more than a thousand beds. Perhaps the most famous is the health resort of Sernovodskii, which has its own mineral water (Sergeievskiye water), its own sulfur springs and its own *kumiss* hospital. Knowledgeable folk on the Raketa told me that the best *kumiss* is to be found closer to the Urals, away from the Volga, at Shafranovskii, where there are up to six hospitals, they weren't sure exactly.

One know-it-all young man, the object of a good deal of nudging and winking from the other travelers, took it on himself to teach me the local facts of life. There was once sandy desert here, he said, before the Volga was reborn, and the caravans from Asia would all stop here to transfer from camels to barges.

"Now, of course, everything is green and verdant," he said, a phrase from the propaganda manual that caused much mirth among his fellow travelers, but he ignored them. "Kuibyshev is rich in oil wells and factories. This is where the Soviet government moved the capital when Hitler was advancing . . ."

"And of course this is where Lenin was parked during the war?" I said.

"Of course . . . And since the Trans-Siberian railway this has been an important industrial town . . ."

At this point I tuned him out. I had little further interest in industry, having had my fill from the preachy Komsomol the previ-ous morning. I passed by Samara without stopping — Old Samara, near the Samara River, and New Samara, spreading out downriver on the left bank. As usual, the right bank was steep and thickly wooded.

Olearius had kept a wary eye out here for Cossacks and other ruffians.

> Because of the thick dark forest that beautifully covers the shore on both sides, this place is very pleasing to the eye. But at the same time it's very dangerous for travelers because of its convenience to brigands. In particular there are high mountains here where approaching people may be seen while far off and a pillaging attack readied. It's said that Cossacks are usually found around this river. Dyevichiya Gora lies on the right, is very high, rising steeply from the shore, and is very pleasant to look at. It presents a series of steps, like benches, one above another, of red, yellow and blue sandstone, and is very much like a series of old walls.

Near the Chagra River (which enters the Volga through a wide inlet on a sparsely populated bluff beyond the town of Davidovka) they'd been told a large force of Cossacks was lying in wait for them, but saw no sign of them.

A few kilometers round the Samara Bend I stopped briefly at the small town of Yekaterinovka, on the left bank, to change boats. Inland from here, about 20 kilometers on the railway, is one of the most famous farms in the Soviet Union, an experimental *sovkhoz* for livestock breeding and the development of new seed grains. Under Brezhnev, foreign correspondents based in Moscow were often flown out on a sweep through this area — a fast tour of the Lada plant at Togliatti, a look at the dairy cows of Bezenchuk, a day on a beach, carefully segregated from any Russian bathers by ropes and armed militia, and back to Moscow . . . I knew several who'd been on the trip and several who'd written glowing reports of the progress at Bezenchuk, though I never knew a Western correspondent who knew the first thing about cows.

Our Raketa stopped briefly at Perevoloki, a small village on the right bank on the "handle" of the shovel. The river is flowing west at this point. Only a few hundred feet to the north it's flowing in the opposite direction, east. The Samara Bend is well named: the river bends back on itself, making almost an island of the Zhiguli Hills. Many of the locals make a day trip of crossing the handle, getting off at Perevoloki and reboarding on the north side, at the railway town of Mezhdurechensk ("between rivers"). A few kilometers downriver, at Pecherskoye, are limestone caverns, for those who like clambering around in the dark.

At the city of Syzran the Volga takes its final and definitive plunge to the south. All the way to Saratov, almost 300 kilometers away, the topography is the same — flat and marshy to the east, with high wooded hills, occasionally with dramatic peaks, to the west. The villages and towns all begin to blur into one another: Novokashpirskii, with its fossil beds and ancient burial mounds; Panshino, Privolzhe, Sofino, Davidovka, Vozrozhdeniye . . . And Khvalinsk, which for centuries had been a stronghold of the Old Believers, and a refuge for bizarre sects of all kinds. There's a *kumiss* sanatorium here, converted from an old monastery. The chalk and limestone Dyevichi Mountains, riddled with deep clefts and bubbling sulfur springs, stretch along the right bank as far as Volsk, a hundred kilometers or so to the south.

Below the town of Balakovo, on the left bank, is a large island called Dyevushkin Ostrov (Maiden's Island), where the Golden Horde once kept a harem. I'd read of it in one of Bruce Chatwin's books; as his cruise ship was passing the island, he'd been told that in early days it was supposed to have been inhabited by Amazons, who made love to their male prisoners before killing them. Only one prisoner ever escaped. His stratagem was brilliantly simple: his last wish was to be made love to "by the ugliest of you." Since none of the Amazons volunteered for this position, they'd perforce had to let him go. This story was recounted to Chatwin by "Svetlana, an Intourist girl with a wonderful curling lip and green come-hither eyes." Alas. I had no Intourist girl, green-eyed or no. The only young girl I could see on the Raketa was enormously fat, with an upper lip that had somehow torn away from her nose. She was carrying a string bag of potatoes and smelled strongly of the soil. But she was sweet and good-natured, and once I heard her singing quietly under her breath to herself, a song, like all Russian songs, that seemed to me filled with melancholy. She got off at a small village, and her family came down to the pier to greet her, and as we pulled away I saw them walking up a muddy path to a ragged village, arms around each other, vanishing into a Russia that hadn't changed much since Catherine the Great sent her colonists down here to plant farms and themselves in the soil of the Mother River.

CHAPTER 19

Kilometer 2,618

Saratov

I stopped my stolid Volga in the middle of a farm road not far from Saratov. There was a rye field to my right, dusty and parched, the crop withered from lack of attention. To my left, in an uncultivated field of stinkweed and burdock, I could see the bony rump of an emaciated cow. I walked a little way into the field; it crackled under my feet and gave off little puffs of yellow dust, the clouds of drought. I went back to the car and spread my maps out on the hood.

Everywhere in this region, the countryside is in ruins. Even the official statistics, which are still mortally shy of the truth, have owned up to 60,000 devastated hectares in the Saratov region. Most people, and many of the newspapers, say the count is higher, much higher. What were once thriving farms — even, let it be said, thriving *collective* farms — were derelict. I could see it for myself: there were eroded gullies everywhere, weeds, great dust bowls. All the stores in the region were empty. In this land of cows, there was no milk. The meat in the stores, what little there was of it, was rancid. Eggs were rationed. Grain was rationed. Even the bread shops at the height of summer were almost empty. People were talking openly of famine.

What brought this about? Blame was everywhere, thick in the air. The *apparat* was blaming perestroika, reformers were blaming hidebound thinking. As usual, Gorbachev was a target of abuse from all sides. Locally, the Volga Germans were popular scapegoats.

This was a most curious piece of blame-laying, for the Volga Germans were conspicuous mostly by their absence, having been deported by Stalin and dispersed into the vast Asiatic hinterland; even the names of their towns and villages had been stripped from the maps. They were being blamed for the mess their (former) farms were in by the very people who had dispossessed them. Some were blaming the Germans for not being there. Others were blaming them for trying to come back, as if the threat of their return had been enough to demoralize the region and turn it into a desert-in-the-making.

In fact, the prospect of Germans returning to Saratov had set off widespread racist hysteria in the region. An ultra-nationalist group had held an ugly demonstration in the city the week before I got there, which was widely reported in the local press. One of the placards waved by a demonstrator said: "What the Kaiser and Hitler Failed to Do, the Volga Germans Will Finish." How so? By demanding back the homes stolen from them by the local Party and its thugs? Moscow is trying to make amends for past injustices, trying to restore the Germans to their ancestral homes — Center, at least, is bent on reparation. Saratov, it seems, won't have it.

I weighted down my maps and guidebooks on the hood of the car with small stones, peering at the pages, trying to make sense of what had happened here from the printed words, trying to find some residual presence of this controversial community. For a decade after the Great October Revolution they seemed to have been left alone, and lived their lives as they had for centuries. My 1926 Volga guidebook has this to say: "On the opposite, meadowy shore below Volsk appear many German settlements with names such as Basel, Zurich, Zoloturn and, among others, Marksstadt. In these settlements, formed after 1762, there are about seventy thousand people, leading an exemplary agricultural life. Their administrative center lies in Pokrovsk city, located on the Volga's left bank, opposite Saratov . . ."

The maps issued by Rechflot in 1990 have a somewhat different story to tell. The word "German" isn't mentioned at all. The towns and villages listed in the early book have been renamed: Plekhani, Georgievka, Zorkino, Mikhailovka, Podlesnoe. Marksstadt has become Marx. The administrative center, Pokrovsk, has become Engels.

I laid the two maps side by side; in the gap between them were many of the dark themes of Russian history: autocratic despotism, pogrom, genocide. And many of the heroic themes: bravery, resistance, adherence to principle, fortitude in exile . . .

Who were these people, these new Huns? The Germans had sailed down the Volga in the 1770s at Catherine the Great's behest. The Empress, a German herself by birth and language, recruited them to stabilize the area, bring it into productive farming, make it into a taxpaying part of the Russian empire. Also, cynically, she wanted them there to take the brunt of the brutish attacks on towns and villages and farms so common in the region. Not of course that she told them that.

The immigrants were promised permission to settle where they wished, freedom of religion, a thirty-year tax holiday, perpetual exemption from military service, interest-free loans for ten years for equipment and tools. In addition, foreign capitalists were granted the right to buy serfs and peasants as well as land. They were to be given free transportation from Germany to their destinations, living allowances, and more.

Almost thirty thousand departed to the Volga, Catherine's first colony. More went later to Ukraine, the Crimea and elsewhere in Russia. There were some two million Volga Germans by the time World War I began; after the Revolution, Lenin set up a Volga German ASSR. By then the Germans had turned Saratov into the largest city on the Volga and the pre-eminent grain port, and the Volga lands were exporting substantial amounts of food to the Russian capital.

The 1927 Party Congress in Moscow, the infamous one that resolved to liquidate private farming, demanded that all farmers join collectives. Most of the German colonists refused. In theory, this was their right under the collectivization law, but in response they were simply taxed out of existence, their taxes soon exceeding the entire value of their farms. In addition, they were asked to make "voluntary" contributions to the "common good." Deportations went on throughout the Thirties, the police vans arriving in the night to take whole families away. Most of them went to the forest camps in northern Russia.

Still, the Volga German community survived, and even thrived, and quietly went about its business. Until Hitler.

After the Soviet-German pact went sour, Stalin banned the teaching of German in regional schools. Many teachers had already been banished to Siberia for being "class enemies," and by the beginning of the 1941-42 school year there were no German children left to teach — they had joined their families in exile, victims of the decision to abolish the Volga German ASSR and all its works and its people; following a decree by Stalin signed by Kalinin in August 1941 the population was herded into cattle cars and scattered through central Asia, Siberia, Altai and the Arctic regions. The German community vanished from Soviet ken and Soviet maps without outcry, without any notice from the international community, just one more injustice among so many.

Until Gorbachev. For the past few years, more than a hundred thousand Volga Germans have migrated back to West Germany, as it was then still called, which received them gratefully: Bonn could always use energetic immigrants to do manual labor, especially if they needed no schooling in the language. I was told in Saratov that the West Germans had declared themselves willing to take up to two million Volga Germans, but I wondered whether this was wishful thinking on the part of the pan-Slavic zealots, who were happy to see them go.

Meanwhile, around Saratov, their old homeland, the barricades were going up and ugly placards were being paraded through the streets.

I'd seen no sign of Germans around Ulyanovsk. However, Viktor Loshak, a reporter for the feisty *Moscow News*, published an excellent piece on the Germans while I was there, detailing not only their hostile reception in Saratov, which I was able to confirm for myself, but a positive response from Ulyanovsk, where there were local authorities with a more generous attitude. The village council of Krasnoe Syandukhovo, for example, looking at the derelict farms around them, overrun by weeds, the buildings falling down, decided that they'd turn the whole thing over to Germans returning from Asian exile — pasture, cattle, barns, cottages, what machinery there was, everything. It was a pattern that was to repeat itself in other parts of the region. The number of offers swelled, encouraged by the Ulyanovsk district council, which knew the desperate need for skilled farmers (or indeed for any kind of farmers, even those of indifferent skills) as the rural population shrank and the farms and villages emptied. By the summer of 1990 twelve districts had accepted or were accepting Germans. These included not only major industrial farms and enterprises, but also individual families. Over 4,000 hectares were being put back into cultivation, and two entirely new settlements planned. Joint ventures with Germany were in the works.

So was this to be a success story for the new era? Would it — will it — work? Are the Germans what the local authorities hope they are — a population insulated from the Russian disease of disaffection? Will they be able to do something with the ruined farmland? Will they be able to get their produce to market? Is this a breeding ground for *kulaks*-to-be or just another experiment in social engineering, as doomed as the others? From all accounts these Germans managed to make a go of their farms in the arid deserts of Asia; a lot of hope is riding on their no doubt exaggerated capacity for coaxing yields from the land.

And in Saratov? Even the local KGB weren't happy with the hysteria. One member even wrote an open letter to Gorbachev claiming that anti-German sentiments were being whipped up by "corrupt quarters trying to stay in power to conceal their economic crimes and abuses of office," and who were "now trying to hide behind the backs of people they themselves have provoked and egged into the flames of ethnic conflict." This letter was never published in Saratov, only in Moscow, and I remained skeptical of its authenticity: it smelled, in its prefabricated phrases and stale imagery, of an old-fashioned put-up job. Even so it demonstrated that there were powerful people not happy with the incompetence and racism of the Saratov authorities.

•　　•　　•

I'd flown to Volgograd from Ulyanovsk, and was retracing my steps upriver by car, first by a "rented" taxi from Volgograd itself, and subsequently in a borrowed car, an elderly Volga, arranged third-hand through a Volgograd taxi driver. Partly, I wanted to see if I could find any Germans — either those who'd escaped deportation or those who'd already returned. This wasn't a systematic quest: I simply pottered along, asking everyone I met whether there was any German presence in the region or whether any of their neighbors was German, and if so could they direct me to one. Mostly I got blank stares, a few shrugs and one rant, this from a farmer who took me for a German and therefore a Russian-killer.

I penetrated the countryside as much as I could, bearing in mind a borrowed car and my continuing nervousness of (a) the GAI and (b) running out of gas. I only occasionally ventured off the main road (pretty fair condition, on the whole) onto some rather more eccentric dirt roads. I did question a collection of farmers, a truck driver having a beer by the side of the road and the driver and passengers of a dirt-encrusted bus that had broken down. It was a magnificent July morning, and this last group were sitting placidly, apparently waiting for divine intervention, having clearly given up on either their own abilities or the abilities of the collectivity to effect repairs. No one knew of any Germans in the neighborhood. Most knew there'd been some, but only in historical times. One or two expressed the notion that it was better thus: no foreigners would be able to understand how Russia worked. And two said they didn't want Germans there. "I know they say these Germans are more Russian, that they're like us, that they're different from Germans in Germany. But a German is a German. It's in the nature of a German to dominate you." I asked them if they'd heard of anti-German rioting in Saratov, with the connivance of the authorities, but no one knew anything about the already infamous banners waved by some "less progressive elements": "Better AIDS Than Germans." Most of the people I met had only a vague idea what AIDS was, in any case. And Rodina, the ultra-nationalist group? Did they agree with it? No one had an opinion.

I stopped the car outside Saratov to scan the local papers. I read, gloomily, about the deteriorating ethnic relations in the region, about the blame-laying and the recriminations. I'll be glad,

I thought, to leave this region. I had a bad feeling about it. There seemed to be so much hatred, so little joy. The landscape depressed me profoundly. It had the same exhausted look I remembered from the photographs of Walker Evans, whose depiction of American sharecroppers in the Thirties was so frightening. The people seemed stiff, sullen, resigned or angry, drunk and slovenly: haunting eyes staring from faces that expressed no curiosity, no emotion, no interest in anything, people who asked no questions and expected nothing. The farms here were rural slums. The machinery I was able to see looked derelict, rusting where the workers left it. Drunks wandered everywhere. Nowhere else in Russia did the population more resemble the louts of classical upper-class Russian literature: vacant, empty of any passions save lust and drunkenness. Somewhat incongruously amidst all these large glooms, I developed a smaller but more urgent worry: there was a strange knocking sound coming from under the Volga's hood.

Just before the car lurched back onto the paved road I passed a short section where there was, in fact, no road at all. They were "repairing" the road but had neglected to build a detour, with the result that vehicles wishing to proceed had to crawl across a drainage ditch and through a field for 150 feet or so. After a rain it would be completely impassable. Once on the paved road I breathed a little easier, and, except for several wary looks at the gas gauge, made it back to the Volga without incident. As I sat waiting for the car's owner at the pre-arranged spot, I began to understand one of the many roles of the Volga in the people's affections: it got them to places, but it also got them away.

The car had been late coming to the rendezvous down by the waterfront terminal. There'd been nothing I could do about it, since I didn't know where it was coming from. After three hours I began to get seriously worried, but after four my contact finally arrived. What had happened? It was an old Soviet story: the car had run out of gas, and so had the gas station.

This happened more often than it should. Sometimes it happened because the refineries weren't producing enough, sometimes because the tankers broke down themselves (on one famous occasion it was because the tanker itself ran out of gas and the crew had nothing readily to hand to siphon it into their motor's tank). More often the tanker was simply sidetracked and its gasoline "disappeared" into the gray market. My contact, Yegor, took his empty jerry can to the nearest house, knowing full well that many houses along the highways, even those where there are no cars, have a supply of bootleg gas in the basement. In this case, he said, he was met only by a stony *nyet*.

"I walked on to the next house," he said, "about a kilometer. There, a very fat woman in a torn dress warned me away. She had a dog, she said, that would take care of me if I didn't leave. A third house also yielded no results."

"What did you do?" I asked.

He laughed. In the end, the tanker had shown up — it had blown a tire and stopped to change it. "I caught it before the gas station did." He laughed again. They had a pump on board but the gasoline came out in great gushes, impossible to put into a narrow-necked can. "So we filled a pothole in the road and I dipped my can in that . . ."

"A pothole that big?"

"Oh," he said cheerfully, "a good meter across and almost as deep."

"But the sand?" I said uneasily. "What if the sand gets into the carburetor?"

"Don't worry," he said. "These old Volgas are impossible to stop."

But of course I did worry. Though the Volga didn't stop.

I'd always wanted to go to the town of Marx, ever since I'd read, during the unlamented Years of Stagnation, that it was one of the happiest, smuggest socialist towns in the Russian republic. A reporter had waxed lyrical, in the style of the day, about how comfortable and prosperous Marx was, how the tractor plant workers put in extra hours without pay for the glory of Socialist Industry and the prosperity of the Motherland. Even for those days, when officially every resident of the Socialist Motherland was happy and prosperous and there were bountiful harvests wherever you looked, his praise seemed excessive — and reading between the lines the reporter himself seemed a bit taken aback, the Marxist-Leninist clichés tripping off the page in a discombobulated way. It read like a prose version of those photographs of smiling peasant harvesters that used to grace the front pages of the national dailies.

In reality, as usual, things were more complicated. I never did get to Marx in those years. The whole region was simply shut to foreigners, as indeed much of it still was in 1990, including Saratov itself. But while I was in the region anyway, I thought it a good idea to pop up to Marx, only 80 or 90 kilometers distant — about an hour's drive if the potholes weren't too alarming.

The trip was something of a disappointment. Marx was founded in 1762, and named Katharinenstadt after Catherine herself. From my 1926 guidebook I discovered that the city had, in addition to the tractor plant, a tobacco factory, a furniture plant and others. The modern Rechflot guidebook, by contrast, simply describes Marx as "a town in the Saratov region since 1918," and says that it contains "many memorials of the various revolutionary struggles and of the Great Patriotic War." Of Engels, which used to be Pokrovsk, the modern book mentions only the trolleybus factory, the fact that Engels was the birthplace "of the Soviet writer L.A. Kassil" and that it's now the location of the Saratov Region Operetta.

So what's there to see in Marx today?

The factory written about so lyrically by the *Socialist Industry* reporter twenty years earlier, then called Vozrozhdeniye (Renaissance), was called Kommunist, a name change contrary to the spirit of perestroika, which didn't seem a good omen. The factory was famous because the very first Soviet tractors had rolled from its gates in the heady post-Revolutionary days, just before Lenin busied himself restoring a market economy "temporarily" after the ravages and absurdities of War Communism. A heady moment indeed! To the star-struck theorists of Communism in faraway Moscow, the peasant was the second sturdy leg on which they would build the awe-inspiring edifice of the New Society (the first leg was the proletariat). One of the prime tasks was to free the peasant from the dual torments of serfdom and primitive implements. The first, they considered, they'd already done by the simple expedient of abolishing the owner class and substituting the collectivity of the people, in the personification of the Party. These new tractors were the embodiment of the second freedom, the implement that would effortlessly cause bountiful harvests to flow from Mother Russia.

Of course, the results are long in. Stalin succeeded only in destroying agriculture and alienating the peasants, driving them into sulky defiance by stripping them of every meager thing they had. The wretched rural land that was to be seen on all sides, even within striking distance of the Kommunist Tractor Factory itself, was testament to the failed technological vision: the god of science had been no match for the stubborn human clay.

Within an hour's drive of Marx, there's a reconstituted Stone Age village, the careful product of Soviet archaeological research (even though this research had been bent, in the days of the Terror, to "demonstrating" the natural Communism of primitive man). It was hard to say which culture seemed more out of date in this place, the Communist or the Stone Age.

I wanted to go to the local Gorkom (the city committee) and ask them whether the earlier praise in the national press had made a difference to the town, but I didn't want to simply show up, a foreign journalist asking impertinent questions. So I tried appearing at the tractor factory gates to see if I could poke about there a bit, but I was refused admission.

I stopped the car near the outskirts of Marx and opened a beer, unwrapping a sausage and cucumber sandwich I'd cobbled together in the market in Saratov. As usual, the car, and the beer, attracted a crowd. One package of Marlboros and a couple of beers later, we workers were having a wonderful time. What did I think of the USSR? What did I think of perestroika? What did I think of Yeltsin? What did I think would happen?

These were the standard questions that I'd learned to finesse. 1. The USSR? I love Russia and the Russians, don't think much of their system. 2. Interesting. 3. Russian politics are too complicated for me, what do *you* think? 4. Everyone I meet seems depressed, what do *you* think?

The slovenly workers of Marx were also part of the Russian political ferment. Even in these far hinterlands, a very long way from Center, the Yeltsin name was magic. They'd all seen him on television, his hulking frame squeezed into his little Moskvich car, and for him they'd do anything. Gorbachev, on the other hand . . . The Man Who Changed the World, as people in Center were calling him, was thought to be "a man of the past, one of the old men," a phrase I'd heard before. Oh yes, perestroika was wonderful, if it worked, if it ever did. So far Gorbachev had made things worse, not better — at least there was no rationing before he started his crazy ride for glory.

They didn't care, they told me, whether the meat they bought came from private plots or a state farm or from a Georgian gangster; they wanted meat for their children and they wanted it to be cheap and plentiful. They wanted clothes for their wives and an end to special stores for the bosses. They wanted the right to go and see for themselves how others did things, without being accused of disloyalty. "All this talk of systems, it's all shit. They should leave us all alone. We can do it without them."

Here I was in Marx, in a car with three Russian sons of toil and others milling about outside, their clothes rank with sweat, their teeth gleaming with steel and gold, unshaven and unkempt, and I felt a huge affection for them. They all wanted to share with me, with anyone, their thoughts, their worries, their food, their drink, their cigarettes, their lapel buttons, whatever they had they wanted me to have. Nor were they simple fools, holy idiots. They'd been taken in by Them, by Center, by politicians and ideologues, repeatedly and for so long that they were wary of promises, and wary of those who made them. There was no trust left. Not just of Center. Also of Pamyat, Rodina, all the utopians and extremists, all the honeyed words or the veiled threats from all the many people who wanted to run their lives.

Whenever I was saddened by the cynicism of Russian life, and by the despair so many Russians expressed about their history and their world, I'd think back to this hour in this car, to these people who reminded me of the long roots of Russian communalism, which in turn had its roots in the family, in the clan and its needs, in the isolated, remote villages, in the harsh climate and the harsh tyrants and the harsh invaders; this communalism that made them sentimental as well as cruel, and more susceptible to the seductive ideas of Communism (and, indeed, gave Communism a better chance in Russia — Stalin was right enough there). This communalism is regarded in Center as a real brake on reform; I'd been told that more than once. It expresses itself in deep resistance to change of any kind and a deeply felt belief that the wealthy are by definition exploiters and that to want to be rich, or richer than others, is by definition an untrustworthy thing.

Gorbachev, for his part, was still impatiently calling for psychological perestroika, and they replied by making catty remarks about his wife, Raisa, who sounded in their prejudiced view not unlike Marie Antoinette. In any case, politics soon palled, and we shared what soccer news we could. (I know very little about the game, but fortunately had caught on Radio Moscow that the next World Cup was to be held in the United States, so I was able to keep my end up all right.) Then they wanted me to explain baseball to them, and we ended up in a weed-strewn field, me demonstrating my admittedly eccentric sidearm pitch with a tennis ball one of them fetched from a truck. Final score: Marx Workers 4, Visitor 0. We parted in great amiability and with many unshaven kisses and hugs.

CHAPTER 20

Kilometer 3,031

Volgograd (Tsaritsyn)

F rom Saratov to Volgograd and east of the Volga to the Urals, the terrain is spare, parched yellow steppe, used by the Soviet space authorities to bring home their cosmonauts. The right bank is bleak and rocky. Stenka Razin is supposed to have climbed yet another cliff somewhere along this dismal land, a cliff that "no one had managed before." I learned another verse of the ballad of Stenka Razin, the Cossack of the Don.

> *There is a high cliff on the Volga*
> *Covered all over with wild moss*
> *From the bottom to the silky top*
> *Only one could climb it, Stenka Razin*

For most of history only "wild tribes" of Kalmyks and Tartars have lived here, people fitted to the terrain. Several days' journey before Volgograd (then called Tsaritsyn) a group of Tartars sent by the Prince Musal visited the Olearius flotilla: "The most important of the Tartars, who spoke for all of them, was a tall yellow man with entirely black hair and a big long beard. He was dressed in a black sheepskin coat with the fur outside, and resembled the devil as he's depicted in paintings. The others, who were dressed in black and brown cotton robes, were scarcely more pleasant to behold."

Only a few kilometers out of Volgograd are the ruins of a town that Tamerlane built of stone, and within which he raised a great pleasure palace called Tsarev Gorod, the site of legendary orgies and great cruelties, a place (according to local legends) "where the beast could retreat, to lick its chops and dream of further conquests." After this town was destroyed, the Russians took most of the stones to Astrakhan and used them to build the city walls, and many of the churches, monasteries and other buildings. As late as the eighteenth century boats were ferrying building stone from the ruins of Tsarev Gorod.

I saw this part of the country backward, as it were. As I've said, I flew to Volgograd and made my way back upriver to Saratov and Marx.

My flight to Volgograd from Ulyanovsk was instructive in the ways of Aeroflot's domestic operations. It was to leave Ulyanovsk at the unusual hour of three in the morning, and was due in at Volgograd sometime before five. I was told to be at the airport by one-thirty. I managed a few hours' sleep after supper, the Intourist bus arrived more or less on time, and on the way to the airport we stopped to pick up Zhina, who'd offered to help me check in. This was just as well, as it turned out. She looked as cheerful as one could, having been turned out of bed at this hour. The airport terminal was a cavernous hall, lit by what seemed like 40-watt bulbs, with no directional signs whatever, anywhere; not even anything so simple as an information booth. Unintelligible announcements echoed over a PA system.

Scattered through the terminal were four or five barricades passing for check-in counters, each with a heaving, scrapping crowd in front of it. Which "counter" was for which flight remained a mystery. After half an hour or so we fought our way to the front of the crowd, and presented my ticket to the clerk. Wrong line. We tried again at the second counter. This time we'd guessed right. The clerk took my ticket, looking dubiously at my large hold-all — a look I didn't at the time understand. She squinted to see whether I'd been assigned a seat — if not, it would have meant another lineup somewhere else. Fortunately, Zhina had thought of this, and had the Intourist office assign me a seat earlier. Then the clerk carefully tore off a stub from my ticket, using a ruler since the paper was not perforated along its dotted lines, which were in any case crooked.

"And my bag?" I asked.

She looked dubious again. "Put it over there," she said, hooking a thumb at a cart of the sort used to truck bags out to airplanes at normal airports.

I heaved the bag into the cart, and waited.

She told me to leave.

I demanded a ticket, which she reluctantly gave me. Would she put the other half on my bag? She would. There was neither a number nor a destination airport on it. I began to half understand the dubious look.

Zhina and the Intourist driver left, and I waited in the "departure hall," which is a wooden bench next to some busy mineral water dispensing machines.

Boarding was relatively easy, except that I was never really sure I was on the right flight — the flight number on the departure gate wasn't the same as the one on my ticket. We got on board, and a scrum for seats began. The numbers on the bulkhead bore no relationship to where the seats actually were — they'd crammed in several extra rows. Finally I sat in what was more or less my seat, and refused to move. This, it appears, is proper procedure. No one pays any attention to seat numbers — you take a vacant seat and stay put and the hell with everyone else. Following this rule on subsequent flights worked well.

At last the doors closed and the plane began to move.

A minute later, the plane stopped, the pilot switched off the engines (and the lights, pitching us into blackness) and came back to open the door to the outside. He swung from the doorpost, peering into the void. He said nothing. No one told us anything. No one asked. No one even grumbled. There was loud snoring from the seat behind me, and in front a baby began the crescendo screeching that was to last for the rest of the flight. I looked around. The plane was going on to Baku, the Soviet oil capital, after Volgograd, and it was full of cheerful swarthy men carrying huge bundles. The aisles were full of packages, suitcases, bags of oranges, cardboard boxes tied with string — two feet deep in baggage. There'd be no room for service personnel to move around the cabin, had there been any service for the service personnel to perform (they did serve mineral water or orangeade in small brown plastic cups halfway through the flight, and the passengers helpfully passed the cups down to the rear). None of the seatbelts worked. The seat next to me was broken, and the fellow in it had to sit upright the whole flight or he would have been in the lap of the man behind him.

A few minutes went by. Eventually, two more passengers got on via a hastily arranged stairway. Shortly thereafter we actually took off. I tried to sleep, but it was impossible. The seats were so jammed together I couldn't get my legs in, and was forced to sit sideways, my feet on someone's bag of oranges, much to her displeasure.

We came in over Volgograd, the morning sun gleaming on the broad, placid waters of Mother Volga; it looked very beautiful from the air. It was about five-thirty in the morning. There was no Intourist office at the airport (well, there was, but I couldn't find it). Nor was there any sign of the car I'd ordered from Ulyanovsk, and paid for in dollars.

The baggage claim room was at the side of the terminal building, and couldn't be reached from inside the terminal — you must go outdoors to get to it. This seemed unnecessary even by Soviet standards of customer service. It wasn't too bad in summer, but in winter it would be unpleasant — it does get down well below freezing in Volgograd. The passengers were not allowed into the baggage claim area until the baggage had actually arrived in it. This took about half an hour, by which time the rest of the passengers, the ones who'd sensibly taken all their bags into the plane, had long gone. While I was waiting a cab driver sidled up and offered to take me anywhere in town for $20 American. He settled for five, still ten times the rate he would have gotten in rubles.

His car was a brand-new Volga. He drove downtown at a tremendous pace, going through red lights when there was no opposing traffic. The city looked lush and green. We were a thousand kilometers south of Ulyanovsk and there were peaches ripening on their trees. Volgograd is at the junction of the steppe grasslands to the west and the arid deserts of Soviet Asia to the east, and is notorious for its sandstorms.

The road from the airport is elevated, built on the ruins of a fortification erected by Peter the Great for a purpose no one remembers. The outskirts are indistinguishable from any other Soviet city: the usual dismal shops with their generic signs, the usual apartment buildings of an irredeemable shabbiness. The central part is pleasant: a little portentous, in the Stalinist mode, but handsome nonetheless. We've distanced ourselves sufficiently from the Stalinist style to develop an appreciation for its wedding-cake excesses, if nothing else, especially when compared with later Soviet efforts, which are boring imitations of an excessively boring International style. There's another reason people like these Stalinist buildings. They're popular because they have high ceilings and the rooms are generously sized, unlike the Khrushchevian orange-crate architecture of the Sixties.

The names of Volgograd's subdivisions are wonderfully resonant of a revolutionary past: Traktorzavodski (Tractor Factory), Krasnooktyabrski (Red October), Soviet, Dzerzhinsky, Kirov and Krasnoarmeiski (Red Army).

There is nothing at all left of the city called Tsaritsyn, founded in 1589, but then Tsaritsyn itself was destroyed several times. The original hamlet was built on an island in the Sary-soo River, which flows into the Volga; it was destroyed in an early peasant war and was rebuilt on the mainland, on the Volga's right bank, in 1615 as a fortress against "thievish Cossacks and their looting expeditions." Razin took the place in 1670, as did Pugachev a hundred years later.

Old Tsaritsyn was built on hills and gullies, and the gullies were used as dumps and sewers. The town was, from all accounts, a hellhole, prone to cholera and typhus, home to brigands and thieves and militant, angry whores who sometimes ran in packs. It was also typical of the way Tsarist Russian towns were laid out: great mansions in the central high ground, odiferous slums elsewhere.

It got worse after the emancipation of the serfs. Until then it had been essentially a sleepy provincial town in Saratov province. Once the railroad came, industry expanded. The French built a steel mill in 1875, and other foreigners followed. By the late nineteenth century Tsaritsyn had became a nightmare of the Industrial Revolution, overlaid and exaggerated by the boyars' uncaring cruelty to the people on whose labor their fortunes were based. The Russian upper classes were dependent on foreigners for their entrepreneurial drive and were, essentially, parasites; it's hard not to feel considerable sympathy with the early revolutionaries whose lives were governed by these people.

By 1916, Tsaritsyn's population of 150,000 was already overwhelmingly proletarian. The city still sprawled without discipline over hills and lowlands, over sandbars and ravines. There was no sewage system. The streets were unpaved.

In 1923, after the Civil War, the city was in ruins.

In 1945, after the war against Hitler, the city was in ruins.

It seems to be a Volgograd litany.

All this has vanished into the past. The modern city is handsomely laid out, if a little too monumental, too widely spaced, to really work at human scale. The planners and builders did a remarkable job of reconstruction, a welcome exception to the dismal Soviet rule, in a land where planners are not renowned for their aesthetic judgment. Sensibly, they've let the broad sweep of the Volga dictate the shape of the city, and tied the streets and parks to river views. Trees and greenery are everywhere, and many of the major thoroughfares have leafy boulevards. Unlike so many American cities, where the railways and the factories dominate the waterfront, Volgograd's industry is inland, in a belt on the arid land to the east. The city proper is therefore an unusual shape: it's about 75 kilometers long and only four or five wide. The planners have divided it into what are essentially four smaller cities, with four downtowns; these four are separated from one another by large wooded parks, which are extensively used by families, even at night. Several hills stand out, and gullies meander through the city; two smaller rivers flow into the Volga, the Tsaritsa and the Mokraya Mechetka. The hills include Mamayev Kurgan, the highest point in Volgograd, a wartime battleground and now the site of a series of immense war memorials. The primary traffic conduits, like the factories, are set back from the river, out of sight. The major arteries near the river (Lenin Street the main one, of course) are more boulevard than highway. The intent of the planners has been to make a large city feel smaller, and they've succeeded admirably.

I arrived at the Intourist Hotel, where I'd reserved a room, before six o'clock. The main door was still locked. I prodded at what looked like a bellpush, but the "push" part of it had fallen off and it gave me a nasty shock. Exasperated, I banged on the door until a sleepy woman came to unlock it. She was pleasant, checked me in, fussed over me, showed me how to use the elevator (not as easy as you might think), clucked over the absence of Intourist's car at the airport and said she was the hotel's administrator and was there to be helpful. I was so taken aback at this solicitousness that I quite forgot to thank her. My room was typically furnished with a grim hard bed and a chuckling refrigerator, but it had high ceilings, large breezy windows and a pleasant view over Fallen Heroes Square, Volgograd's main plaza. The bathroom was typical — no plug for the tub, a shower that didn't work. Still, there was a towel, and plenty of hot water. I went down to breakfast at eight, as instructed. The restaurant staff seemed astonished to have a customer, for some reason, but they were amiable all the same. The restaurant was in an attractive columned room, circular in shape, that had the distinct feel of the pre-Revolutionary era, though the hotel was built in the Fifties. A waitress indicated a small table by a window, and said it would be mine for the rest of my stay. I was taken aback again — remembering the brawls to get fed elsewhere — though this time I was properly effusive. The room was elegant — linen napkins on the tables. Breakfast was soft-boiled eggs, fresh bread and excellent coffee. I wanted to stay forever.

Volgograd is a multicultural society, in the modern jargon. Kazakhs live here, of course, since the western border of Kazakhstan is only a hundred or so kilometers into the eastern desert. So do many Georgians, Gypsies, Armenians, Poles and others. My first morning in town a giggling busload of Kazakh girls went by, touring the monuments of the city — I later caught up with them and photographed a few, to their delight; in their colorful national dress they looked like a cageful of tropical birds. Officially Volgograd is 90-percent Russian, but judging from the street crowds, the true figure is probably much lower.

At the railway station, which resembled the Moscow river terminal in its Stalinist grandness, there's a bustling informal market:
people with small pickle jars of raspberries, gooseberries, currants,
apricots. Lots of apricots, though most of them looked green. The
stores contained none of this stuff, only cucumbers — is a city of a
million to be fed from peasant pickle jars?

Fallen Heroes Square used to be a thriving bazaar in the
Tsaritsyn days, with dozens of stalls and shops. Maurice Hindus
visited it in 1923: "The immense sandblown market teemed with
caravans of carts, drawn by ox, horse or camel and loaded with all
manner of produce, including pork, beef and mutton — on the
hoof. NEP had struck its stride, and trade was booming in the
bazaars and the shops." Now the square is a park, somewhat sterile
and solemn, except for a sentimental plaque on the only tree to
have survived the Nazi bombardment. The bazaar has shifted 300
feet north to the station square. Kiosks stand in rows along one
side of the square, and scattered elsewhere.

These kiosks are one of the oddities of Russian retailing, and in
a way represent one of the few flexible responses to consumer
demand. They've been cropping up for years in odd locations. The
entrance to a zoo might have a little kiosk selling ice cream, for
instance. Newsstand kiosks are located on many corners.
Elsewhere, kiosks sell souvenirs outside tourist attractions. Oddly,
there are kiosks outside shops that are a kind of digest version of
the shop itself, selling the same merchandise, thereby saving the
shop the bother of opening itself to the public. The kiosk is usually
a small prefabricated building glazed on one side with either a
grille or a sliding window for pushing money through and asking
questions. If the kiosk staffer doesn't want to talk to you, she (usually a she) simply slides the window closed and ignores you.

Kiosks sell everything from leather belts to beer, and they're
multiplying all the time. There were even kiosks in the pristine
square outside the Lenin museum in Ulyanovsk. These kiosks never
made much sense to me. Dozens of massive shops are available,
mostly empty — why not use those? Especially in winter, when
kiosk customers stand around in the frost, shivering, fumbling with
gloved hands for change. In Volgograd, enough kiosks were clus-
tered in one place to become a version of an older tradition, the

bazaar. They're eminently adaptable to "individual enterprise," as the phrase goes. Small "entrepreneurs" could rent one of these kiosks cheaply and set up in business. Whether this is deliberate policy or not I never discovered. Hindus reported in 1923 on the swiftness with which the city was recovering from the death and wreckage of the Civil War; perhaps these kiosks, and the enterprises that flower in them, might witness a similar swift recovery after the wreckage of the Years of Stagnation?

In 1940 this city was still called Stalingrad. The Volga here is only 60 kilometers from the Don, but, as a Volgograd civic pamphlet put it, "these were perhaps the longest and most fatal kilometers the German army ever traversed." In one of the museums in this museum-prone city there's a note from a young soldier, a private, a hurried scribble: "Without the Volga, Russia is a body without a soul. Sacred to us is this great Russian river and it shall remain unpolluted. We dare not allow the Germans to reach the Volga." And so Stalingrad, which Hitler sought to turn into a synonym for catastrophe to all Russians, became instead a symbol of glorious resistance.

The assault on Stalingrad was a disaster for the Nazis. It was perhaps the decisive battle of World War II. One of Khrushchev's sons was killed here. So was Mikoyan's son, and the son of La Pasionaria of Spain. Walter Ulbricht, the German Communist leader, fought here. The epic phase of the city's defense lasted fifty-three days in a hundred separate sieges in neighborhoods, houses and factories; 85 percent of the city's buildings were demolished.

Reminders of the war can be seen all over Volgograd. On the Volga embankment is a place where a platoon of girls held a post until they were wiped out. The so-called Pavlov House garrison, which held a small house for an incredible month against continuous bombardment, consisted of several Russians and Ukrainians, two Georgians, one Tartar, one Jew, one Kazakh, one Uzbek and one Tadjik, a paradigm of the Soviet Union's optimistic future.

It's said that the peasants in the dugouts and trenches refused to use the word "German," whether from superstitious dread or hatred is not clear. They used the word "he" instead. Whatever their emotions, they did not give in. They simply endured. They waited in the frosts and died, and then their brothers moved into the places where they'd been, and died in their stead, to the fury, then the panic, then the despair of the German commanders.

Of all the many monuments in this city to the Great Patriotic War, the most effective is the ruined factory they've left standing as a mute reminder of how bad it really was. It's not as large as Mamayev Kurgan, the "main" war memorial, and they've surrounded it with false grandiosity, huge frescoes of fierce Red Army heroes, solemn colonnades, arches, statues, and a banal museum, together with several tanks, machine guns and airplanes somewhat the worse for wear. None of that detracts in any way from the hulk of the ruined factory, its vacant windows gloomy and brooding, looking exactly like old documentary photographs of the war, so that it's easy to imagine the brutal boom of the bombardment, and the shells that destroyed the fabric of the city but left its heart intact. After the war, Volgograd was so ruined that plans were drawn up to preserve the whole monstrous, smoldering pit just as it was, as a gigantic war memorial, with a series of hotels on the periphery from which schoolchildren could tour to see what men are capable of doing to each other. Fortunately, sense prevailed, and the city was rebuilt.

Ulyanovsk, Lenin's birthplace, is a theme park to a mummified idea; Volgograd could easily have been a theme park to war. They've avoided the traps, however, concentrating the overt sentimentality in a few places — the Pavlov House, the Mamayev Kurgan and one or two more. They're getting on with life. Of all the cities of Soviet Russia, Volgograd is the least sad, the most optimistic, the most confident, the most buoyant.

The following day I ran into eight old fellows on the Volga embankment, near the Mamayev Kurgan. They were all dressed in bright blue sweatsuits cut to look like pajamas. Some wore slippers, some shoes with no socks. One defiant old bird had his slippers on a string around his neck and was padding about in his socks. This was the day-uniform of the sanatorium where they were resident, and they'd been brought down to the river for an outing, "to be aired," as one of them put it. They were all veterans of the Volga front against the Nazis. I'd spent the day among memorials to the war, and was brooding on the long history of blood that had been let along the Volga; when Russian writers speak of the land groaning under the weight of the dead they seem, at least here, to be speaking the literal truth. I leaned on the railing with the old soldiers and studied them covertly. Many were wearing campaign ribbons pinned to their pajamas — still a common practice here. They were of varying degrees of decrepitude, but most looked tough in the fiber. They were mostly unshaven, with sunken cheeks, blotchy of skin, though lively enough in the eye. I asked what their ribbons meant, and after they saw I wasn't making mockery of old men they recited the names: Poltava, Kursk, Lvov, Rostov, Stalingrad . . . Stalingrad, always Stalingrad. The name has a heaviness in the Russian heart, but it's also the root of a fierce and chauvinistic patriotism: *It was here that we stopped the beast.* We. Always we. *At the cost of our sons, we did it.* I wanted to talk to the old men about politics, but they wouldn't. They wanted to talk about the Volga itself, and though none of them remembered it before it was tamed, they all agreed it was better now. Better for all: for ships and small boats and kids on the beach. So a few small towns got drowned. So what? Russia has lots of small towns no one wants. No one would miss them if they drowned a few more.

"And a lot of people, too," one of the old codgers interjected.

"Did you notice that there are sailboats again?" another asked. "I haven't seen young people sailing in small boats since I was a boy myself."

"In the time of Catherine II," said another, somewhat snidely.

It wasn't until they were about to be herded back to their bus that one of them turned back and said, "It's all been a fiasco. Everything since the war has been a fiasco. We fought for . . . what we fought for, and now we hear on television that it was all for nothing, that we might as well have let the Germans win, that they were no worse than we've been."

He shook his head. "I was wounded, twice, and left to die in the mud. Some nurses found me and took me away. These were Soviet nurses, these young women, it was for them we fought . . . They took me away and I recovered and for what? It was all a lie, a great fiasco."

He looked sad, then fierce, then resigned. "You're a foreigner, you can never understand. None of us know what to think any more. But never mind. We'll all be dead soon."

With that cheerful thought, he shuffled off. They were filled with self-pity, these old men, the sentimental self-pity that is the Russian disease. But self-pity aside, it's a genuine tragedy: millions of veterans are still alive in the Soviet Union. They are a fraction of the number who died, sacrificed for an ideal that never came to pass, for a squalid and brutal tyranny, but it's not an inconsiderable number. For years they lived the lie, half believing it, half believing that things would get better, but perestroika has made self-deception impossible, and all these old men are being forced in their last years to confront the dreadful reality: that the system they fought for so bravely had been corrupt to its very heart.

Later I walked up to the memorial at Mamayev Kurgan and was filled with sadness. Oh, there's kitsch here — the portentous music that plays from tinny loudspeakers at odd intervals, the phony "scribbles" in the concrete trying to pass as the thoughts of dying soldiers. But . . . the Motherland statue, a gigantic version of Delacroix's *Liberty Leading the People*, is fine and moving and the kitsch faded into irrelevancy. I would have liked to come up here with the old men, but none of them were interested. Few memorials interested them. "Except I like the idea that the children go," one said, "as long as they go in the right spirit." What this spirit was, he wouldn't say.

I was curious about the people at Mamayev Kurgan. I was there on a Saturday — who goes to war memorials on summer Saturdays? There appeared to be three different groups: bus tours, usually out-of-towners or schoolkids, wedding parties and young couples with children. The kids were generally bored, more interested in being photographed, or in the goose-stepping young soldiers who changed the guard on the hour. I tried to talk to one of these as he was leaving duty, but he refused. He looked about sixteen, though he was likely older. The Mamayev Kurgan guard unit is supposed to be an elite corps, and probably is. They seem well drilled.

I stopped to chat to a woman at the top of the hill, by Motherland's toes, where there's a superb view of the Volga. Tanya was a tour guide by occupation, and was there with her husband, who came from Alma-Ata in Kazakhstan. She pointed to a cluster of houses below the hill, unusual because it looked like an American suburb, if less maniacally regular, and with more trees.

"They're all single houses, private houses," she said. "After the battle" — she meant Stalingrad, of course — "there was nothing left of the city, and because they needed to get things going in a hurry, they allowed people to build these houses with whatever materials they could find."

I visited these houses later. Most were in the usual atrocious condition. They were little wooden cottages with a central wood-stove, with decorated windows and eaves. When left to their own devices, freed from the strictures of the urban planning institutes and their banal architects with their banal copies of banal Western buildings, the Russian soldiers reverted to the folk vernacular, with the result that this area, neglected as it is, has a great deal of character. Not, however, for much longer. Almost half of them had been demolished when I visited, to make way for the kind of high-rises being built from Minsk to Murmansk.

I asked about the housing problems in Volgograd, and Tanya explained her own situation. Her father, who'd fought in the battle of Stalingrad, was one of those to build a small individual cottage. She lived with him while she completed school. After her marriage, she and her husband applied for an apartment of their own. They were optimistic. Her husband was a mason with plenty of seniority, and the enterprise at which he worked had promised them a flat as soon as possible.

"When did you get it?" I asked.

"After thirteen years," she said.

"Thirteen years? What did you do in the meantime?"

"We stayed with my father. He paid 10,000 rubles and enlarged the cottage. My husband, my daughter, my sister and I lived with my mother and father for all of those thirteen years. My mother died in 1982 and my father in 1988. That year, we finally got our flat."

Many people are still waiting for theirs. Cooperative flats are being erected in various parts of the city, and can be purchased for 30,000 rubles for three rooms. There's a queue for those too, even if it's much shorter: about five years. No medium- or low-density housing is being built anywhere. I wondered why the local authorities, instead of demolishing the small individual houses, didn't try some variant of the urban homesteading idea. Why not give the residents these small houses, free, on condition they fixed them up?

I tried this theory on Tanya and her Kazakh husband, and she looked at me pityingly.

"All you Westerners like these houses," she said. "You think they're picturesque. But consider: they're small and dark, with low ceilings and small windows. There's no running water — yes, I know your theory, that the residents could pay for installing it, but wait. If I get one of these houses for myself, what can I do? In order to survive, my husband and I work, and we have little money left over. In order to get food, we must queue for hours every day after work. When will we have time to fix up our house? And if I need some wooden planks, where will I get them? Shops for planks, as you have in the West, don't exist here. And nails? Where do I buy them? And bricks? You cannot just buy bricks. Bricks are a monopoly of the city central construction department, and they're needed to make new houses. They won't sell me bricks, and if they do someone will make a scandal. You can get these things, of course, if you have *blat*, or if someone owes you a favor. You know this word *blat*?"

I said I'd heard of its existence. She smiled grimly.

"We have so many problems in our country," she said quietly. "You cannot change one thing without changing them all, but you cannot change everything at once."

I thought that was a neat formulation of the dilemma that had been vexing policymakers at Center for several years.

And then she said, expressing the other half of Center's problem: "And if I do get my planks or my bricks and I fix up my house, other people will say it's unfair because I'll have something they don't. We want to end unfair, not make more of it."

I mentioned to her husband that I'd met two other masons on my travels through the Soviet Union. One had returned to school to take an engineering degree, and the other was about to.

"Ah yes," he said, "no one wants to be the proletariat any more. They all want to be of the *apparat*. How do you say that in English?"

"Bureaucrats?" I suggested.

"Yes," he said. "And who can blame them? You get more influence if you direct people than if you're a worker. No more workers in our country . . . All engineers."

Apart from the pitiful food supply, housing remains the most nagging grievance of ordinary people. Many of them feel they'll never get a place of their own, that the system is falling further and further behind as people flood into the cities from drought-starved villages and the ruined countryside.

I was interested to note, though, that the griping was aimed at the system and the complaints at officials, and that the severe shortages didn't seem to have set off ethnic tensions. At least in Volgograd, unlike Saratov and Kazan, the Russians hadn't resorted to blaming "ethnics" for their problems, which seemed to me a sign that something was working right. The day before, I'd fallen into conversation with a fellow from Tashkent, a young man who rather resembled Lenin. We were both strolling along the quay, and he helped chase away a persistent flock of small boys demanding bubble gum, which I didn't have. He was a worker in the traditional mode: Lenin cap, coveralls, boots. He said he was living in Tashkent but was really from Siberia. He named the town. I didn't catch it, except that it was near Novosibirsk. He couldn't wait to get back home. People were human beings there, he said, not dogs. In the cities, all they wanted was to get something for themselves. But the Russians and the others got on pretty well, he thought.

After the war memorials, I went to visit the factories — one excitement after another. The Red October Steel Mill and the Dzerzhinsky Tractor Plant are truly immense by any standards, stretching literally for kilometers. In the Soviet period, official propaganda has always glorified the factory as the symbol of Soviet power. Until the Eighties, Soviet posters would often include a belching chimney as a shorthand way of signaling industrial might; black smoke was looked upon approvingly as a sign that everything was unfolding as it should. Even now there's some ambivalence. The rise of the Green movement, and a dawning consciousness of the damage unchecked development is doing to the environment, has forced some rethinking. Smoke has fallen out of favor as a positive symbol, and more people are examining with growing skepticism and alarm the air in the industrial areas. But otherwise sophisticated people will often suggest that you visit such-and-such a plant, such-and-such a factory, as if they were still synonyms for progress. Many people actually seem to know how many factories there are in their city, and can reel off their statistics of production — so many tonnes of this and square meters of that . . . Is there anyone in the West outside small single-industry towns who can do the same?

Some simple explanations exist. For one thing, the number of factories in any one Soviet city is relatively small, and the factories themselves are immense, so their impact is much greater. More interesting is the complete absence in the Soviet Union of the small, quickly built private enterprises that are the engines of contemporary capitalist economies — the industrial equivalent of the mom-and-pop store. On the outskirts of every American city are endless small businesses, which spring from the enterprise and drive of individuals determined to find a personal niche in a complex economy. Businesses like these come and go all the time. Some fail, some succeed and grow. Who'd think to count them, except the tax collectors? Who'd notice another one coming, or another going?

I took a picture of the grandiose entrance to the Dzerzhinsky Tractor Plant, which calls itself the first Soviet tractor manufacturer — I wondered if the folks in Marx knew about this. It's an imposing thing, colonnaded left and right, flanked by Socialist Realist mosaics of brave workers, brave peasants, brave tractors . . .

There are differences between American and Soviet enterprises other than size and flexibility. These immense factories are important for more than jobs. They also provide food, housing, furniture, holidays, even travel. To some degree the empty stores in the "official" economy are misleading. Most people use the gray market and also rely on the welfare bureaucracies in these large factories for goods and services. Daycare services, for example, and clinics are provided at work. Most new apartments are assigned to workers through the factories. Generally, if you want to furnish your flat, your place of work will have a furniture outlet, or at least access to one. And food, too: there's hardly a factory of any size outside Moscow that doesn't operate a pig farm, even if the factory makes industrial machinery with no connection to agriculture. Most large enterprises operate holiday camps for kids and resorts for workers and their families. They even arrange trips abroad for favored employees, especially to the Bulgarian Riviera, which is very popular with Russians. In these not inconsiderable ways, workers' lives are more orderly, more protected, than those of the intelligentsia.

Late one afternoon the cab driver who'd gotten such a good deal bringing me in from the airport came by the hotel to see if I wanted to sample some Russian nightlife. By this time I had some experience in what the Russians considered nightlife, and I wasn't keen. I suspected, falsely, that Vasilii was more interested in a commission than in giving me a good time. I also suspected that whatever it was, it would be very loud and very drunken. Well, I was wrong on the first, at least. He wanted no money. That night he took me to an anonymous building not far from the central railway station, opened the door and plunged into a thicket of beefy bodies just inside, calling out "It's pay as you go" as he disappeared into the crush. Leaving me with this cryptic message, he wasn't seen again.

Since I was there, I pressed on. Even at the door, the din was tremendous. Not just because too many people were crammed into too small a space, but because a very good stereo system was cranked up to a component-damaging volume. Mostly rap music, in what passed for English. Once I'd broached the beef hedge at the door, things thinned out somewhat. A number of small bars were scattered through the room, stocked mostly with vodka and brandy and Soviet champagne; but also with bottles of something bright green, and one huge bottle of Remy Martin. At first, I saw mostly men. Hard-looking men of a Georgian cast, army brass, a few militiamen, lots of older men in shiny suits. Young women made up about a quarter of the crowd, and I suddenly noticed that many of them were bare-breasted; at the end of the room, on a small elevated stage, there was a clumsy and thoroughly naked chorus line. One of the topless young women wanted me to dance, but I offered her a glass of champagne instead, and she drifted quickly away. I felt quite out of my depth. I'd become reasonably adept at dealing

with most aspects of Soviet life, with strategies for hostile militiamen, hostile Soviet gas stations, hostile Soviet restaurant staff. I'd
even learned to cope with Leningrad street gangs (cigarettes calm
them down). But a high-decibel Soviet brothel disconcerted me
utterly. Within a few minutes of arriving I found myself retreating
to the door. The beefy men in the entranceway at first didn't want
to let me through — maybe I hadn't spent enough money — and
one grabbed for the pocket where I kept my wallet. "Out of my
goddamn way," I yelled in English, loud enough to penetrate even
this din, and that startled them sufficiently for me to squeeze
through and to emerge on the deserted street, thoroughly panicked.

Presumably someone with more savoir-faire would have stayed
to make notes, or at least had a better look around before fleeing. I
did have a vague impression that other salons existed, and possibly
a second floor — there must have been an upstairs, given the
nature of the business. Still, this was no discreet, mellow New
Orleans bordello, all flocked velvet and tinkling piano. This was
more Coney Island, this was midway, this was bargoon day at
Bargain Boris's, this was noise and drunks and lots of sweat, some
of it quite rank. I walked back to the Intourist Hotel — fortunately
the railway station is a good landmark, especially at night when the
red star on its spire is lit up, and I was in bed by one.

There's a legend that says seven thousand rivers and streams run
into the Volga, but only one runs out. This is a stream called the
Akhtuba. "Stubborn as a mule is the Akhtuba," the folk saying
goes. "All her sisters go one way and she goes another." The map
showed that about 20 kilometers north of Volgograd the Akhtuba
flows eastward out of the Volga, then turns south and runs alongside its parent for 500 kilometers, finally emptying, as the Volga
itself does, into the Caspian Sea. The usual legends exist about the
name, the most popular of which involves a beautiful princess
named Tuba, who drowns herself for love; but it probably derives
from the Tartar *ak-tube*, or white hills, a prosaic description of the
landscape in these parts. More practically, the Akhtuba forms the
real boundary between steppe and desert; the hot winds from the
east break here, and it shields the Volga embankment from all but
the worst of the desert storms.

All the way to the delta at Astrakhan the two rivers are linked by hundreds of shifting channels; and where there's no water the land is marvelously fertile, consisting of silt as rich as that of the Nile. The Volga Akhtuba Water Meadow, as this area is called, has been diked and tamed, just like the Volga itself; 85 tonnes of vegetables per hectare are produced in the irrigated fields of the meadow, phenomenal by the standards of the Soviet Union, where a quarter of that is the norm. And yet the Akhtuba is still the spawning ground for herring, bream, roach and other Caspian fish. This area has more frost-free days than anywhere else in European Russia, so the local propaganda calls it "the national garden" (people in Moscow I asked about this had never heard of it).

But the Akhtuba isn't, after all, the only effluent of the Volga. In addition, the Volga and the Akhtuba intersect many times. So this notion of the stubborn sister, of the mulish little stream going its own way, is nothing more than a charming folk tale.

When I went to the "source" of the Akhtuba, it was no longer there — it had been engineered out of existence to make way for a massive hydroelectric scheme across the Volga with the old-style moniker of Twenty-second Congress of the CPSU Dam. I was quite taken with this dam. A brochure in its visitors' office still describes it as a "miracle of Communist Construction," which in these days could be given a considerably more sardonic meaning than the one intended. The brochure goes on in great detail to list the tons of "ferro-concrete" that built the thing and how very big it is ("Each of the 22 turbines puts out twice the power needed by Volgograd itself"). And so on. Soviet publicists always refer to "ferro-concrete" as if Western tourists would know what that is. The dam and its works looked impressive enough to me, but then so do Boulder Dam and the James Bay project. The dam this particular barrage created is almost 1,000 kilometers long and up to 20 wide. Some 100,000 hectares were flooded and fourteen thousand buildings submerged. This was done in the usual peremptory Soviet way: the residents of those buildings were simply told the water was coming and they'd better be off, and off they went. On balance, this dam is probably a good thing. It did drown some farmland, but it made possible the cultivation of far more land that had been barren; it has stabilized agriculture in an area notorious for debilitating droughts and has allowed cultivation of huge tracts of otherwise unusable land, in the process bringing life to the desert.

I finally found the Akhtuba's beginnings a short distance downstream. It didn't look much like a river any more, just a tame canal cut by the hydro engineers, its "ferro-concrete walls," much of their ferro showing, alas, a sad simulacrum of the real thing. Never mind, downstream it would be fine, I was sure.

The town of Volzhski, which began as temporary shelter for the workers building the Twenty-second Congress dam, has spread along the upper reaches of this new tame Akhtuba. It's now a city of more than three hundred thousand people, and it's one of the most depressing places I've ever seen.

It was begun in the Fifties to "a general plan drawn up by the State Institute of Urban Planning" in faraway Moscow, which ought to have been warning enough. The "old part" of town follows the familiar Soviet pattern of large blocks of flats strung along overly wide avenues. The newer part, the city's own propaganda says, is built "on a system of free planning," which on personal inspection appears to mean scattering those same blocks into random "aesthetic" clusters, each with its food store, polyclinic and the rest, leaving vast tracts of wasteland ("park") between them, and enormous distances to go to catch a bus or buy a loaf of bread. In one of these complexes the social engineers had concocted one of their loonier models. In their Ivory tower innocence, they asserted that to be truly happy people need "zones of silence" (private spaces) as well as "zones of contact" (communal spaces). As a result, they built an apartment complex whose apartments lacked kitchens. Cooking would be done in the "zones of contact," one to a floor, where a professional cook would be on hand to supervise and advise. The results were predictable: after a year of squabbling and acrimony, the residents bought stoves anyway, set them up in the living areas and washed their dishes in the bathtub.

There's not a distinguished or even interesting building in the whole town, not a vista that doesn't depress the soul. Everything is banal: the flats, the "scientific institutes," the schools, the Palace of Sports, the Palace of Culture, the moviehouses, the inevitable monument to Lenin. Worse, the northern half of the city is a sprawling, hellish chemical complex. It produces synthetic fibers, synthetic rubber, synthetic cattle feed and other synthetics too boring to list. All these are no doubt worthy. What would it be like to work and live in this tangle of pipes and smoking chimneys and suspiciously gushing discharge pipes steaming into open sewer channels? This nightmare landscape made me fear not only for the health of the people who live here and the future of the children who grow up here, but also for the health of the Caspian itself, into which all this ultimately flows, not to mention the health of the few remaining beluga that swim to the Akhtuba for spawning and that produce the caviar we eat in all the expensive restaurants in the Great Outside. I fled back to the city.

But I couldn't stay away. I spent my last morning in Volgograd leaning on the railing at the fish elevator at the Twenty-second Congress of the CPSU Dam, watching for sturgeon. That I didn't see any wasn't so surprising. This wasn't the spawning season. And even if it had been . . .

The Volga and its tributaries have always been spawning grounds for the Caspian sturgeon, among many other species: Mother Volga was mother to caviar too. The dams of the Volga Cascade threatened to disrupt these ancient rhythms, breaking the breeding cycle. What were the fish to make of these barricades, especially this one, the first in from the sea? Fish moving upriver to spawn navigate by sensing the current flow, and locks confuse them. So the dam's engineers provided a large movable chamber containing a turbine, which was surrounded by a fine mesh to prevent damage to the fish. The turbine propels the water at exactly the speed of the Volga current, and when the fish get to the dam they dart about until they find where this "current" is coming from. They swim into the chamber, are caught, elevated the 40 feet or so to the upper dam, and released . . .

That's the theory, anyway, but the Volga is now so polluted that the effort to preserve it as a hatchery in these parts has been abandoned. The elevator is still there, still going up and down, still manned, still working, still carrying no doubt bewildered fish into the Volgograd Sea, but no one pays much attention.

"So why is it still in use?" I asked a grizzled worker I found near the elevator's gates.

"Why not?" he replied.

"How often does the hoist operate?"

"As often as need be," he said. "We don't hoist for one fish, but in the spawning season we're going up and down all the time."

He smirked. "I wouldn't eat the caviar from one of these in any case. None too clean around here: you should see what else floats into the chamber." He laughed humorlessly. "And God knows what's in here you *can't* see."

He peered down into the water. The railing on which he was leaning was polished smooth.

I said, "So your job is to watch for fish, and raise the elevator when you see some? Even if no one believes in the Volga sturgeon fishery any more?"

"Yes," he said, "that's what I do."

"Not a bad way of making a living," I said, "watching for fish all year."

The old man spat into the tank. "It's a job," he said.

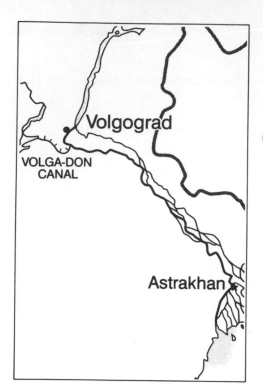

CHAPTER 21

Kilometer 3,500

Astrakhan

rom Volgograd, the Volga takes a sharp left turn and then plunges, without any more fuss, southeast to the Caspian Sea. By its side, like a sulky child, runs the Akhtuba, and between them are channels and runnels and rivulets that make up what the geographers call the Water Meadows, where marsh grasses and reeds grow as tall as a horse among narrow, shifting channels, a damp and secretive place between the desolate arid plains of the Kalmyk homeland to the west and the endless deserts of central Asia to the east; in Kalmyk legend the "betweenness" of the rivers is referred to in explicitly sexual imagery as the birth canal of the people.

In more recent centuries the Meadows were a stronghold of the Cossacks, who preyed on the trading vessels picking their way between the channels. Just below Volgograd is Sarpinski Island, where the burghers of Tsaritsyn once pastured their cattle. Olearius, who by this stage of his journey had developed a paranoid fear of anything Cossack (his party opened fire every time they spotted anyone resembling one), recounts how one day, as the "wives and daughters of the *streltsi* [soldiers] milked the cows there, the Cossacks lay in wait, seized them, had their way with them and then sent them back unharmed."

About 80 kilometers from Volgograd there's a long flat mountain on the right bank, and opposite it a similarly long flat island, both called Nasonovski. Close by are other small mountains and hills, and many more islands and shallows, coves and wandering channels complicate the river's course. Wild licorice grows in the shrubbery on both sides of the river. As the Olearius flotilla lay at anchor in its lee, fishermen brought them a fat carp weighing over 30 pounds, and eight sizable pike. They wouldn't take money, "arguing that certain Moscow merchants who leased this part of the Volga had sent them there to fish, and that they would have to pay dearly if it were learned that they had sold the least little fish. They were more concerned about vodka, and after receiving half a tankard, delightedly went off with many thanks." Other fishermen brought them *chiberik*, a "large fish like a Polish mottled dog," and *sterliad*, "which are like a sturgeon and very abundant in the Volga."

I, too, was looking for fish. I was looking for a place called Rechnoe, which was supposed to be near the town of Zavolzhskoe. Rechnoe wasn't marked on any map I'd seen until then (though it was on a more detailed regional map I acquired in Astrakhan), but I'd been told by the fish hoist man at the Twenty-second Congress of the CPSU Dam that there was a fish farm there, whose job was to seed the critical species back into the Volga. Not just the noble sturgeon, which is what foodies in the West are interested in, but also the more mundane species, like Caspian herring, which is generally what you buy in Soviet fish stores when you acquire what is simply called "fish." Also *sudak*, a sweet fish greatly prized by Russians, an essential ingredient of *ukha*, a fish soup that I was told all along the Volga was "world famous," though no restaurant ever served it. This fish farm, if I could find it, would be the Volgograd Sturgeon Hatchery. I'd read elsewhere that it produced over seventy-five million fingerlings a year, releasing them at thirty-five days of age into the Volga and its tributaries.

I'd left Volgograd by car, bound for Astrakhan, the end of the river and my final destination. This car was acquired in the now-familiar way — I'd asked my Volgograd contact, the bordello-fancier, whether he'd drive me the 450-odd kilometers to the Caspian and back, but he wasn't interested. However, he'd found a friend of a friend who was prepared to strike a deal, and I "rented" his taxi in return for a shopping spree in a *valyuta* store, which ended up costing $180, a bargain. The car, a peppy red Volga of recent vintage, was marked with the checkered squares that denoted a taxi, but no one ever tried to flag me down, the GAI ignored me, and I made good time.

I poked about where Rechnoe should have been, on the banks of the Volga itself, but I saw nothing resembling a town or a fish farm, and after a while I gave up. No one in nearby Zavolzhskoe seemed to know anything about it either, so I backtracked towards the Akhtuba, to the village of Volnoe, on a small road more like a rutted farm track than a highway. I stopped at a rickety bridge over a creek, where a cluster of fishermen were leaning over the railing, staring at the water. Below the bridge, a number of powerboats were moored. After a fruitless discussion about fish farms, I persuaded one of the fishermen, Arkady, to take me into the Water Meadows, the method of persuasion being a great pile of rubles.

Arkady said six words all afternoon, *nyet* being four of them, but he obviously knew the channels and which ones ended in swamp and which ones didn't. After about half an hour of twisting and turning, he cut his motor and motioned me to silence. The boat glided on slowly. The channel here was only about ten feet across; marsh grasses and swamp trees and something that looked like jacaranda were dense on both sides. The grass itself was taller than a man. There was no wind. No birds sang. There were no splashes, no insects, no movement at all. I've never been in a stiller place. The water itself was a murky green, filled with leaves and grass seeds. The whole place made me really uneasy, and dark thoughts filled my head. Why was this man so quiet? What was he thinking? Why had he brought me here? The claustrophobic pressure grew so severe that I quite forgot I'd been the one to insist on coming. What had caused this unnatural stillness — had there been some ecological catastrophe? One of the fishermen explained later, when we got back to the bridge, that it was all perfectly natural, that it was always like that in the Meadows in the early afternoon. The fish were sleeping under the grassy banks, away from the hot sun, and would do so until the insects came out at dusk. At dusk and in the dawn's early light there was plenty of life.

But I don't think my feeling of claustrophobia was all just foolish paranoia. There's something of the Louisiana bayou country about this place, a shut-in feeling, a secretiveness, a cloying claustrophobia, as if people could be hidden for centuries in these swamps and never change. It wouldn't have surprised me at all to see a representative of the Tartar Khans waiting at the bridge by my car, a relic of the extraordinary past. It was easy, gliding about the secret channels, to fill the mind with legends. To the left are the endless deserts, stretching to the horizons out of which appeared the Golden Horde. To the right are the great Russian plains that produced the Cossacks, the legendary soldiers-for-hire, secure for centuries in their Zaporozhets Fastness, as their steppeland refuge was called, until Catherine the Great sent in volunteers to "clean out the nest" and tame them at last.

In the Meadows life went on: the Golden Horde came and went, as did centuries of peasant revolts. Finally Kirov the Bolshevik arrived, and near this place he decisively defeated the White Guards, an important battle in the Civil War that had ended the Great Tyranny forever. (Or so it was fondly believed at the time. Now, of course, even the Soviet propaganda machine has grown tired of this line, and it's only found on the forgotten shelves of sleepy provincial towns and in dusty outposts of empire like Cuba.)

Life went on in other ways too. The pitted, scarred old sturgeon, many of them more than fifty years old and weighing 1,200 pounds, their bellies filled to overflowing with black gold, came into the Water Meadows to spawn, as they'd been doing since the beginning, and men in small boats pulled them aboard and ashore. I'd read many stories of barges full of caviar making their way up the Volga in the old days; the Tsars used to ship sturgeon to Moscow by cart, keeping the fish alive for the month-long journey by packing them in wet hay and smothering them in vodka. Drunk but alive, they were sold in the fish markets of the capital. Later, I saw some wonderful old pictures in the Astrakhan museum of these laconic fishermen, leaning on their oars for the unknown photographer, the captured sturgeon almost as big as their boats. Where have they gone, those great fish, those laconic men? Some of the men still pole about the Meadows despite the stiff fines for poaching, and still scoop the 50 pounds or more of caviar from the slit bellies of the females, but most of them have departed. Some have joined the fleets plying the world's oceans, and can be found pulling codfish from the Grand Banks off Newfoundland and in the chilly waters of the South Atlantic near Tristan da Cunha, a very long way from home. Others are in Astrakhan, or in Volgograd at the Red October Tractor Factory, a restless proletariat waiting for their apartments, their consumer goods, their food, waiting for the fulfillment of promises made and never kept.

The main Volgograd-Astrakhan highway is on the right bank, on the opposite side of the Volga from the Akhtuba. I ignored it and stayed in the Meadows, taking a small road south on the desert side, following the Akhtuba's banks closely for a hundred kilometers or so, passing through the villages of Komsomolskii and then Seitovka, which is set on a narrow peninsula between the Akhtuba and a minor Volga channel called the Buzan. Seitovka is a wonderfully picturesque but falling-down little village inhabited mostly by fishermen. At Krasnii Yar I joined another main highway to Astrakhan, this one coming from the east.

I was wondering whether I'd get to eat any caviar in Astrakhan. I wasn't optimistic. Caviar had become as scarce as camel's milk in the Soviet Union. Twenty years earlier in Moscow you could still buy the stuff by the handful. Once I bought half a kilo at a fish store, getting some dry ice from an ice cream vendor and air-expressing it to friends in Canada, more or less as a lark. Now, it's not to be had at all in stores where Russians shop, only at the Beriozka chain of foreign-currency stores at ripoff prices, and there's not very much of it there. If you're Russian, you can still get it, but you need *blat*. You can also buy caviar from black marketeers, though you need to be careful. The one time I did so it wasn't caviar at all, but an artificial substitute made of petroleum derivatives.

Actually, this polymer caviar is not at all bad, and many tourists would never know the difference — it's greatly superior to lumpfish caviar. Years before I'd spent a few hours at the Moscow Institute of Chemistry, which made the stuff, mostly as a byproduct of its research into flavors. I sat in the office of the director and he cracked a small jar of *ikra* (caviar) and another jar of *iskra* (a joke: it means spark, and was the name of one of Lenin's early newspapers). *Iskra*, the artificial stuff, was agreeable though hardly the real thing: they'd got the flavor down pat but hadn't been able to duplicate the texture, the delicious pop fresh caviar makes when you bite down on it.

I once watched a fisherman slit a huge sturgeon and scoop out the caviar with gloved hands, and the profligacy of the thing got to me at the time (those could all have been little sturgeon, and suddenly they were on their way to a Georgetown reception for the Ambassador from Qatar . . .). But I soon got over that. Besides, the fish wasn't wasted: how many *zakuski* at how many parties did that fish provide, how many accompaniments to how many glasses of vodka, drunk to how many toasts to eternal friendship and amity? Delicately smoked, sturgeon is in its way as delicious as caviar itself. I was still ruminating on these pleasing matters as Astrakhan appeared. As expected, I found no caviar there.

I drove in along the embankment in the late afternoon, passing the city's kremlin, which has for so long been a witness to extraordinary events: the overthrow of Tartar rule, the sacking of the town by Razin and Pugachev, the Cossack revolts . . . The twin of Kazan's, it's a rather prim fortress, whitewashed and austere, with square, squat towers, but it did the job in its day, and those who patrolled its walls saw many a rogue sail down the Volga and into the Caspian Sea.

I stumbled on the city market and stopped to buy fresh apricots, which I ate steadily from a cone of newspaper. Astrakhan has always been a city famous for its markets. The Russians had theirs, of course, but so did the Persians, and the Indians. Olearius reported further: "Since the Bokharans of Central Asia, the Crimean and Nogai Tartars and the Armenians, a Christian people, also carry on a great traffic with all sorts of goods, the city is said annually to bring his Tsarist Majesty a large sum, as much as 12,000 rubles in duties alone." In the city markets, the travelers found:

. . . marvelous fruits, better even than we found in Persia. They have apples, quinces, walnuts, large yellow melons, watermelons which are very juicy, sugary sweet and have black seeds. Formerly they had no grapes here, but now there are grapes everywhere, for in 1613 some monk laid out a proper vineyard by the order of the Grand Prince. The monk I mentioned was 105 years old, an Austrian by birth, taken captive in war and brought to Russia while still a boy. Here he converted to the Russian faith . . . While we were there he still had the management of the whole monastery in his hands. He was still gay in temper. After he had two cups of vodka, he began to show his strength by dancing without the help of a stick, though his legs wobbled. He said that the region was healthful and boasted many extremely old people.

The markets are less exotic now, though the ethnic mix is as complex. As I wandered about, I found Gypsies and Georgians, Armenians and Kalmyks, Russians aplenty. There were Tartars too, very unlike the Tartars of Kazan, who seemed by contrast very European. These were short, stout people, with broad faces and small twinkling eyes. Their skin was a dark yellow, like vintage parchment, and the men and women alike were wizened and wrinkled, so they looked like cheerful little walnuts. I bought a second kilo of apricots from one of them, and as she poured it into a twist of the local *Pravda* she bade me good health and asked me where I'd come from. Ah, Canada! she said. Hamilton! It turned out she had a relative in Hamilton, Ontario, 70 kilometers or so from Toronto.

I'd been wondering what had happened to the Tartars Olearius described, who were "partly Nogai and partly Crimean, and were not permitted to settle in the city but only in designated places outside. . . They are often attacked and plundered by their permanent enemies, the Kalmyks, who are scattered . . . from here to Saratov." The apricot lady's neighbor was a Kalmyk who spoke neither Russian nor Tartar, but who smiled a golden smile at everyone who spoke to her, and had a small heap of pomegranates on the table before her. Hamilton, Ontario, never appeared on television in Astrakhan, the apricot lady said, but she got letters from her relative who said things were going well there. As for herself, one cannot complain, and the television was a great comfort . . . There were no grapes in the market, and no melons, only pathetic piles of vegetables and fruits in small individual heaps; this was surely not enough to feed a city?

"Are there other markets?" I asked.

"Oh, yes, many," she said, "but not as big as this one."

"Where do people get their food, from markets or from the stores?"

"There's nothing in the shops," she said. "Most people come here, or get food from the farms, or from their jobs."

I'd heard in Moscow that Astrakhan had become politically liberal, not to say populist, not to say radical, and that its First Secretary was one of the most accessible officials in the Soviet Union; Misha Lyubimov had suggested I give him a call. Later that morning I debated whether to put this to the test. On the one hand, I wasn't supposed to be in this city at all. On the other, I wasn't expressly forbidden to be here, and Astrakhan is an "open" city in the singular and peculiarly Soviet sense that it isn't forbidden to foreigners. On the one hand, the First Secretary might see some merit in spending a few moments with a visiting journalist. On the other, I didn't have a journalist's visa. I decided in the end to assume that his reputation was correct. I'd passed the Gorkom building earlier, so I returned there, pushed past the surly guard at the door and asked for the First Secretary's phone number. Somewhat to my surprise, they gave it to me — one gold star for the Secretary. I went around the corner and found a public phone that worked. This was easier than it may seem; a much higher proportion of public phones work in the Soviet Union than in, say, New York. I called the Gorkom office.

I went through three levels of stalling before I reached the Secretary's office. A very correct male voice answered, which switched to English as soon as it heard me speak. Second gold star for the Secretary.

I explained my intention. I was visiting from Canada, I liked his city, I'd heard remarkable things about his boss (true) and I'd like to take a few minutes of his time.

"Why?"

"Well, I've heard he's an interesting person . . ."

"He is that," the voice answered, dryly. "Unfortunately, he's in Moscow, preparing for the Party Congress."

"Oh of course," I said, "the Twenty-fourth Congress . . . That's next week, isn't it?"

"Right."

"Well, thank you."

"You're very welcome," the smooth voice answered, exactly like a receptionist at a Wall Street law firm.

For the rest, Astrakhan struck me as being unremarkable, with no more and no less the feeling of a port than any other Volga city, and in many ways indistinguishable from them. The usual mix: splendid parks, empty food stores, drunks under the trees, banal public art. But there was one nice touch: the monument to the murdered Bolshevik hero Kirov, a statue in the clichéd Socialist Realist style, was completely overgrown with a tangle of wild roses, blood-red blooms in a profusion that gave the earnest bronze figure the air of being hung with celebratory bunting. Kirov looked gay and colorful, as if he should have been playing a kazoo instead of clutching a tome of Lenin's thought . . .

The Astrakhan papers had reported earlier that the Caspian was becoming seriously polluted. Oil slicks had been sighted in unexpected places. Communities east of the Akhtuba had closed their beaches to swimming; analysis of the water had found all kinds of contaminants, chemical and human. Sewage accounted for a good deal of this, but the chemical wastes that were being poured into 3,000 kilometers of river were turning parts of the Caspian into a sinister stew that endangered the lives of fish and human. The authorities are alive to the danger, and the eco-movement in places like Volgograd is having a greening effect on the *apparat*. I'd heard several times that ships were forbidden to dump anything into the river, and indeed Rechflot seemed to be a model corporate citizen — I often saw their sewage boats pumping out ships' holding tanks. But I'd myself witnessed the steaming ditches that poured into the Volga unchecked from hundreds of factories, and in an economic crisis who has the money and the energy for pollution abatement, when the unrest in the cities makes increased production an urgent necessity? On the one

hand the Russians love the Volga with a fierceness and a protec-
tiveness, and maybe they'll find a way. On the other hand . . . what
is this problem among so many others?

When I got home I looked up my files from twenty years earlier,
when I'd lived in the Soviet Union. The file marked "Pollution"
was filled with clippings. Many of them dealt with the Volga. They
made dispiriting reading, especially since the Astrakhan papers in
1990 were triumphantly "discovering" bad news that had already
been commonplace in 1970.

For symbolic reasons I wanted to see the place where the Volga
actually empties into the sea. I'd always assumed this was at
Astrakhan itself. But when I bought a detailed map of the region at
a news kiosk, I saw the city was a good 30 or 40 kilometers from
the nearest open water. From the way it was drawn on the map,
the delta itself was an intricate array of mud flats, shifting channels, sandbars, rock outcroppings and flood basins. A shipping
channel was kept open to the west; further east the Akhtuba itself
finally emptied into the Caspian, having taken a last-minute turn
away from its mother. In between was a chaotic network of small
muddy channels, too unstable to be worth mapping in any serious
way; the cartographers, giving up the attempt, simply made
scratching motions with their pens to indicate to mariners they
should stay away.

Some of the sand banks had names: the Belda and the Kutum
and, lower down, the Tsarova, Tsagan, Birul and others. The vast
alluvial peninsula projecting into the Caspian is at least 250 kilometers around. There are reckoned to be altogether about two
hundred "mouths," most of them shifting streams choked with
mud. From early accounts, the navigable channel once flowed due
east from Astrakhan; since then it has shifted more towards the
right bank and now runs south-southwest.

How to make my way through all this?

I figured there must be local mariners able to pilot through the
confusion. People still pulled large sturgeon into small boats, in
defiance of common sense and regulation, and I could surely find
someone who could schlep along a tourist as deadweight, either a
fisherman or simply a local enthusiast, someone who loved the

place and had got to know it in an intimate way. I'd found such a person in the Water Meadows. Why not here?

I saw nobody on the Volga embankment in town who looked promising. There were no small boats at all, only commercial pleasure craft, tugboats and anonymous vessels that looked like they were on nasty official business. Some of the pleasure craft made daily excursions to the Caspian, but I thought I'd hold them in reserve. It somehow didn't seem right to be ending a journey of 3,500 kilometers with a bunch of jolly Russian day-trippers singing "Moscow Nights" to the accompaniment of a rubber piano on the ship's PA system . . . In retrospect, I think I was wrong. The symbolism would have been quite nice, and the company of jolly Russians, while wearing, would surely have been considerably more entertaining than mucking about in a too-small boat.

At the time, though, I was in a sentimental mood, and preferred to seek the quieter company of some philosophic son of toil. So I searched further, without much luck, before it occurred to me that near every Volga city is an embankment used by the locals to moor small motorboats. Sure enough, near one of those soulless New Town highrise complexes that blight every Soviet city, there they were.

It took me a while to find my man, since most of the boats were out on the water, their proprietors apparently snoozing, fishing lines dangling over the side. Finally I found him.

He wasn't exactly what I had in mind, but he did have a boat with an outboard, even if overlarge to my inexperienced eye. He had a spare canister of gasoline, a stash of kolbasa, and no visible sign of vodka, all of which was reassuring. On the other hand, he himself seemed . . . odd. Not seriously odd — I wouldn't have gone along if I'd suspected serious dementia — but he seemed somehow overly . . . gleeful. Still, we set off.

The Astrakhan Reservation is one of the richest sources of bird life in the USSR, and a resting place on the migration routes from the Arctic to Cape Town. What I hadn't known is that there are dozens of small settlements south of Astrakhan; we skirted these and roared down the channel, stirring up quite a wake and a number of angry shouts. My pilot was grinning ferociously to himself and humming under his breath. We made our way generally southeastward, along a few broad channels and a few minor ones, and some that didn't seem to be there at all, and I was soon, not unexpectedly, hopelessly lost.

I looked down at the muddy water sliding by a few inches below. There was no eelgrass in the delta, no marsh reeds, the boat had a sputtering outboard instead of oars, and I was a long way from the Valdai Hills, but . . . my journey was ending pretty much as it began, in a small boat, at some hazard, with a burly Russian for company — a nice piece of symmetry. More than 3,500 kilometers of Russia lie between the Valdai uplands and the Astrakhan Delta, a Russia that's steeped in cynicism, confused about what it wants and where it's been and, when I was there, teetering on the edge of chaos, a Russia immense and depthless, at times cruel and cold, and at the same time a Russia alive and inquiring, conscious that it had grasped the attention of the world, a Russia too small for the generous spirit that inhabits it. My journey through this larger-than-life Russia started in a swamp, in a small boat, and here I was again, messing around outside Astrakhan in a boat that seemed too small, with someone whose seamanship I had no way of judging. The last time it was a swamp we'd thought it was the Volga, and this time . . .

It was about an hour later that he abruptly cut the motor and stood up. Remembering what had happened the last time someone stood up in a small boat, I told him not to be an ass and to sit down. This water looked a good deal less hospitable than the swamps of the Valdai. It could have been a hundred fathoms deep, for all I knew.

"Here it is," he said. "We're in it."

"In what?"

"The Caspian Sea," he said impatiently. "Where you want to go."

"How do you know?" I asked, looking around. True, there was no longer much land, or even mud, to be seen, but the water was the same murky brown it had been since Astrakhan. And off to the left I saw floating what looked like a plastic Javex bottle.

He scooped some water up with his hand.

"Smell it," he urged.

I smelled it. It didn't smell of anything much.

"You can smell the sea," he said, sniffing deeply, and chuckling inappropriately. "There's a lot of mud here, it's true, but this is definitely sea water."

I scooped some for myself, rocking the little boat perilously. I was skeptical. I'd heard that almost a third of the Caspian was fresh water anyway, and most of its northerly waters were fresh — so how did he know? As I scooped, I saw for the first time that one of the boat's plywood seams was parting, or coming unglued, though there was as yet no water in the boat. I smelled carefully. Faintly, faintly, I could smell the sea, and I asked him to turn around and take me back to shore.

AFTERWORD

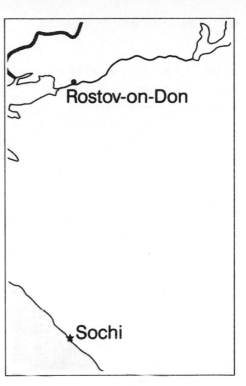

Rostov-on-Don

Sochi

Sochi

I flew to this lush Black Sea resort for a little R&R after my Volga journey was over, and it was almost as if I was going Out, as the Russians call the strange world of non-Russia, wheels up into the outside air, a lightening of the spirit. It was only a short flight, an hour, but the griminess and grimness of "Russia" was suddenly entirely absent, the little Aeroflot plane bounding into the air with its forty-odd passengers, schoolchildren on holiday in the front chanting some version of "going to see, to see the sea," which I remembered from my own childhood, while two soldiers smiled indulgently and hummed along and two young women out for a good time giggled and elbowed each other. Even the stewardess smiled as she handed out the sugar-water pacifiers in brown plastic cups, and when we landed at Sochi, everyone cheered.

Sochi is not at all part of "Russia," the Russia of anyone's imagination. It's at once part of and not part of the Soviet Union; it owns a sultry decadence that's more suited to the children of the southern Mediterranean than to the stolid comrades of Novorossirsk. It's a subtropical resort, attractively sited, with lush green hills steep to the sea, snowcapped peaks not far away, health spas, holiday camps, resort hotels, clean stone beaches. My hotel, the Pearl, was a huge complex with its own beach, lots of chaises for lounging, umbrellas, bars, cafés, piles of watermelons in the shade of the jacarandas.

This isn't Yalta, where Westerners used to summer, nor is it the Crimea, which is a kind of subtropical St. Petersburg, a bizarre mix of the classical amidst the palms. Sochi is newer, a Soviet invention. It was to be a paradise for proletarians, a reward for the toils of Socialist Construction, where workers from the gigantic tractor factories and machine tool manufacturies of the industrial north could disport, having earned, by their labor for the People, their three weeks in the sun. Well, it's a worthy idea, and there are worse places.

I liked Sochi. I liked the unselfconscious bodily enjoyment of Russians at last liberated from winter swaddling. I liked the landscape, which is every bit as beautiful as that of the Côte d'Azur, but more lush, fecund, with a sultry air. There are none of the corniche roads, and the food (while relatively plentiful here) is hardly to be tolerated, but the surroundings are wonderful. In some ways Sochi doesn't feel like a town at all. It stretches for lazy kilometers along the lazy coast, most of its buildings hidden in the lush greenery.

There are worse ways to spend a day or two. I lay on the beach in the sun, while a procession of young people approached me, looking for small favors, a cigarette, a souvenir, something Western, some words from an outsider, or to share some story, some gloomy anecdote . . . Two of them came to my room one night, a young couple, sweet and nervous, and we sat on the bed and talked as the setting sun turned the sea a glittering gold; they cried a little as we talked, for they wanted so badly to get Out; and I was sad for them, for they had no idea what Out was like.

A young man gave me a religious medal as a souvenir. Many of the younger women had crosses on chains around their necks. Another young man asked an innocuous question about politics, pulled a Bible from his pack and read me a long, rambling passage in the sonorous and archaic language of Byzantium, none of which I understood. A group of young people formed a circle on the sand and began to pray, their chanting heard clearly above the drunken laughter of the Finnish tourists.

Also on the beach were a good many hard-looking men who one informant told me were KGB security "watching everyone, listening all the time," but who to me looked to be of a more obvious calling, for they had the unmistakable air of the parasitic pimp. In reality, I guess, they were probably both these things, looking for a fast score as well as watching for the "politically immature," which was KGB jargon for anyone at all different — leftover hippies, *metallistii* (heavy-metal rockers), the leather-and-chains dissidents, democrats, churchgoers, anarchists . . . Some of the new Soviet rich and famous come here to the beach. There was an elderly-looking young man with a dissolute air, a top Soviet rock star; just before lunch he made love to a young woman standing up in the Black Sea, but no one paid much attention. There were many people from the movie community there too, and a camera crew from Mosfilm, the Moscow Film Studios.

Even on the beach the anxiety that people were feeling for their own future and for their country followed them. The first exhilaration of that spiritual revolution called glasnost, the guilty pleasure of being able at last to pick at the scabs as well as the thrill of shouting out loud whatever you please, had subsided, and apart from the journalists, who were still generally having a wonderful time, gray disillusion had set in. In Moscow the journalists and the politicians and the intellectuals still argued about politics and constitution-making, but the Volga was the Russian heartland, and the heartland was sick, sick in the fiber and sick at heart, a sadness at themselves and their fate welling up in every conversation.

On one level the questions were purely political: Could the Center hold? Would it all fly apart? Did anyone any longer care, for the grand and noble idea of Union, of disparate peoples united into one mighty country? Would the economy collapse utterly? Why were the people once again talking of famine, of revolt and revolution . . .? On another level the questions dealt with matters of meaning and moment, with the soul, with the realization that so much of their history had been, in the word I kept hearing over and over, disgusting, and with the despair of ever recapturing a sense of themselves that contained optimism, humor and joy.

I remembered the old man in Uglich, who lamented the lack of faith he saw all around him; the judge in Yaroslavl, who'd been surprised at and ashamed of her earlier self; the man on the log in Cheboksari, who spoke of the long nightmare and the chilly shadows and who was bitter at the West for having nothing better to offer than smug self-congratulation; Zhina in Ulyanovsk, who cried because it was all so unfair, because simple human relations had turned to sly calculation and greed; the war veteran at the Mamayev Kurgan who'd woken in his last years to the "fiasco," how it had all come to nothing, nothing but the bitter taste of ashes; the *kolkhoznik* who was convinced that "they" would confiscate anything anyone accomplished; Tanya, the tour guide at the Motherland statue, who'd said, quietly: "We have so many problems in our country. You cannot change one thing without changing them all, but you cannot change everything at once." And then she'd said, a simple truth that was very poignant: "We want to end unfair, not make more of it."

The Pamyat people in Tver had lamented the long history of Russian wars, and how the Russians always bore the brunt of defending European civilization; now Russia was faced with the prospect of endless little wars within itself as the center cracked and the ethnic spokes of the Russian wheel went flying off into the Great Darkness . . . People felt abandoned by their history, confused, rootless, insecure; I remembered the judge, crying, the professor, crying, the man on the log, crying, the old man in Bolgari, crying, Zhina crying, crying for what they'd been and not been and for what they could have been . . . Tears, tears everywhere, and shame.

And in the countryside, why were Razin and Pugachev once again at the forefront of the slow, steady, unblinking Russian imagination? What was the Russian countryside thinking, these no-longer-peasants who were patient and slow to anger but who could, in the phrase of the country, "think their way through a brick wall in time"? Would the worst fears of the intellectuals in Moscow be realized, would they — "they" the people — follow another Iron Man if one emerged, some Yeltsin figure without Yeltsin's heart? Underlying this deep sadness, behind the shame, there's a restlessness that's truly dangerous. They'd lost their past, that was bad enough. Now they felt they were in danger of losing their future too. The heartland was preparing itself for another assault, this time as much from within as from without; their anger is banked, smoldering, red hot.

On the beach people were talking about the recent riots in Bucharest as prophecy and warning; they were toasting in the Black Sea sun, but their prediction for their own country was somber, not to say alarmist: hunger, riots, starvation, civil war . . . Many bitter jokes about the Motherland circulated. More than one person told me that the Volga lands, always prone to drought and to revolt, were once more on the verge of famine. Famine! It should be a word from the distant past, but here it is again, the specter of mass hunger, with the farms producing food all around, rotting on the way to market . . . One of my informants was from Gorky and, as he said, "a Russian, not rootless like the Jews, with the *rodina*, the motherland, in my blood"; he'd given up on the future and was looking forward to fleeing, getting Out, anywhere. Russians are patient, he said, but remember Razin! He's still a hero to us all.

I returned to Moscow to a heat wave (over 100° F) on a Friday night. Everyone at Vnukovo Airport was irritable. The crowds were crushing, the smell indescribable, the heat paralyzing, the anger bruising, the traffic jams debilitating: every Friday night in summer the exodus to the country is like . . . well, like Manhattan on a Friday in August. Do they really want the consumer society? Certainly the Russians will be eager consumers of the automobile, and the over-massive scale of their housing developments can only encourage them in this folly.

But by this time I was weary of it all. I made a reservation at one of Moscow's trendy "private" hard-currency restaurants, the Strasnoy, which is a pretty room, and quiet, and mostly empty, and where the food is by Western standards unexceptional but by Soviet standards magnificent, and spent what was a month's wage for a Russian in self-indulgence. I took Misha, my tame ex-KGB colonel, to supper, and we gossiped about journalists and politicians and shared dire predictions as we ate smoked sturgeon and drank Belgian beer, and the crowd across the way, joint-venture bureaucrats and Westerners smelling of excessive profits and expensive cologne, ate red caviar and drank champagne. And so it ended.

•   •   •

May 1991
Well, in the subsequent months Shevardnadze resigned, the Kremlin "liberals" went into shock (and many into obscurity), Gorbachev sent the tanks into Lithuania and Armenia (or let the tanks be sent, which may be worse), and his government ineffectually "cracked down" left and right, but hardly anyone seemed to be listening.

In the West, Gorbachev remained secure as a figure of historic dimensions, though there was considerable disillusionment with his policies. This is a correct estimate in my view, not because he ripped the blinkers from Russian eyes but because he allowed the Russians to do it themselves, a crucial difference, a radical turning point.

In the Russian countryside, though, they didn't need the collapse of Communist ideology to tell them the system (even in its reformist incarnations) wasn't working — they could see it in every waking hour for themselves, as their lives stretched out into endless, endless monotonous queuing. A year after my trip the Jews are still lining up at the exit counters (their ears fearfully straining for the thunder of distant pogrom), the miners are striking, whatever "economic reforms" are put forward are ridiculed and discounted, every day new crackpot theories about how the economy can be dragged into some form of market-driven enterprise are presented. The economy teeters from one "terminal" crisis to another.

The "revolt" against Gorbachev is not really a revolt, nor just a matter of alienated workers or "Black Colonels" of the reactionary right: everyone wants stability, but no one knows where it can be found. Russians have rejected Gorbachev in their hearts but they have no one of his size to fit into his place.

Maybe the students in Kazan were right: it needs another generation to make reform work. And almost certainly by then the Soviet Union will be a very different place. It will be Russia again, ethnically less diverse, considerably smaller in girth and in population and in ambition, possibly sunken into stupefied repression but, with any luck at all, freer and more vigorous, and all the greater in spirit: there is still a largeness to that great, sloppy, sentimental, flawed Russian heart, and I'm hopeful for it.

The Volga seems to me to typify that Russian heart, and the Volga will still be there at the end, when the Last History is written. Russia endures, and will endure, and out of those many small meetings and debates and rallies in provincial towns like Yaroslavl, out of those many yearnings on all those many *kolkhozes* across the Russian heartland, out of the work of all those journalists and writers and filmmakers, there is a chance that some genuinely "new way" (to use that optimistic Russian cliché) will be found and the lumbering aircraft of reform will finally lurch off the runway into the free air. Perhaps perestroika will shrivel and glasnost turn opaque — no one yet knows. Perhaps Gorbachev will disappear into obscurity — no one yet knows that either, or knows his final place in history. But despite the Russian heartland's disillusionment with his politics, I believe Russians will in the end remember that he gave them a mirror in which to see the possibility of a very different and more hopeful future.

SOURCES

Whatat follows is a short list of some of the many books I have used, consulted and relied on. I have made no attempt here to list all the general and particular histories of Russia available, nor the voluminous publications available on Soviet current events and recent history; I mention only a few with a point of view that I found interesting or unusual.

All the quotations from Russian-language books, magazines and newspapers are my translations unless otherwise noted here. In a few instances I had some translating assistance from Alex Shkolnikov in Toronto, but any errors are my own.

TRAVEL AND GEOGRAPHY

The Volga Lands: A Guidebook to the Volga, the Oka, the Vyatka and the Byeloi Rivers. The Volga State Shipping and Transport Authority, Leningrad, 1926. In Russian. Conversational in tone, containing a number of discursive essays on the peoples and customs of the Volga lands as seen in the first flush of Bolshevik enthusiasm.

The Volga Lands: Travel Information and Guidebook. The Central Committee of the Water Transport Authority, Moscow, 1932. In Russian. Aimed specifically at Russian tourists, filled with must-see sights of Revolutionary history. Includes schedules and maps.

Places Associated With Lenin in the Volga Region. Planeta, Moscow, 1987. In Russian. Guidebook in the dreadful Socialist Realist style, useful mostly as an example of contemporary cant.

Journey For Our Time, by the Marquis de Custine. English translation by Phyllis Penn Kohler. Gateway, 1951. Custine's acid portrait of tyrannical Russia in 1839 was rediscovered in the West in Cold War times. Despite that, he remains an acute, if dyspeptic, observer.

The Voyages and Travels of the Ambassadors from the Duke of Holstein to the Great Duke of Muscovy and the King of Persia, by Adam Olearius. Translated and edited by Samuel H. Baron. Stamford University Press. Sycophantic towards his own superiors, Olearius was nevertheless an interested and interesting observer of seventeenth-century Russia. First published in English in 1662.

Russia in the Thaw, by Aldo Garzanti. Norton, 1964. This thaw was the short-lived Khrushchevian one; the Brezhnevian freeze was still to come. An amusing recounting of Russian travels in the Sixties. It includes a short account of a voyage down the Volga.

Guide to St. Petersburg and Other Chief Towns of Russia, by Otto Keller. Siegle Hill and Co., London, 1914. Keller seems to have translated this himself from the German original; it is full of misspellings, malapropisms and typographical errors, but is still a fascinating glimpse of Russia on the brink of revolution.

GENERAL HISTORIES

History of Russia, by Vasilii Klyuchevsky. State Publishing House, Moscow, 1957. In Russian. This massive history was Klyuchevsky's life's work. It was grudgingly published recently in the Soviet Union. Magisterial and complete, with the best available retelling of the Russian Chronicles.

A History of Russia, by Bernard Pares. University Paperbacks (Methuen, London), 1962 edition. This is the most passionate and involved of outsider histories. Pares, a British academic, became so obsessed with Russia that he moved there permanently in his last years.

THE PEOPLES OF THE SOVIET UNION

The Empire of the Steppe: A History of Central Asia, by René Grousset. Translated from the French by Naomi Walford. Rutgers University Press, 1970. The most complete and objective history of the Golden Horde of Baku and Tamerlane.

The Slavs, by Roger Portal. Translated from the French by Patrick Evans. Weidenfeld and Nicolson, 1965. Exhaustive and occasionally exhausting. Well regarded by Russian historians in Moscow.

The Tatar Yoke, by Charles Halperin. Slavica Publishers, Columbus, Ohio, 1986. A short, somewhat eccentric dissertation, but interesting for its recounting of the various revisionist theories.

The Nationalities of the Soviet Union, by Viktor Kozlov. Moscow, 1982. In Russian. Available in English as *The Peoples of the Soviet Union*. The Second World Series, Hutchinson, 1988. Boring but a good reference.

Soviet Nationalities Policy in Practice. Edited by Robert Conquest. Soviet Studies Series. One of a long series of specialist papers in the series published through the Sixties and Seventies, it is particularly useful in setting theory against practice.

The Volga Germans, by Fred C. Koch. Pennsylvania State University Press, 1977. Engagingly written, told relentlessly from the Volga German point of view. More complete than any general reader would want, unless you're family.

Across Russia From the Baltic to the Danube, by C.A. Stoddard. Scribner, 1891. Not very enlightening, but does include a vivid description of the fair at Nizhni Novgorod.

The Volga Falls to the Caspian Sea, by Boris Pilniak. Publishing data unavailable. In Russian. Useful geographic and ethnographic notes.

From the Banks of the Volga, by A.I. Roskin. A life of Maxim Gorky. In Russian. Altogether too respectful, even reverential, but if you can ignore the tone, there are good bits on Gorky's sojourns in the town that was to bear his name.

Through Starving Russia, by C.E.B. Roberts. Published in 1921, it contains a grim recounting of the famine years in the post-Revolutionary chaos.

A Trip Up the Volga to the Fair at Nijni Novgorod, by Henry Alexander. 1902. Very good on everyday life in provincial Russian towns of the period.

Lake Seliger, by V.Z. Isakov. 1978. Handbook. In Russian. Aims to be a tourist manual, but reads like a geological textbook. Mostly useful for specialists.

REVOLUTIONARY HISTORY

History of the Russian Revolution, by Leon Trotsky. Translated by Max Eastman. Victor Gollancz, 1965. A polemic, a self-justification (self-glorification), but also acute, insightful, wonderfully well written.

Leon Trotsky, by Isaac Deutscher. Oxford University Press, 1954. Where I have quoted Trotsky in the text I have generally used this edition's translation. This is still the best portrait of Trotsky.

The God That Failed: Six Studies in Communism. Edited and with an introduction by Richard Crossman. Hamish Hamilton, 1950. This is an exemplary examination of the Western intellectuals' fatal fascination with Communism. The quotes in the text by Arthur Koestler, Ignazio Silone and André Gide are from this book.

The Great Terror, by Robert Conquest. Macmillan, 1968. Still the best recounting of the hold Stalin had over his country.

Stalin in Power, by Robert C. Tucker. Norton, 1991. Better than Conquest in his understanding of how Stalinism became possible.

The New Russia, by Dorothy Thompson. Jonathan Cape, 1929. A journalist's observations of the new society, sometimes acute, always well written, seldom credulous.

Mother Russia, by Maurice Hindus. Collins, London, 1944. Often credulous, usually over-written, now mostly amusing for its acceptance of propaganda for fact.

CURRENT EVENTS

Inside Perestroika, by Abel Aganbegyan. Translated by Helen Szamuely. Harper and Row, 1989. An insider's view, now mostly interesting to see why it all started to go wrong.

Getting Russia Wrong, by Patrick Cockburn. Verso, New York, 1989. Iconoclastic, clear-eyed and useful, a thorough demolishing of "Kremlinology."

The Man Who Changed the World, by Gail Sheehy. HarperCollins, 1990. Biography on the run by an accomplished journalist. Best recounting yet of the rise to power of Gorbachev. Not at all credulous.

Fatal Half Measures, by Yevgeny Yevtushenko. Little Brown, 1991. Odd and disjointed and self-serving as this book is, it contains many useful insights, often as throwaway lines.

Breaking With History, by Lawrence Martin. Doubleday, 1989. Martin was lucky to be on the spot as a Moscow correspondent during Gorbachev's accession to power. An excited, somewhat breathless account of those days.

Soviet Women: Walking the Tightrope, by Francine du Plessix Gray. Doubleday, 1990. A useful book, one of the first to provide a view of Soviet feminists and what troubles them. Passionate and angry.

Moscow and Beyond, by Andrei Sakharov. Knopf, 1991. Encounters with Gorbachev. Sakharov's luminous intelligence is present on every page, in even the most mundane observation.

INDEX
of
PLACE NAMES

Z

W

Y